Praise for *Ancestral W*

"Ben Simpson's extensive knowledge and experience of
and depth. Full of fascinating and diverse examples of l
approach is never prescriptive. Through insightful journal prompts and a r
ration of the challenges and blessings, *Ancestral Whispers* encourages the reader to get to
the root of what a meaningful and authentic relationship with their ancestors might be."

—Philip Carr-Gomm, author of *Druid Mysteries*

"An important, intelligent book that beautifully and profoundly articulates the nature of
the ancestors. Simpson leaves no stone unturned in his examination of ancestral concepts and practices, ancient and modern, and in doing so he reveals a depth to ancestor
work that is new, challenging, and refreshing. His comprehensive examination of ancestral concepts is both fascinating and illuminating....If you buy any book on working with
the ancestors, it needs to be this one."

—Kristoffer Hughes, Head of the Anglesey Druid Order, author of *Cerridwen*

"If you are drawn to working with your ancestors but only have a vague idea of how this
might take shape, *Ancestral Whispers* will prove to be an invaluable resource in helping the
reader to craft deep and respectful connections to those who have gone before. Intelligently
written with great insight and sensitivity, Ben Simpson's book illuminates the importance
of our ancestral bonds and empowers us to be the very best ancestors for those yet to come."

—Eimear Burke, Chosen Chief of the Order of Bards, Ovates & Druids

"*Ancestral Whispers* offers what many other books don't: a discussion of every aspect of
ancestor veneration from what it is and why it's important to how and where it can be done.
With practical tips for how to actively connect to ancestors as well as engaging questions
that challenge readers to define those connections for themselves, this book gives us a
holistic look at what relationships with those who've come before have been and can be."

—Morgan Daimler, author of *21st Century Fairy*

"Ben Simpson offers us a thoughtful and in-depth guide to forming relationships with
our ancestors. Filled with practical, hands-on approaches, this book will act as a leaping
board for those who wish to approach this often-inaccessible aspect of spiritual practice.
Thoughtful, practical, and immensely personal, Ben has gifted us with a book that I am
certain many will treasure for years to come."

—Mhara Starling, author of *Welsh Witchcraft*

"A heartfelt journey into the world of ancestral veneration, masterfully weaving together
timeless wisdom and personal experience. Ben Stimpson's captivating guide transcends
cultural boundaries, providing a solid foundation for building authentic ancestral practices
rooted in cultural understanding and personal exploration. With its compassionate approach
and extensive knowledge, this book is an essential addition to anyone's spiritual library."

—Mat Auryn, bestselling author of *Psychic Witch* and *Mastering Magick*

"Exploring ancestor veneration from various cultures around the world...Stimpson situates his exploration of this complex subject in thorough academic research as well as insights from a multitude of individual perspectives, including BIPOC and LGBTQ+.... Stimpson explores the idea of ancestors from the widest perspective, including adoptive relatives, lineage ancestors, ancestors of group affinity and precursor species, deities and mythological forebears....This book is a rare treasure on a subject that is close to my heart and on which there are far too few good resources. Written with a great depth of insight, excellent research, and a can't-put-downable ease and flow, this is a book I really enjoyed reading, and a resource I'll be returning to again and again."

—Danu Forest, MA (Celtic Studies), traditional
seer and wisewoman, author of *Wild Magic*

"Ben Stimpson lays out a simple, direct, and very effective set of foundational techniques and practices to assist anyone in communicating with the ancestors....A deep respect and attention to detail make this an excellent work for any beginner in ancestor veneration, as well as anyone who just wants to think about their connections to the rest of the people in our universe....Ben has done a great service in writing this book, not only for his own ancestors but for all of the ancestors. I am deeply grateful this book exists in the world, and I will recommend it to everyone without hesitation."

—Mambo Chita Tann, author of *Haitian Vodou*

"Timely, personal, and intersectional, this book is everything you need to build meaningful connection to your ancestors and claim the gifts that such a practice brings to your spirit."

—Nicholas Pearson, author of *Crystal Basics* and
Flower Essences from the Witch's Garden

"A comprehensive guide that lays a strong foundation for building a meaningful and authentic ancestral veneration practice. Stimpson challenges us to consider the legacy we are creating through our own engagement with ancestral reverence and invites us to contemplate the transformational powers we possess in our roles as 'ancestors-in-waiting.'"
—Jhenah Telyndru, MA (Celtic Studies), founder of the Sisterhood of Avalon and author
of *The Ninefold Way of Avalon*

"In this easy-to-access guidebook, Ben Stimpson offers a deeply personal, psychologically grounded, and culturally mindful roadmap for reclaiming one's place in the larger human community."

—Daniel Foor, PhD, author of *Ancestral Medicine*

"It is a great pleasure to find a book about an important topic that is erudite, thoughtful, original, wide-ranging and multicultural, and yet also deeply personal. This is such a book."

—Ronald Hutton, historian and author of *The Triumph of the Moon*

ANCESTRAL WHISPERS

About the Author

Ben Stimpson (he/they/them) is a therapist, student, and spiritual director. Ben has developed courses on a variety of topics, including ancestor veneration, the power of story, and folklore. When not working with clients or writing, Ben is engaged with his areas of study: religious studies, medieval and classical studies, folklore, and spirituality. Learn more at BenStimpson.com.

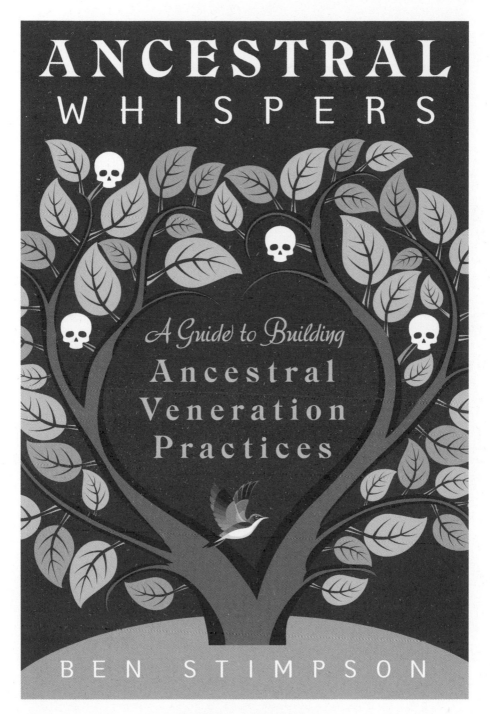

ANCESTRAL WHISPERS

A Guide to Building

Ancestral Veneration Practices

BEN STIMPSON

Llewellyn Publications
Woodbury, Minnesota

FIRST EDITION
First Printing, 2023

Book design by Samantha Peterson
Cover design by Kevin R. Brown

Photography is used for illustrative purposes only. The persons depicted may not endorse or represent the book's subject.

Llewellyn Publications is a registered trademark of Llewellyn Worldwide Ltd.

Library of Congress Cataloging-in-Publication Data (Pending)
ISBN: 978-0-7387-7472-5

Llewellyn Worldwide Ltd. does not participate in, endorse, or have any authority or responsibility concerning private business transactions between our authors and the public.

All mail addressed to the author is forwarded but the publisher cannot, unless specifically instructed by the author, give out an address or phone number.

Any internet references contained in this work are current at publication time, but the publisher cannot guarantee that a specific location will continue to be maintained. Please refer to the publisher's website for links to authors' websites and other sources.

Llewellyn Publications
A Division of Llewellyn Worldwide Ltd.
2143 Wooddale Drive
Woodbury, MN 55125-2989
www.llewellyn.com

Printed in the United States of America

To Mum and Dad,
The more I look in the mirror,
the more I see you both looking right back out at me.

Contents

Territorial Acknowledgment   xi

Acknowledgments   xiii

Introduction   1

Part One: The Living and the Dead

Exercise One: Encountering the Tree of Life and Death   10

Chapter One: The Nature of the Living   11

Chapter Two: The Nature of the Dead   27

Chapter Three: Who Are the Ancestors?   43

Chapter Four: Expanding the Concept of Ancestor   55

Exercise Two: Exploring Conceptual Ancestors   72

Chapter Five: Defining Ancestor Veneration   73

Chapter Six: Ancestor Veneration and Personal Story   87

Exercise Three: Exploring Ancestor Story   98

Chapter Seven: Ancestor Veneration and the Community   99

Part Two: Forming a Living Practice

Chapter Eight: Conceptualizing Lived Practice   115

Chapter Nine: Physicality of Sacred Space   131

Chapter Ten: The Use of Color   141

Chapter Eleven: Physical Representations   151

Chapter Twelve: Objects of Power   171

Chapter Thirteen: Offerings   183

Chapter Fourteen: Ritual   193

Chapter Fifteen: Communication   203

Chapter Sixteen: Pilgrimage   217

Conclusion   229

Resources and Further Reading   231

Bibliography   241

Index   249

Territorial Acknowledgment

I take this opportunity to acknowledge the ancestors of those who for countless generations lived in relationship with the land that I write this book on, which is situated in the Haldimand Tract, the unceded land that is part of the traditional homelands of the Haudenosaunee, Anishinaabe, and eradicated Chonnonton peoples. In writing this work on this land, I pay my respect to both the ancestors and the living communities of these peoples. May all readers of this book incorporate the important work of reconciliation efforts into their ancestral spiritual work as we build a better future for all our descendants.

Acknowledgments

As we embark on this journey, the concept of relationship will come up again and again. Just as we are the product of relationships between our ancestors, so, too, are we products of the many relationships we have in our lives. I am blessed in that I have had a lot of support during various points in this process. These friends and teachers have been there to listen, challenge, offer feedback, inspire, and give encouragement along the way. They are my lineage of teachers that contributed to this book.

My absolute gratitude to Tiffany Lazic, who has been a teacher, mentor, landlady, and friend at various parts of my journey. When I decided to take the leap and start this journey in late 2020, Tiff gave me valuable advice from her own experience. Our friend and colleague Carrie Lee was a major presence of inspiration and encouragement and was always there to offer wise words and gentle pushes.

To the community of students who embarked on the journey in "Ancestral Whispers: The Course!": Gail, Cecelia, Martha, Jackie, Anita, Krista, Josie, and Larissa. We shared a lot of laughter, some tears, and many "aha" moments over the span of those intense eight weeks.

To my former godfather in the Lukumi tradition, M. David Goodwin, Oshunnike, and the guiding hand of his tutelary orisha, Oshun. While I did not initiate into Lukumi, the experiences that he facilitated form an important cornerstone of my personal practice. A big nod to my former godfather's partner, who supported and put up with us both while living together as roommates.

To the staff of Words Worth Books, the bookstore in Uptown Waterloo that I worked at during the bulk of writing this book. Owners Mandy and Dave seriously educated me about the bookselling world, and my fellow coworkers listened with enthusiasm as I talked about this project. Similarly, my coworkers Michelle and Alyssa, who I worked with at a little bakery in Ancaster, enthusiastically shared with me their love of genealogy and family story as I wrote up very early notes that would become this book.

I would be remiss if I didn't point out those other supporters in my life or important people who have been on this journey with me the past few years:

To Baba Ogbe Di for helping to keep me grounded and sane through this process by wit and the sharing of many memes. His patience for my "tendency to write epistles the length of Romans 1 and 2 at the least excuse" was most appreciated.

To one of my best friends Finnley, who has journeyed with me these past six years and whom I bonded originally with over ancestral magic. Finn kindly beta tested the course that evolved into this book. I cherish and deeply respect her thoughtfulness, compassion, and vulnerability.

To the community of Tribal Hearth, who at a pivotal moment in my life reintroduced me to my spirituality: Allison, Gomer, Tracy, Fallon, Rebecca, Wendy, Allegonda, Connie, Jessica, Brian, Robin, Edmund, Jynx, Mars, Rae Lynn, Jim, Bryce, Misty, Sandi, and Barry. I wish to thank Adam particularly for being the architect of the rituals of Tribal Hearth and for being an exceptional polymath and spiritual worker. I respect each of you deeply. You have affected my life in ways you'll never fully know. The Tribal Hearth experience came at a time in my life when I was lost; the community tasked me to be their Seeker, and I sought. Part of that seeking led me to writing this book.

While developing the many revisions of this work, I relied heavily on my queer practitioner friends for reassuring words and inspiration: Clinton Burn, Dakota Goodrich, Chris Lung, Aven, Aaron, and so many others. Your presence in my life is something I treasure, and I've grown from knowing each of you. In a similar feeling, to fellow authors who made me feel welcome in the community, in particular Mhara Starling and Morgan Daimler for pep talks and frequent sage words of advice, and to all the authors who wrote endorsements for me and encouraged me along the way: I thank you all.

I would like to thank the team at Llewellyn Worldwide for shepherding me through my experience of writing my first book: my editors Elysia Gallo and Hanna Grimson for their excellent guidance in the revision process, my publicist Markus Ironwood, my copywriter Alisha Bjorklund, and Bill Krause, Shira Atakpu, Tom Lund, and all the other team members who worked on this project. I would also like to thank the sensitivity readers from some of the communities who are spoken of in this book, and who graciously took time to read through the manuscript and offer opinions on appropriateness of characterizations. Thank you all!

Finally, and most importantly of all, I would like to thank my parents, the lineage bearers of my ancestors. Through some turbulent times in my life, they never abandoned me. It is from their lips that I heard the stories of my grandparents and great-grandparents. While they may not understand my personal spiritual beliefs, they appreciate my deep interest in our family and ancestral story. My mum sat down with me often as I asked about the family stories, and my dad added all the missing bits. My mum is one of the strongest women I know, and my dad is one of the most creative forces in my life. In writing this book, I hope to both honor my parents and all of our shared ancestors.

Introduction

It is the night of Halloween, and my apartment smells divine with the rich aromas of baked goods and my favorite scented candles. The film *Practical Magic* is playing on the television, and outside, the sky is darkening as kids begin to take to the streets in their costumes. My attention is drawn to a collection of framed photographs on a sideboard, each with a candle flickering in front of them. The faces of my ancestors and departed loved ones smile out at me as I place a plate of food down onto the sideboard in front of them, an offering on this night of the dead. Some believe that on this night the veil between worlds is thinnest, and I spend the rest of the evening enjoying the company of my dead as I watch some of my favorite Halloween movies. I take time to honor my ancestors and reflect on my own life up to this point.

Ancestor veneration or *worship* is the honoring of one's ancestral dead through a system of spiritual expression. Many cultures around the world have systems of honoring the dead, whether through organized religion or through less-formal community traditions. Veneration is predicated on the idea that the dead still have some connection with the world of the living, and through a ritual practice, the living can form relationships that benefit the individual and whole community. Essentially, ancestor veneration states that death is not an end.

The word *death* conjures up some of our deepest fears. That single inescapable reality of death is unavoidable and unchangeable. Despite human advancement, death is the one absolute that we have no control over. All religions grapple with this reality, both explaining and preparing us for the experience in some way. In the West, I would argue we have a deeply unhealthy relationship with death. When someone dies, the body is whisked away by professional mortuary attendants or the coroner, and the next time we see it, it is inside a gorgeous coffin or wrapped in a shroud ready to be cremated. The image most people, I think, have in their minds is of either the person as they were alive or the person shut away in a box and soon buried in the ground. The unhealthy ways our society grieves have evolved in such a way as to banish social fear of death by also banishing the person who has experienced that death. Particularly in the West, we create in our collective grief abstract holes in the shapes of people we once knew and loved because our culture doesn't allow us to do anything different without fear of triggering social awkwardness.

I have noticed our culture has begun to shift toward talking about and exploring these topics with less shame or taboo. Over the past couple of decades, a growing collection of critically acclaimed television series and movies have challenged the Western relationship with death and the dead. Movies such as Pixar's *Coco* (2017) or *Soul* (2020) and television series such as *Six Feet Under* (2001–2005), *Dead Like Me* (2003–2004), *Pushing Daisies* (2007–2009), *Being Human* (2008–2013), *The Good Place* (2016–2020), and most recently *Upload* (2020–) all grapple with themes of meaningful existence and continued relationships after death. These themes are not new and speak to the human condition. The same questions explored in these titles have been explored through ancestral traditions for centuries.

Ancestral work is often portrayed or conceptualized in popular Western media as death-focused. While it includes the dead, ancestral veneration is about life as well. My ancestral work transcends simply honoring the dead and informs how I show up in the world, my preparation as an ancestor-in-waiting, and my own eventual death. I'm at an age now where I have had enough life experience to be able to put things into clearer perspective, and while I still make mistakes, I appreciate a lot more what my ancestors went through in their own lives.

As I age, my spirituality and my relationships with my gods and spirits have shifted. My spiritual journey has taken me all over the place, but in writing this book, I realized how much of that journey has reoriented me back toward home. I'm originally from North Wales, and my family emigrated in the mid-1990s to a small rural town in Ontario, Canada. For years I felt completely out of place among my Canadian peers, because unlike them, I didn't have any connection to that place. I drive through the town now and have nostalgic love for my time spent there, but it isn't home. I was bullied badly because of my accent and being different, and I longed to return to a sense of belonging. It might sound strange, but I was not British until I came to Canada. Coming to Canada suddenly marked me as different, and in suddenly being different, I latched on to anything that reminded me of the UK—anything that would make me feel normal again. Therapy has helped me to understand that what I was probably experiencing was a form of trauma connected to being uprooted at such an early age. Part of my journey has been to let go of the anger I developed by realizing that it was no one's fault, and that no one in my life could have predicted that I'd feel this way.

In my early teens, I started to explore alternative spirituality, probably to gain some sense of power in my life. To a backdrop of media like *Buffy the Vampire Slayer*, *Harry Potter*, *The Worst Witch*, *The Mists of Avalon*, and the infamous *The Craft*, I started to explore Paganism and witchcraft. A lot of the literature available to me online or in the few books I owned was centered on the goddess spirituality movement and British folklore. Around that time, I started to understand I was queer, and the association I formed between goddess-centric spirituality and my British background helped me to feel a sense of belonging in a town that was predominantly Christian. I started to connect with other queer people my age online who were involved in Paganism or magic, and through them I developed a deeper interest in the esoteric.

As I entered my twenties, I studied Hinduism, Buddhism, the Western Mystery traditions, magic, and comparative religion. Hinduism became very important to me, particularly the traditions of Shiva and the non-dual philosophy of Vedanta. Despite the positive direction of my life, I had a deep feeling of disconnect, and truth be told, I was miserable. In 2010, after fifteen years of living in Canada, I had a chance to work during a summer at the satellite campus of a Canadian university located in East Sussex, UK.

I spent four glorious months working, traveling, and spending time with family. When I returned to Canada, I fell into a dark period of my life, one that took many years to recover from.

In 2015, I entered a renaissance and took ownership of my practice again. I started working with a group called Tribal Hearth, who worked with the hero's journey theory of Joseph Campbell to develop a series of ritual Mystery play experiences. At the first event I attended, I was chosen to play a primary role in that shared story. I can't quite describe the impact the Tribal Hearth events had on my renaissance, but through this group, I connected in a very substantial way with the Neopagan community. While not all of the people I connected with through Neopaganism were necessarily healthy, the strong relationships I built are treasures for me. It was around this same time that I also met my friend Tiffany Lazic at a local psychic fair and began taking classes with her. When I met her, she told me about some classes she was starting at her center in Kitchener, and at the time, I was living an hour and a half away.

We will talk about intuition in other parts of the book, but I got a feeling that some big things were starting to occur, and I had a choice. So I made the choice to drive to Kitchener, sometimes in dreadful weather, and eventually that process led me to retrain in psychotherapy. The courses helped me to become alive again after a very long time of entropy. Thinking back on it now, a key moment of recognition in all of this was that when I met both Tiffany and the people of Tribal Hearth, not only did they recognize that I was Welsh by something I had said, but they actively celebrated it. Up until that point, there was no one who had been savvy enough to recognize that, and I was othered as "just British." Many of these people had not only been to the UK and loved it, but they actively worked with spiritualities connected to that landscape.

The period of 2015–2020 saw a revolution in how I showed up for my life. All sorts of coincidences and synchronicities conspired to put me into the orbit of people who would change my life forever. I cannot do justice in this short introduction to all these influences, but suffice to say, in the span of five years my whole life changed. I started dating a guy who was a practicing Vodouisant (a practitioner of Haitian Vodou) who introduced me to other practitioners of several African Traditional Religions. I met my now-former godfather in

Lukumi (also called Regla de Ocha or Santería), the Afro-Cuban tradition centered on the Yoruba spirits called the orisha, and I joined his spiritual house as a godchild. Around that time, I went back to school in Toronto to retrain in psychotherapy, and, to help support that work, I moved in with my former godfather and his partner to be closer to the school. All the people I was interacting with were living in relationship to the cultures of their spiritual practices. My former godfather, who is a crowned priest of Oshun, seriously lives his relationship to Oshun every day. Tiffany is solidly grounded in her spirituality that has, frankly, been an inspiration as she navigated the peaks and valleys of her own journey. The friends of Tribal Hearth and others I've bonded with all inspired and challenged me to take ownership of my relationships to my spirits and deities.

My experiences in the Lukumi *Ile* tangibly demonstrated how my ancestors showed up in my life, and I felt a major pull to reconnect in a substantive way with my ancestral story. I began to explore the traditions of my homeland, and this led me to modern Celtic spiritual traditions, where I began studying through the Order of Bards, Ovates & Druids (OBOD). This focus on my homeland's spiritual traditions coincided with a heavy exploration of my ancestors' history and story. I was assigned a major project in my psychotherapy training to look at my family history, and so I sat down with my mum and dad to do a deep dive into our family's past. These various threads over the span of five years all eventually wove together to unveil a road map into the future, and a consistent message from spirit was, "Don't live in the past; you don't belong there." The ancestors did not whisper—they bellowed, and their directive was to simply "live."

As of right now, I have various spiritual traditions that I draw inspiration from or am connected to. I look to Advaita Saiva Hinduism, I practice magic, I belonged to a Lukumi house as an *aleyo* (an uninitiated person), I practice *espiritismo* (a Caribbean form of French Spiritism), I am studying the Bardic tradition through OBOD, and I am reconnecting with the folk practices of my British ancestors. All these streams feed a different part of my soul and inform how I move in the world, but they also pose certain problems for me. I am a white, queer individual from the UK, and though I have been deeply impacted by my time with my former godfather and his Oshun, I am not initiated into that tradition, and there are large aspects of it that are closed to me for now. Similarly, I am not South Asian, and so there are various cultural aspects of Hinduism that I do not have a right to involve myself with. It is my responsibility to understand and respect the boundaries of these traditions while also honoring their deep impact on my journey so far. My ancestral work, though influenced by Lukumi and espiritismo, is one of those spaces that is 100 percent my responsibility.

I feel fortunate to have been taught several different approaches to working with ancestors, but what if I had never encountered the above traditions? Part of my ancestral journey has been to develop parts of my ancestral practice that relate particularly to my own ancestors and the cultures they belonged to. Often, I hear from people who have the desire to connect with their own background but have no idea where to begin. This is the reason I decided to write this book.

However, this book is not written to be a definitive guidebook, nor is it meant to teach you a tradition to follow. Instead, it is a handy road map to help you explore the terrain of your relationship to your ancestors. This book isn't here to sell ancestral veneration as a spiritual practice to you, but to give an overview of how this form of spirituality impacts the daily lives of so many around the planet. Likewise, nothing in this book is here to tell you what to believe or do, but to challenge you to really explore your practice and take ownership of it.

For me, spiritual work is not about theorizing alone, but putting into practice and doing. In the same way that reading about a movie is not the same as watching said movie, I encourage you to involve yourself in your work. A basic formula for my spiritual life has been: thinking + doing = being. For too long I sat in an armchair thinking about my life and not experiencing it. Part one of this book is the "thinking," while part two is all about the "doing." There are some exercises for you to do, but there are many more journal prompts. As you go through this book, I recommend reflecting on the content using three specific questions: How do I relate to what I'm reading? Do I agree or disagree with what I'm reading? What more do I want to know about this topic? I have also included robust resources at the back to assist you in going deeper. To help you further, there are four key words you will see repeated throughout: process, relationship, tradition, and intentionality. For me, these four foundational concepts are the backbone of not only ancestral veneration, but all spiritual work. Before diving into the content to come, I'd challenge you to think about what these words mean to you both individually and collectively.

I would like to make one final note: Throughout this work I offer many examples from traditions I do not belong to, and in no capacity am I trying to speak for these traditions. I rely on primary and secondary sources to inform me about the content of these lived practices, but in no way am I claiming to be an insider to these traditions. While I have striven to be respectful of how I use examples to support my assertions in this book, as an outsider I don't have that nuanced relationship. While I try to approach my writing with sensitivity in mind, I would like to apologize for any errors or mischaracterizations I might inadvertently include in this book. I encourage readers to listen to the voices of insiders in describing their traditions and worldviews and respecting the boundaries of closed traditions, especially of those communities who have been marginalized and oppressed.

Ancestor work has changed my life, and I hope that it does yours as well. If this book is your first introduction to this form of spirituality, then I hope that it is useful for you. No one book will give you everything you need. As with any form of spirituality, the threads of the tapestry of your relationship are numerous, but I hope this content will be useful to you in some way. If only one question in this entire book causes you to deepen your relationship to your ancestors, then it has done its job. I invite you to take a deep breath, close your eyes, and open yourself to hearing the whispered words of the ancestors.

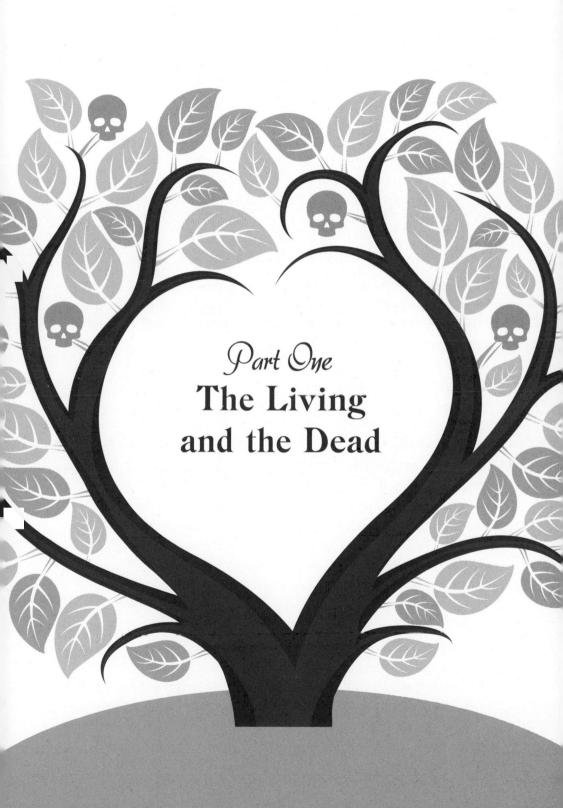

Part One

The Living
and the Dead

Section Introduction

In part one, we are going to lay the foundation for building your ancestor veneration practice by exploring worldview, beliefs, and conceptualizing the ancestors. It is my strong opinion that building a spiritual practice must correspond to or be reconcilable with your underlying beliefs; otherwise, your practice can become confused and ineffective. The following topics are offered as food for thought and not as beliefs to follow. Consider how some of these topics relate to you and how you see the world; use them to deepen or challenge your held beliefs.

Exercise One
ENCOUNTERING THE TREE OF LIFE AND DEATH

The front cover of this book, beautifully rendered by the Llewellyn art department, is of a tree containing symbols of life and skulls of the dead. To begin working through the content of this book, I invite you to meditate upon this tree of life and death.

Find a quiet place to sit comfortably. Closing your eyes, take a couple of deep breaths, inhaling for a count of seven, holding for a count of three, and exhaling for a count of ten. With each exhale, allow any tension in your body to drop away. Feel your feet planted firmly on the ground, connecting you to the earth. Continue to take deep breaths in this manner until your breathing naturally settles into a steady rhythm.

Visualize yourself within a great forest, the myriad trees surrounding you extending out as far as the mind's eye can see. Travel through this forest, allowing yourself to forge your own path through the underbrush. As you walk through this forest, visualize yourself coming to a large open space. In the center of this space is a tree larger than any others, its branches reaching up into the sky and its gnarled roots firmly planted into the earth. At the base of its trunk, you see candles and plates of food arranged. As you sit at the base of this great tree and look up into its branches, you notice the lovingly placed skulls of all those who came before. This is the tree of life and death, a tree we are all born from and eventually return to when we die. Spend time at the base of this tree, and if it is helpful, as you work through the following content, come back to this visualization to help ground you in your work.

Chapter One
The Nature of the Living

As we begin our exploration of the concept of "the ancestors," I think we need to understand for ourselves how we view the living. Death is most often popularly defined as an absence of life, but what is life, exactly? In this chapter, we look briefly at the connection between the concepts of living and state of personhood and their relationship with the identity of spirit. We will also look at the concept of prelife and some other related questions. While we work through these topics, we'll also be discussing how our use of language affects our beliefs.

All these issues are good background information for the work around ancestor veneration coming up in later chapters. Later in this section, we will discuss from a cross-cultural perspective the dead as a category of being and elaborate on themes that show up again and again. We will expand on various beliefs about personhood and what happens after death. We will then dive into how the dead are understood, the categories of dead spirits and their potential for transformation, and how these beliefs determine or are determined by the perceived dwelling place of these beings. We will essentially be looking at how worldview and belief shape our understandings of the identity and experiences of the dead when they transition, setting ourselves up for further discussion on how those core beliefs affect how we relate to the dead as ancestors in veneration practices.

What constitutes a person or the self is a central question for most spiritual traditions. How we relate to and define others often relies on how we define ourselves. Among the diversity of humanity, we will find many beliefs about what can claim the title of personhood. In this section, we are going to explore several related topics that, in my opinion, are foundational to developing relationships with the dead, namely personhood, self, and spirit.

Personhood is a social status of being recognized as an individual and person, *self* is our innate identity, and *spirit* is the animating force, which in some cultures exists as an underlying element and at other times a bearer of personhood. In many traditions, all three are present at birth simultaneously, while in some other traditions, parts of selfhood are gained through initiation or rites of passage. In some traditions, personhood and self can be far more complex and affect how we relate to one another.

Most traditions I have come across tend to view humans as being composed of a physical body and some spiritual animating force. This is a difficult topic to cover due to its sheer variety, but below are some examples that demonstrate how different cultures take up this question. The important thing here is not to take up a particular viewpoint but to become aware of and critically reflect on how you already answer the question of personhood and self, and how that belief might affect your relationships to your ancestors.

In the West, our popular view of personhood arguably stems from the Christian concept of self. There is a deeper history stemming from Greco-Roman tradition, but for all intents and purposes, Christianity specifically has impacted our current cultural paradigm. In this system, a person is made up of three aspects: the body, the mind, and the soul. The body is the physical vehicle, the mind is the mental function bound to reason and logic, and the soul or spirit is that transcendental animating force. In many ways, this concept of the person mirrors the trinitarian doctrine of Jesus the Son as the physical body, God the Father as the mental aspect, and the Holy Spirit as the spiritual aspect.

The concept of the soul in Christian thought has evolved over the past two thousand years and originally developed from Greek philosophers like Socrates, Plato, Aristotle, and Plotinus. The pre-Christian Hellenic approaches to understanding self were introduced into Christian scholasticism by Saint Gregory of Nyssa (ca. 335 CE–ca. 395 CE), Saint Augustine of Hippo (354 CE–430 CE), and the later Saint Thomas Aquinas (ca. 1224 CE–1274 CE). The early church fathers saw no contradiction between what the Neoplatonic school of Hellenic philosophy taught and what was revealed within biblical literature. Both groups of philosophers cast a long shadow on the Christian orthodox understanding of the self. We find many of their views in our modern popular understanding of the soul, even 1,600 years since Saint Gregory and Saint Augustine.

According to the Neoplatonic and Augustinian views, the soul is an immutable aspect of self that is connected to but distinct from the material body. In the Neoplatonic view, the soul is described as going through multiple bodies as if putting on a new cloak and taking off an old one.[1] That is to say, the essence of an individual is not tied directly to or defined by the physical body. Platonic thinking suggests immortality as an essential attribute of the soul, and death is a recurring experience that does not inherently lead to a soul's extinguishment.

The Christian view as suggested by Augustine is that the soul is not inherently immortal and capable of transmigrating to a new body on earth by itself. It is through God's resurrective intervention that new life is granted in an afterlife. This also underscores the belief that a soul gets one life in a body and not multiple lives in multiple new bodies.

This might sound like a small distinction, but it is a pivotal one because it underscores so many Christian rituals and beliefs around the dead, such as praying for the soul, preservation of bodily remains, and belief in the resurrection of an individual through faith in God. The relationship between mind and soul is close—the mind tends to follow the soul into that after-death state, whereas the body breaks down and remains in the physical world, waiting to be reunited with the spirit at the Last Judgment.[2]

While I am writing a lot of this book with Western readers in mind, there are many multicultural societies around the world where dominant cultures influence minority religions and views. The point I want to make—and challenge you to consider—is how dominant culture impacts your personal views, whether that is a dominant culture derived from your own religious

---

1. Plato, *Phaedo*, translated by G. M. A. Grube. In *Classics of Western Philosophy*, ed. Steven M. Cahn, 8th ed. (Indianapolis, IN: Hackett Publishing Company, 2012), 47–79.

2. Hiroshi Obayashi, ed., *Death and Afterlife: Perspectives of World Religions* (New York: Praeger, 1992), 111.

faith or not. As we move into developing an ancestral practice, what I hope you will be empowered to do is develop your practice as an organic extension of your beliefs, which you can invite your ancestors into. However, becoming aware of what you believe in the first place is important. Reflect on how you see and understand the self and how that belief then might translate into how you see the dead and your relationships to them. Below we will explore some of the more dominant human worldviews and assumptions of how the self is defined, with comments on how those worldviews then impact cultural and individual relationships to the dead. It is crucial to note that these are overviews only. Beliefs are usually spectrums, and even within these worldviews there will be many differences among those who hold these views.

Animism

Animism is a broad anthropological term to refer to a large range of different but similar cultural expressions. Dr. Graham Harvey, scholar of animism and contemporary Paganism, says, "In the most general terms, animism concerns the nature of human-being and the nature of our world…addressed in specific relationships, etiquettes, activities, ideas and encounters."[3]

In an animist worldview, the nature of the world is that of an animating spiritual force that permeates everything. Sometimes that spiritual essence coalesces into individuated identity, and we get animals, spirits, and human beings. Other times the identity of spirit is far more subtle and fluid, a form of intelligence that is not like our own but is nonetheless intelligent and holds presence. In animism, sometimes the spirits of the world are deity-like and at other times are explained as containers for information that we build relationships with. Sometimes individuals are manifestations of the underlying spiritual power, and at other times they are envisioned like eddies in the flow of a river, anomalies that exist and then dissipate.

Personhood in animism encompasses the whole world, as a person is any form of life. And as life is in everything, so is personhood. Harvey sums this worldview up, saying, "the world is full of persons, only some of whom are human, and that life is always lived in relationship with others."[4] In animist

---

3. Graham Harvey, ed., *Handbook of Contemporary Animism* (London: Routledge, 2013), 1.

4. Graham Harvey, *Animism: Respecting the Living World* (London: Hurst & Co. 2005), xi.

cultures, animals, plants, and minerals are members of a large family or community and are referred to in familial terms. Since there is no separation of self and environment, in quite a few traditions the dead are regarded as very much a part of the environment and not in some distant and inaccessible place. In this worldview, there is no set state of personhood or self, as depending upon the culture, the possibility and ability to transform and become something else is always present.

In Shinto, the pre-Buddhist tradition of Japan, the world is seen as imbued with *musuhi*, a creative spiritual force that binds the world together. From musuhi emerge the kami, the divine spirits and embodiments of the world. Kami are the individuated forms of musuhi and are the personalities of their various domains, whether they be physical or social. Often, the word *kami* has been translated into English as "gods," but this is an oversimplification and shows the way translation can infer external cultural notions into indigenous understanding. Kami and other forms of spirits in Japanese traditions are the personifications of qualities, emotions, and places that are each composed of spiritual power. The greater kami (such as Amaterasu, Hachiman, Susanoo, etc.) are venerated because they exemplify certain qualities or goals that are spiritually desirable and are understood to have universal significance, while lesser kami are venerated as part of relationship with place.[5] By entering into relationship with and honoring the kami, individuals are affirming a grand universal order that in other forms of Japanese spirituality is understood as *onmyō*.[6]

Japanese popular media such as manga and anime are filled with the essentially animistic worldview of the culture. For centuries, the Japanese have reveled in tales of *yokai*, a shifting category of the supernatural that describes individual beings such as monsters as well as unexplained occurrences that have a spiritual dimension. Yokai and the supernatural form a robust aspect of the culture, as evidenced by yokai themes showing up often in modern anime and manga. Yokai and other tales of the supernatural tell us a lot about the essentially animist way of viewing the world, how all things have a potential to form

---

5. Bret W. Davis, ed., *The Oxford Handbook of Japanese Philosophy* (Oxford; New York: Oxford University Press, 2020), 98.

6. *Onmyō*: The Japanese term for the philosophy of yin and yang, incorporated into Japan from China as early as the seventh century.

intelligence and act on their own agendas. For example, a recurring belief connected to the supernatural is that as something ages it can develop more spiritual power, which makes it both worthy of respect and potentially dangerous. For example, there is a class of yokai called *tsukumogami*, which are everyday objects such as fans, scrolls, or umbrellas that have reached the age of one hundred and become enlivened, taking on spiritual powers and personality.

A common story of tsukumogami is that after a century of faithful use, an object is thrown away as trash and comes back to haunt or take revenge on its former owner. This belief has given rise in recent years to funerals for objects that are no longer wanted, such as traditional dolls. In recent years, temples began to offer *ningyo kuyo* ceremonies to put to rest the potentially vengeful spirits of dolls and say goodbye in a respectful and dignified manner.[7] This concern over objects or individuals of great age gaining power and transformative abilities is also in folklore about the elderly (elderly women in particular are feared to become *yama uba*, or mountain hags). Other yokai such as *kitsune* (foxes) or *nekomata* (cats) are believed to grow or develop extra tails as they gain spiritual power.[8]

The Japanese culture of animism is certainly not the only culture that views the entirety of the world as being composed of spirit. Many cultures have concepts of a unifying energy permeating reality like musuhi: *ashe* (Yoruba), *mana* (Polynesians), *orenda* (Haudenosaunee), and *manitou* (Algonquian cultures). While each of these terms have nuance, they all point to permeating animating force. Extending this, most traditions have a sense of an energy that exists as an integral part of the universe, for example: *chi* in China, *prana* in India, and *silap inua* among Siberian and Northern American Inuit peoples.[9]

An animistic worldview can pervade not only beliefs about things but how one even speaks of various parts of the world. In her seminal work *Braiding*

---

7. Heather Greene, "Japanese Temples Are Holding Funerals For Unwanted Dolls," *Religion Unplugged*, The Media Project, November 5, 2021, https://religionunplugged.com/news/2021/11/5/japanese-temples-are-holding-funerals-for-unwanted-dolls.

8. Michael Dylan Foster, *The Book of Yōkai: Mysterious Creatures of Japanese Folklore*, illustrated by Kijin Shinonome (Oakland, CA: University of California Press, 2015), n.p.

9. Daniel Merkur, "Breath-Soul and Wind Owner: The Many and the One in Inuit Religion," *American Indian Quarterly* 7, no. 3 (Summer 1983): 23-39, https://doi.org/10.2307/1184255.

Sweetgrass, botanist Dr. Robin Wall Kimmerer speaks about the process of learning her native Potawatomi language. She noted that there are only about 30 percent nouns versus 70 percent verbs, and that an important aspect of the language affecting conjugation and tense is whether something is animate or inanimate. She noted how frustrating it was to try to understand why there were so many verbs, until she suddenly had a spark of inspiration and understood how closely connected the beingness of what would be a noun in other languages was to animacy. She gives the example of the word for *bay*, which is a verb because water itself is a living entity. Being a bay means the bay is in a relationship with the water that flows. Interestingly, Dr. Kimmerer notes that the list of nouns tends to be man-made objects and thus essentially dead, versus verbs, which are natural and alive.[10] These two different cultures—Japanese and Potawatomi—both reflect an essential view that the world is inherently animated with spirit, and this understanding creates the foundations for how individuals relate to one another and the world around them.

The Spirit as Divine Spark (Dualism and Nondualism)

The spirit as a divine spark is a widespread concept found in multiple major traditions categorized as *mysticism*. This point of view suggests that every individual spirit is an emanation of a creator and ultimately is working toward a goal of reunion or direct personal relationship with the source. This is very different from animist traditions where the relationship to spirituality is more about going with the flow of a natural order. The divine spark viewpoint is expressed in very similar language in such major mystical traditions as Christian mysticism, Jewish Kabbalah, Islamic Sufism, Hindu and Buddhist yoga dharma, Tantra, Daoism, and Sikhism to name a few. A general summation of the approach of mystical traditions is that the creator or source can be experienced now without the need to wait until death, and with the proper tools and techniques practiced, an individual can engage with mystical states of consciousness.

---

10. Robin Wall Kimmerer. *Braiding Sweetgrass: Indigenous Wisdom, Scientific Knowledge, and the Teachings of Plants* (Minneapolis, MN: Milkweed Editions, 2020), 54.

In this worldview, the search for self is the search for source and becomes an inward journey of self-discovery over a materialist externalism. The question of selfhood in this worldview can be taken up differently depending upon two major approaches: dualism and nondualism. Simply put, dualism suggests a continued separation between creator and created where the goal is eternal relationship, whereas nondualism suggests the appearance of separation caused by a delusional state of separation between creator and created and the goal is eternal reunion.

The goal of both non-dualistic and dualistic traditions is to transcend the limited bounds of individuated mundane existence and reach out to experience the divine source and attain an understanding, even if just temporary, with a sense of higher Self. Realization of greater Self is achieved by means of asceticism, deep inner exploration of awareness through meditation, and striving to pierce the veil of mundane perception by entering altered states of consciousness. Ideas of personal identity and selfhood start to break down, and expansion of self becomes an inclusive process. Personhood in this worldview is not about "I," but the quest for "we." Or, as the Israeli philosopher and mystic Martin Buber puts it in his seminal work *I and Thou*, the quest is to transition from an "I-It" relationship with others and the Divine, where other is seen as an object to be experienced only, to an "I-Thou" relationship, where other is related to in a mutually holistic way that underscores mutual sovereignty.[11]

Mystical traditions would say that anyone is capable of momentary experiences of mystical union with the creator, and it is through the experience that an understanding of self and relationship is gained. The nineteenth-century Western mystic and psychologist William James describes mystical experiences as having four primary qualities: "passivity," "ineffability," "noetic quality," and "transiency."[12] He describes mystical states as temporary experiences of being "grasped and held by a superior power" without the ability to adequately describe the experience in human language.[13] This experience can

---

11. Martin Buber, *I and Thou*, trans. Ronald Gregor Smith (Edinburgh, UK: T. & T. Clark, 1937), 84.

12. William James, *The Varieties of Religious Experience: A Study in Human Nature* (Scribere Semper et Legere, 2021), 380–81.

13. James, *Varieties of Religious Experience*, 381.

impart a sense of deep universal truth and considerably impact the individual going forward.

When viewing the writings of well-known mystics from various traditions, such as Rumi, Julian of Norwich, Saint Hildegard of Bingen, Milarepa, Chaitanya Mahaprabhu, Lao Tzu, Sri Ramakrishna, and Mirabai, they all speak about the Divine in language of deep longing and love. Experiencing divinity directly is likened to the bliss state of the peak of sexual orgasm: momentary, ecstatic, blissful, and deeply impactful. Following the peak there is a pause, and as contemporary mystic Mirabai Starr puts it, "ecstasy empties into stillness."[14] That stillness is the moment of peace where individual consciousness dissolves. Anyone who has experienced that peak of orgasm or that truly intimate place of connection with someone else has probably experienced that state of no self, where for the briefest of moments there is no individuality. This feeling of union is at the heart of and is the prolonged goal of the mystical experience.

Mystic traditions have often centered on extreme ritual, prayer, and contemplation—pushing the body to extremes as a way of gaining mastery over it to focus and direct one's attention away from momentary and fleeting needs of comfort or discomfort. This is sometimes attained through sleep deprivation, prolonged repetition of prayer, denial of comforts, breathwork, and meditation techniques. There are traditions that have also included the use of psychotropic substances to enter altered states of consciousness. The *sadhus* of India, for example, spend their lives devoted to the cause of spiritual liberation through extreme ascetic practices and self-denial and routinely smoke cannabis. Other plant medicines such as ayahuasca, peyote, or psilocybin mushrooms have been used for similar purposes. Altered states of consciousness, whether from extreme practices or partaking of substances, are believed to lead to the experience of dissolution of personal ego and states of bliss. These experiences challenge the concept of Self that we routinely exist within in everyday life.

If we consider what we believe to be essential qualities of self, what implications does the mystical worldview have on how we perceive the state of

---

14. Mirabai Starr, *Wild Mercy: Living the Fierce and Tender Wisdom of the Women Mystics* (Boulder, CO: Sounds True, 2019), 41.

the dead? If we are all on journeys to join in personal union or become one with the Divine, how might this impact our view of the state of the soul in an afterlife?

Soul Multiplicity: Spirit Formed by Multiple Aspects

Next to the concept of an individuated soul, there are many historical and contemporary traditions that see the essential self as being made up of various parts. Essentially, the belief speaks to a person's identity and sense of self as being composed of multiple parts instead of a single component. Those multiple parts are all required to recognize someone as a complete person.

This conception of personhood is best exemplified through the ancient Egyptian conception of the self. The ancient Egyptians are well known for their funerary traditions, such as mummification and the building of pyramids. The funerary traditions of the culture were varied, as Egyptian religion was a series of cults centered at sites spanning their territory. In some Egyptian beliefs, an individual was made up of, depending upon the era, as many as nine integrated components. These component aspects came together at birth and after death either disappeared or continued to perform a function for the individual.[15] Some of the components that appeared over time were the physical body, the spiritual body, the heart, the vital essence, the personality, the shadow, the form, the personal name, and the intellect.

According to this view, each of these various components have interdependent relationships with each other. For example, the physical body was required so that the spiritual body would have form; the heart was needed as a repository of thought, will, intention, and emotion; and the personality is what would go on in the afterlife existing much as it did in life. Mortuary temples were essential technologies to guarantee the continued existence of the various parts of the body so that the individual could continue into an immortal existence, which was jeopardized if any of these parts were lost. One reason why mummification and preservation of the body was so important was the belief that the personality in the underworld still required a physical body in the world to continue to exist.

---

15. Clifton D. Bryant and Dennis L. Peck, eds., *Encyclopedia of Death and the Human Experience* (London: SAGE, 2009), 399.

The vital essence (*ka*) and the personality (*ba*) interacted with each other in the afterlife, but the ba (which was often depicted as a human-headed bird) flew back to interact with the living and take up offerings and prayers left at the tomb. In this worldview, death was not a one-directional state. Personhood was not dependent upon any one part of self, but all components were important. The fear of many Egyptians in certain periods was that their heart might be devoured by the crocodile-headed being Ammit in the Hall of Truth, a space in some versions of the Egyptian underworld.

While the Egyptian example is one of the most elaborate forms of this view of the self, comparable views exist both historically and contemporarily. In Chinese traditions connected to Daoism, the spirit of an individual is composed of two types of souls called *hun* and *po*, which are both connected to the *yin* and *yang* dualism of the universal order. Upon death, hun spirits ascend to the spirit world while po spirits remain tied to the body. Every individual is believed to have a number of hun and po souls within their body, the exact number dependent upon the specific tradition or time period.

The concept of multiplicity begs some interesting questions related to how we view self. Even in the Western modern sense, we see self as being composed of three parts: the body, mind, and spirit. The Egyptians developed a complex system of working with their dead, supplying each of the various components with their needs so that the individual would continue to survive in the afterlife. What implications might a view of self like this have in working with the dead? In some contemporary spiritual reconstructionist and New Age traditions that have introduced reincarnation into their worldviews, there are some who are proposing a multiplicity of self as a way of reconciling an afterlife with reincarnation, most notably the idea that there is a part of the soul that remains in an afterlife state while another part of the soul reincarnates. What would the implications be for working with the dead if you yourself believe in both an afterlife and reincarnation on earth?

Spirit as Divine Double

There are traditions in the world that state that a person has both an earthly form and simultaneously a higher self, a divine double that exists in the spiritual realms.[16] This is different from traditions where the spirit is incarnate and embodied, as this higher self is a more expansive part of us that has access to a wider field of vision but is remote or cut off from this plane. Communication between our earthly and celestial selves can be attained through divination, omens, or intuition. The belief in some of these traditions is that while we exist here on earth, our temporal selves are in contact with this celestial or spiritually higher self. In this worldview, the spiritual double acts as a guardian or guide for their earthly counterpart, capable of interceding with other spiritual beings or directly impacting the life of the earthly counterpart. For many readers coming from a New Age or Pagan background, this concept will not be new, as it has been within these two traditions for a long time, and writers like Deepak Chopra and Carl Jung have much to say on it. But you may find it surprising to know how ancient this concept actually is.

In orisha traditions, which have their roots among the Yoruba of West Africa and continue among the diaspora communities, there exists the concept of the *ori*, a celestial double that dwells in the heavenly realm of *orun* (named in the Lukumi tradition). I was taught that the ori is created by the supreme deity, and its job is to negotiate a blueprint of our earthly lives with the divine regent, Olofin. This blueprint of our life on earth outlines the healthiest and most content life path for us. I was taught that the ori, which translates to "head" but which has deeper implications, is both present with us on earth and in Orun. In Lukumi theology, I was taught that the world is seen as a marketplace, a place of both danger and opportunity. While on earth we might theoretically live a perfect life, but a more realistic outcome is that we are compelled to negotiate, compromise, haggle, and trade due to situations and life experiences. Because of this, the blueprint formed by the ori before we are born is not perfectly realized. At the end of a person's life, their ori, Olofin, and the earthly form of the individual engage in a life review of how closely we realized that preplanned blueprint.

---

16. Specific traditions include: Theosophy, Spiritualism, many African Traditional Religions (particularly orisha traditions), and some forms of Espiritismo (influenced by Lukumi).

Every action and reaction are carefully considered, and judgment is passed based on how closely we align with the plan. To mitigate the potential damage that misalignment from the ori can hold, the tradition offers all manner of counterbalances: spiritual readings with the orisha, cleansings, ancestor work, offerings and sacrifices to orisha, and ceremonies specifically geared toward ori. One of the most powerful avenues of realigning someone to their ori is the process of initiation (in Lukumi this is called crowning), where an individual discovers the identity of their tutelary orisha, literally the keeper of their head, and through that process enters a lifelong partnership with that orisha. This orisha is the one who can best assist the individual with staying in close alignment with their ori and reaching a place of contentment and health in life.

This view that there might be a divine double—an aspect of self that exists within the higher realms with a much broader view of reality—is not confined to Yoruba traditions, and traces of this view can be found in various ancient cultures from around the Mediterranean, Near East, and South Asia. Dr. Charles M. Stang of Harvard Divinity School produced a fascinating study of the divine double in ancient Greco-Roman and Gnostic traditions, which suggests that the belief in the divine double existing on earth was prolific, and that it is our destiny to one day meet this twin.[17] What are the implications of seeing self in this way? How might personhood extend to higher realms, and what implications does that have for physical death? How might understanding ourselves in this way affect how we navigate our lives?

Soulless Traditions

In contrast to the above worldviews, there are traditions that essentially posit a no-self or nonessential aspect. Within these traditions, there is no immortal, essential aspect of self that carries on, and part of the spiritual journey is, ironically, to realize this. Buddhism is the ultimate example of this, but other traditions have popped up in world history that took on this view as well (particularly the Greek philosophical school of Pyrrho). The reader might be asking themselves how a spiritual tradition can essentially put forward a worldview where there is no self, and the answer really lies in the details.

---

17. Charles M. Stang, *Our Divine Double* (Cambridge, MA: Harvard University Press, 2016), n.p.

The Buddhist concept of "no soul" (Sanskrit: *anatman*, Pali: *anatta*) has been contested even within Buddhism over the millennia and is difficult at times for Westerners to grapple with. Whereas in Hinduism there is the belief in an essential soul with multitudes of personalities lain over it from life to life, Buddhism suggests that what we think is a self is merely a coagulation of ultimately transient and impermanent attributes that are finite. For example, a candle flame is a series of chemical interactions that produce light, heat, and plasma, which when extinguished cease to be a flame. The flame exists for a time and then disappears when its constituent components cease interacting. So, like a candle flame, Buddhism suggests that what we call the soul is formed by the interaction of various components that by themselves do not constitute a self.

The delusion of self leads us to cling to the material world—which Buddhists see as the cause of all suffering—instead of work toward understanding the nature of reality and minimizing the karmic interactions that lock us into cycles of rebirth. The Buddhist spiritual goal of Nirvana isn't to not exist, but to realize that there is no essential self to begin with. When working with the dead and all beings, Buddhists pray for and work toward the upliftment of all beings, that they may eventually find themselves in a place where they can realize the impermanent nature of reality and find peace in that realization.

Buddhism stands in contrast to the various other South Asian traditions it evolved around, such as Jainism and Upanishadic Hinduism. The dominant philosophies of Hinduism and Jainism both teach the existence of an immortal, essential self, while Buddhism teaches there is no essential self. While it may seem a nihilistic tradition to Western eyes, the reality of Buddhism is complex, and there has been historical disagreement within the tradition on what exactly the teaching of "no self" means.

Journal Prompts

- How do you view personhood? What defines a person?

- What are your thoughts on the nature of the soul? What does it mean to be alive?

- Do you have a sense of a higher self? What qualities define that higher self?

- How might recognizing personhood in nonhumans affect your relationship to them?

- In what ways are you a reflection of the Divine? Is the Divine reflected in the world, and if so, in what ways?

- How does your use of language affect your beliefs or worldview? How is it informed by your beliefs?

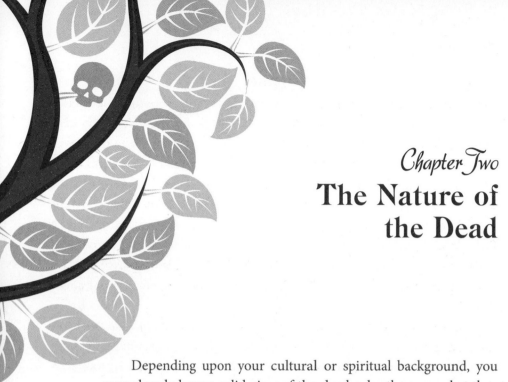

Chapter Two

The Nature of
the Dead

Depending upon your cultural or spiritual background, you may already have a solid view of the dead: who they are, what they do, and where they dwell. The question of personhood brought up in the previous chapter leads us into the question of death and the dead, because death is often seen as a transformative experience. In most cultures, the process of death transforms individuals into something else, and this affects their status of personhood. For some, death means a diminishment, while for others it means an expansion into a much larger form of self. I'd like to discuss three interrelated beliefs: prelife, afterlife, and reincarnation, and explore how these different forms of existence or processes affect how we can relate to and connect with ancestors.

As we move through the material in this chapter, keep in mind that the goal is not to accept any of these worldviews but to reflect on your own viewpoint. Ask yourself how those beliefs color your relationship to the world of spirits and the dead. Keep these insights in mind as we move into the sections about building a veneration practice, and consider how your underlying beliefs will impact your practice and approach to developing a relationship to your ancestors.

Prelife

While I was preparing to write this book, Disney's Pixar outdid themselves again and came out with a gorgeous movie called *Soul* (2020). The story centers on Joe Gardner, a middle school teacher from New York who dreams of being a professional jazz musician. Joe decides to take a chance and auditions for a show, gaining a gig in the band of a local legend. As he leaves the audition, he falls down a manhole and finds himself plummeting toward the afterlife, only instead of dying, he is redirected to the Great Before. The Great Before is a place souls exist before life on earth, where they take on personalities and talents before living. In the movie, Joe is accidentally assigned to a new soul named 22 to mentor as they choose who to become in their soon-to-be life.

While the details of *Soul*'s cosmology are written to fit with the story, the underlying idea of a before-life as well as an afterlife is grounded in many world traditions, as is the concept of being mentored or guided. In some traditions there are spaces between life and final death, spaces between reincarnations, and spaces of prelife where the eternal spirit can take time to pause and reflect on the lessons learned or yet to be learned. Depending upon the tradition, the nature of prelife spaces differs. Some traditions view the prelife setting as an in-between space where souls rest for a while before taking on a new body via reincarnation, while other traditions see the space as the origin point of souls where they plan out their coming lives on earth. Based on my studies, I've identified three broad categories of where different traditions seem to fit on this issue of a before-life:

- Traditions where souls exist before life, particularly in reincarnation-based traditions or in religions such as Mormonism where all souls were created at the beginning of the universe and wait for a corporeal body to house them.
- Traditions where the soul is created and delivered upon conception or birth.
- Traditions where the soul or parts of the soul are given at a point within life, such as in the Egyptian example in chapter one. Other examples here include various animistic traditions where rites of passage are also

times when aspects of personhood are attained through rites such as naming ceremonies, vision quests, confirmations, and initiations.

In traditions where the soul exists before life, we can see concepts of preparing or creating a plan for the life to come, such as we previously discussed in Lukumi and the journey of the ori, or as exemplified by the plot of Pixar's *Soul*. Traditions that espouse reincarnation often see this before-life state of existence as a space to work through traumas from the previous life and prepare for the coming one. A good example is the Summerland, an afterlife espoused by some Neopagan traditions, which acts like the Tibetan Buddhist *bardo* state and is envisioned as a place of rest and reflection between lives.

Traditions where the soul is delivered to or created in the body upon conception or birth may disagree at times on exactly when a soul is created, but the relationship between personhood and physical body is an interesting one. In early Christianity, the church father Origen suggested that souls were created prior to conception and birth, but this concept was condemned as heresy by one of the church councils, and so now most Christian denominations reject preexistence.[18] In Islam it is taught that all souls were created in adult form at the same time as the first man, Adam, and exist before life, waiting to be born. The soul is delivered to the body at birth by God and develops into a living human.[19]

As was discussed in the previous chapter, those traditions that see a soul as a multiplicity of parts may view certain parts as preexisting while others are formed at birth. For example, concepts of Norse and Egyptian personhood speak of multiple components of the person joining, such as the name and the shadow when one is born or goes through another rite of passage. Interpretations of Native American "vision quests," various forms of naming ceremonies, and other rites of passage from around the world could be read as pieces of personhood being added after physical birth.[20] Indeed, initiations

---

18. Lindsay Jones, Mircea Eliade, and Charles J. Adams, "Soul," in *Encyclopedia of Religion*, 2nd ed., vol. 2 (Detroit, MI: Macmillan Reference USA, 2005), 8563.

19. Jones, Eliade, and Adams, "Soul," 8567.

20. Suzanne J. Crawford and Dennis F. Kelley, *American Indian Religious Traditions: An Encyclopedia*, vol. 3 (Santa Barbara, CA: ABC-CLIO, 2005), 1128.

of many kinds are often thought of as rebirthing ceremonies, where the individual is reborn into their new state of being after the initiation is completed. For example, consider the popular language used around baptism in Christianity, of being "born again." Initiation often has connotations of a death and rebirth, where part of an individual dies to give rise to a new individual.

Between Life and Death

In some traditions, there is a time between life and death when the individual is still tied to their body but is not considered fully alive. This state might be in the time between physical death and the funeral or for a period where the spirit lingers until moving on to their next life. In such traditions, no matter how decomposed the body may be, the etiquette of the culture is for the individual to still be treated as if alive in some way. Among Tibetans and Mongolians (and other cultures associated with Vajrayana Buddhism) the spirits of the dead are often believed to remain for forty-nine days in their bodies until certain rites are performed, and then the physical body is removed and delivered to the burial grounds. These rites include being read to from the *Bardo Thödol*, the *Tibetan Book of the Dead*. Instructions on what the deceased can expect in this in-between time before reincarnation are read, as well as practical guidance on how to move into a better life or seek liberation.[21] The body is washed and swaddled in a white funerary cloth, then is removed and disposed of. Only after the completion of the funerary ritual is the individual considered free of this life and dead.

Likewise, due to religious and cultural beliefs, the Torajan people of Indonesia's South Sulawesi region keep the bodies of dead loved ones at home in bed until it is possible to perform a lavish funeral, and the bodies are often treated as if they are sleeping or ill but very much alive. These elaborate funerals can sometimes take up to twenty years to occur, as the family must raise enough money to put on a spectacle, especially if the deceased was a notable member of society. In the intervening time, the body of the deceased stays in the home with the family and is treated as if they were alive. A

---

21. Bryant and Peck, eds., *Encyclopedia of Death and the Human Experience*, 952; Hiroaki Mori, Yukari Hayashi, Barrie McLean, *The Tibetan Book of the Dead: The Great Liberation*, National Film Board of Canada, 1994, 45 min., https://www.nfb.ca/film/tibetan_book_of _the_dead_the_great_liberation/.

householder might say to their family, "Grandfather is ill today. Don't disturb him; he needs his sleep," or when seeing food offerings left uneaten, might say, "Grandfather must not have liked today's meal." The Torajan people are Christians, having been converted in the last century, but a sizeable number remain connected with their indigenous faith called Aluk To Dolo.[22] In Torajan tradition, the dead dwell in necropolises located close enough to the village to be visited but far enough away that the boundary between life and death is respected. The bodies are preserved and routinely taken care of, often also represented by elaborate carvings, which sit together and are visited frequently by the living. There is a specific moment in funeral services when the individual transitions from being alive to being dead.[23] Despite the nominal acceptance of Christianity, indigenous traditions thrive and form an important part of how the Torajans negotiate with death.

Afterlife

The most widespread belief is that after the physical process of death, part of a human transitions into an afterlife stage or place. Even those traditions that espouse reincarnation often have spaces between lives where the spirit might dwell for a time. The state of being dead is often conflated with what we believe the dead do and where they dwell. In quite a few worldviews, the final dwelling places inform us of the moral character of the deceased, as well as what existence they experience now. A very good example of this is in Christian and Islamic theology, which teaches that good people go to heaven or paradise, while bad people go to hell.

When I was five years old, my Grandma Poplar died. I had been closer to her than my grandmother Stimpson and had spent several weeks living with her and my grandfather the previous summer. As a five-year-old, the concept of death was alien to me, and I remember I kept asking, "But where has Grandma gone?" My parents and older siblings kept saying, "She's gone somewhere better," "She's gone away for a while," and "She needed to go away."

---

22. Kathleen M. Adams, "Club Dead, Not Club Med: Staging Death in Contemporary Tana Toraja (Indonesia)," *Southeast Asian Journal of Social Science* 21, no. 2 (1993): 62–72, http://dx.doi.org/10.1163/030382493X00116.

23. "The Fascinating Death Ritual of the Toraja People | SLICE," SLICE, YouTube video, 25:25, August 21, 2022, https://www.youtube.com/watch?v=EuN5W6_jQK8.

Explaining death to a five-year-old is a difficult task in and of itself, but these answers cemented for me an idea that to die was to go somewhere else.

There are roughly four major worldviews I have been able to uncover that speak to where the dead are believed to go after death, chiefly: below the earth (underworld) or in the sky (heaven); in the same physical space as humans; a particular known location in the landscape; and some remote space completely inaccessible to the living.

Where do you believe the dead go after death? This may seem pedantic, but as we will see with ancestor veneration later in the book, where you believe the dead exist and what you believe their existences are like impacts how you interact with them in a substantive way, both through ritual and even in how you conceptualize them. Likewise, what kind of existence we believe the dead have impacts how we access them and what we believe their needs are. For example, if you believe that the dead dwell in the earth, then it doesn't make sense to place offerings up high. If the dead dwell in an inaccessible afterlife, then communication with them may be through divination or by proxy. If you believe that the dead can hear you at specific places, such as their graves, then that underlying assumption can be utilized for your practice. For example, the Chinese believe that the dead are in a spirit world and so burn offerings, as fire is seen as translating the offering into spirit, whereas many African traditions see the dead as dwelling in the earth, and so offerings are placed onto the ground or buried so they can be accessed.

Identification of the dead with physical locations in the landscape, which act as either a gateway to or the permanent dwelling place of the dead, is a universal belief found on all inhabited continents. These physical spaces become part of funerary and ancestral ritual and often become taboo to visit outside of ritual settings. In 1960, Roberto Bosi wrote about groups of Sámi in Northern Scandinavia taking their dead to isolated islets on frozen lakes and abandoning them. The belief was that the water surrounding the island prevented the deceased spirit from returning to camp and potentially harming the living. The Sámi in these regions called their ancestors the *saivo-olmak* ("happy men"), who sit in judgment over new arrivals and decide whether they should be allowed to join the ranks of the ancestors.[24] This belief by the Sámi that

---

24. Roberto Bosi, *The Lapps*, trans. James Cadell (Westport, CT: Greenwood Press, 1976), 137.

the dead are connected to features in the landscape is shared by many, even secular Westerners. Church graveyards in urban and rural settings are places of the dead, and we have an abundance of ritual, folklore, and custom around these spaces.

Sometimes traditions had a bleak and unappetizing view of the afterlife. In the Greek religion, the afterlife was a place of endless shadow. After paying the ferryman Charon to take you across the underworld river Styx, the dead drank of waters that relieved them of their memories. The dead were then sent to different parts of the underworld based on the experience of their lives on earth. The vast majority went to the Asphodel Fields, dwelling place of the completely unremarkable. Tartarus was the place of punishment for the truly wicked, and many stories in mythology recount the punishments meted out to those dwelling there. The Elysian Fields were a paradisial place, but only a very select few were sent there.

These places are not analogous to Christian conceptions of heaven and hell. To the ancient Greeks, existence in the underworld was meaningless, and so emphasis on life on earth was more important. This is one reason why in the golden age of Greece (around 500 BCE) salvation cults such as the Eleusinian Mysteries, Orphic Mysteries, and the Dionysian Mysteries had such a wide appeal. Likewise, in the Roman era after 146 BCE, when mainland Greece became a protectorate of Rome and the region later became integrated as provinces, the Eastern Mystery cults of the Egyptian goddess Isis, Persian god Mithras, and eventually also Christianity appealed and proliferated. The Greeks were not the only ones to hold such a bleak view; many ancient cultures saw existence in death as a bleak prospect. The Norse conceptualized the realm of the dead as cold and barren unless you were one of the lucky few to be chosen to feast in Odin's hall, Valhalla. In the Middle East, the story of the goddess Inanna's descent into the underworld paints a vivid image of a bleak cavern where the only sustenance is dust.

Conceptions of the afterlife vary too greatly to do them all justice in this small volume, but they tell us a great deal about how cultures and individuals view themselves. What we hope for in an existence outside the bounds of corporeal life informs us of what is important to us. Even cultures that see an afterlife as bleak inform us that the cultures value experiencing life. Consider for yourself how you see the afterlife and what that tells you of your desires and needs.

Reincarnation versus Singular Lives

There are two major views connected to death present in the world, sometimes even interacting with each other—namely, the belief in reincarnation and the belief that we have a singular existence. In my spiritual communities, both views are prevalent and cause a great deal of debate about how they might be reconciled with each other. The very basic belief of reincarnation is that an individual's essence is reborn in a new body in what is called transmigration or metempsychosis. While at the outset this concept might seem to contradict or nullify the idea of a set of dead ancestors who exist somewhere and are accessible in an afterlife, as has been stated, there are individuals and traditions who reconcile both views.

One interesting view that I have seen emerging in Neopaganism and being spoken about by writers such as Starhawk is the simultaneous belief in both reincarnation and an afterlife. In this view, different layers of a person simultaneously exist in an afterlife and others are reincarnated on earth.[25] If we were to expand on this further, how it might look is that the personality formed during a lifetime exists in an afterlife while a different level of the soul is reborn to animate a new body and experience life as a new personality. The personality of previous incarnations is tied to their families as ancestors, while the soul is freed to continue a spiritual journey. I have heard some who espouse this viewpoint say that at the end of a soul's journey, all the previous personalities and lives are reintegrated. This view sees the essential Self as multidimensional and not bound by the linear rules of our corporeal world.

This view of multiple layers of soul opens up the opportunity for another interesting take I have seen being asked and talked about by community members in several of the spiritual spheres I operate in—that we can, through reincarnation, be our own ancestors due to having lived a life as them. This raises some interesting questions on the nature of self and questions of how we would work with our previous selves through ancestor ven-

---

25. Starhawk, M. Macha NightMare, and the Reclaiming Collective, *The Pagan Book of Living and Dying* (New York: HarperCollins, 2013), 157.

eration practices. For example, if I am the reincarnation of my own great-great-grandmother and that information was proven somehow, then what if through my ancestral practice I connect with her and interact with her? What am I interacting with if I'm living now? What I think might happen in that case is that my persona in this life is connecting with her persona, while our shared common soul is present in the here and now.

This might sound strange and very meta, but there are hints of such a view historically in older cultures. For example, the Norse had a concept and part of the soul called the *hamingja*, often described as appearing in visions as a womanly spectral figure. The *hamingja* was both an essential part of self but also seemingly independent of an individual. It was essentially a power connected to valor and manifested in victory and battle. When a Norse warrior died, as spoken of in Norse literature, the dead warrior's *hamingja* sought a new body to "follow."[26] There has been a long debate as to whether this constituted transmigration of souls as understood in the Eastern religious sense, but rebirth of parts of self in newer generations seems to be the case. To ensure that the hamingja of a certain warrior would "follow" a descendant, the full name or aspects of it would be given to newborns in the hope that certain traits of the ancestor would be reborn. This tendency seems to have been only after someone had died, as giving a person's name while they still lived did not seem to happen. In this way, parts of the previous individual could be reborn in some form, and the newborn would be anchored into the family unit.[27]

If your worldview does not include both singular lives and reincarnation, this issue is a moot point. If your worldview does include both in some way, whether because of the tradition you follow or because the belief resonates with you, then this raises some interesting questions about how you might navigate between the two in developing an ancestral practice.

What the Dead Do

I have noticed that when reading about the beliefs of the dead, the identity of the dead is heavily connected with where they dwell and what they do there. Consider how you conceptualize the dead: is it based on what you think they're

---

26. H. R. Ellis Davidson, *The Road to Hel; A Study of the Conception of the Dead in Old Norse Literature* (New York: Greenwood Press, 1968), 132.

27. Davidson, *The Road to Hel*, 146.

doing wherever they are? I think part of the identification of dead individuals with the state of being dead is the living trying to grapple with questions about what our futures as dead people will be. As mentioned previously, some afterlifes are shadowy and vague places, while others are worlds very similar to our own. Whether death is a shadowy place of rest or we wake up in an expanded world much like our own is ultimately something we will all find out one day. However, different traditions have developed different ideas about this afterlife state and have extrapolated ideas about the dead because of it.

Identifying the dwelling place of the dead with morality as a defining feature is very familiar to the majority of the world, as the afterlife is often determined on moral character in most of the world's largest traditions (Christianity, Judaism, Islam, etc.). This is a very old concept and can be found in both ancient and contemporary religious belief. Whether you are good or bad in life determines whether you are rewarded or punished after death. However, what is considered good or bad in various cultural contexts has meant anything from being honorable, nonattached, nonviolent, or in harmony with the world.

To the ancient Norse, a seat in the god Odin's hall of Valhalla was afforded to the bravest and most honorable who died in glorious battle, while most regular people could only look forward to a somber and cold existence in the goddess Hel's hall in Niflheim.[28] Being morally good was connected to individual strength and glory rather than righteousness of character.[29] To the ancient Egyptians, on the other hand, being a good person was having a heart unweighted with the sin of going against divine order, and if judged to have a heart lighter than the feather of Ma'at, an individual would be rewarded with a perpetual existence in a place much like their own home on earth. But if they were considered to have a heart weighed down by sin, they would be cast into the jaws of the monstrous Ammit, and their existence would end completely.[30] To the dharmic traditions, which espouse reincarnation, the circumstance of the next life is determined by your actions in this

---

28. John Lindow, *Norse Mythology: A Guide to the Gods, Heroes, Rituals, and Beliefs* (New York: Oxford University Press, 2002), 172.

29. Sveinbjorn Johnson, "Old Norse and Ancient Greek Ideals," *Ethics* 49, no. 1 (October 1938): 18–36, https://www.jstor.org/stable/2988773.

30. Obayashi, ed., *Death and Afterlife*, 43.

one. The concepts of karma and dharma interact to determine some of the circumstances and contexts you will be born into. Even within these traditions, there are potential lives incarnated in planes of paradise as gods or torment as demons. If you visit a Sri Lankan Buddhist temple, for example, the various hell planes you might find yourself in for certain immoral actions are vividly painted on the walls for all to see.

Quite separate from a moral approach to identifying the dead's state of experience in the spirit world is the approach that the living continue to improve and keep up the existence of the dead through continual offerings and veneration rituals. In Chinese tradition, and by extension many other Southeast Asian traditions, the spirit world is viewed as a place much like our own, and the needs of the dead are similar to our own. In this worldview, goods from our world can be sent as offerings to the world of the dead for their immediate use. A widespread practice is the burning of paper money, the belief being that the flame will transport the money into the spirit realm and make it accessible to the ancestors. This belief has led to an entire industry of paper goods for gifts to the ancestors. Paper clothing, appliances, houses, even cars have been created for families to offer to and appease the dead.[31] In this cultural worldview, the realm of the living and dead are separate but not inaccessible to each other, and both living and dead rely on each other. This worldview is widely dispersed and can be found on all inhabited continents, even buried in morality-focused traditions.

Keeping in mind cosmological rules of every being in their proper place, a widespread approach to defining the dead is to qualify their relationships as transactional and service based. This is where questions of ancestor veneration come into play, as many traditions that work with ancestors see the dead as very capable, if appeased, to intercede on behalf of the living in the cosmological order. Take for example the Chinese grandfather offered a car for his use in the spirit world. This form of offering is not just for use by a beloved grandfather but is understood as creating the opportunity for reciprocal benefits to the living. By appeasing Grandfather with the gift of a new car, he may look favorably on his living descendants and use his powers of

---

31. Paul Williams and Patrice Ladwig, eds., *Buddhist Funeral Cultures of Southeast Asia and China* (Cambridge, UK: Cambridge University Press, 2012), n.p.

influence positively as opposed to becoming bitter and lashing out. The relationship between offering, appeasement, and blessings is strongly tied to ancestor veneration traditions worldwide.

Hazards to the Dead

As the dead are identified with their resting places, in most traditions there are beliefs about what could potentially jeopardize that continued existence. These hazards impact the continuation of the dead in one form or another, possibly leading them to forgetting their humanity and lashing out at the living. Transformation of dead humans into "other" is a recurring theme throughout the world's lore around ghosts, monsters, and evil spirits. Below are some of the major hazards I have noticed in my studies and ones that are addressed in disparate traditions.

- **Violating the boundary between life and death:** Even in traditions where the dead communicate often with the living through divination, spirit possession, or necromancy, a recurring theme throughout world traditions is the expectation that every being is expected to be in their cosmologically defined spaces. Breaking these cosmological rules, as defined by each cultural context, creates fear and potentially misfortune and disease. All cultures have stories involving ghosts and spirits that haunt places in the world, causing mischief or direct harm. When dead spirits violate the spaces of the living, there are many stories of ghosts transforming into monsters who are no longer considered human, which makes them even sadder and more dangerous. Humans have developed several ways to protect themselves from the restless dead and to assist those dead spirits with moving where they need to be. Ensuring that proper burial rites are performed, tending to any unfinished business, continuing to honor through rituals of ancestor veneration, and using magical wards and spells to protect are just a few of these measures. Indeed, not receiving the last rites or having proper funerary rituals enacted make up a great deal of the reasons why dead spirits come back to haunt us in most ghost stories.
- **Being forgotten:** One of the major apprehensions in quite a few traditions is losing our personal identity and being forgotten. Unfortunately,

it is a reality that all of us will eventually pass out of living memory, and most of us will be forgotten. In the Pixar movie *Coco*, this eventuality is one of the major plot points. To counteract being forgotten, elaborate ways of detailing genealogy and remembering the dead are employed in prayer, record, and memorials around the world. In some other traditions it is a given that an individual will be forgotten and their identity subsumed into the collective identity of ancestors, and so elaborate ritual is employed to help the individual transition to this further stage of death. In Haitian Vodou, there is an entire grouping of spirits called the Gede Lwa, which is composed of those forgotten dead who are honored as a collective. In some lineages of Haitian Vodou, the belief is that to some degree all people become Lwa when they die, and many of the more powerful Lwa in the pantheon lived lives on earth. Like many African spiritual traditions, it is important for the family in Haitian Vodou to honor their ancestors to keep the spirits healthy through ancestral veneration. But what happens to those spirits who no longer have living relatives to remember them or carry out the rites? These spirits of the dead are gathered by two specific Lwa (Baron Samedi and his wife Manman Brijit) and become part of the collective Gede who are communally honored through the entire month of November during *Fèt Gede*.[32] In some traditions, the apprehension of being forgotten is not that the dead will disappear, but that instead the dead will become uncontrollable because they no longer have living connections to stabilize them or their needs are no longer being met by living relatives. Then they lash out, seeking that service.

- **Transformation into ghosts:** A similar uncanny tale of the deceased turning into ghosts—those earthbound spirits who haunt a place or a person—is found throughout the world. Often, certain types of deaths, incomplete rites, or unfinished business will doom an individual to be transformed into a monster or trapped on earth. Violent and unnatural deaths are often blamed for the existence of certain types of ghosts, as is dying in moments that normally should be moments of life. For example, we see stories of women who die in childbirth turning into vicious

---

32. Mambo Chita Tann, "The Gede Lwa," in *Haitian Vodou: An Introduction to Haiti's Indigenous Spiritual Traditions* (Woodbury, Mn: Llewellyn Publications, 2012), 154.

and monstrous spirits who attack and lash out in their grief. It should be noted that transformation into monstrous spirits by women points to the inherent patriarchal and misogynistic nature of many of the world's cultures. What the society sees as dangerous are often the parts that the society tries to control. This is also why we often see types of ghosts and monsters connected to executed individuals, or the reports of hauntings of sites of execution. To prevent the potential for ghosts or monsters to be created, many cultures have developed spells, wards, or rites to safeguard both the community and the individual from being transformed and returning to do harm.

- **Evoking and speaking of the dead:** In some cultures, certain taboos or etiquette of referring to the dead are employed so as not to disturb them unnecessarily. In Lukumi, when speaking of the dead, we utter the word *ibae* after their name out of respect and to not incur their wrath. Among Indigenous Australian cultures, it is taboo to see a picture or utter the name of a deceased person, and it is common on Australian television to see content warnings before broadcasts warning viewers. We see this belief of not invoking the dead through specific ritual practice among the Sámi of northern Scandinavia, who despite living in a landscape where the northern lights are frequently visible, do not often sing about them. One proposed explanation is that some Sámi view the aurora borealis as being the place of or connected to the ancestors and either will not sing or do not see a need to sing of the phenomenon.[33] However, it should be noted that even within cultures, traditions around disturbing the dead are not set in stone, and there are variances of opinion. Other communities of Sámi, for example, see *joiking* about the dead differently, as evidenced by contemporary Sámi singer Jon Henrik Fjällgren winning *Sweden's Got Talent* in 2014 with a *joik* to his deceased friend Daniel. Names are powerful, and in every culture, we find custom and superstition to avoid needlessly calling the attention of the dead or disturbing their rest.

---

33. Stéphane Aubinet, "The Craft of Yoiking: Philosophical Variations on Sámi Chants" (master's thesis, University of Oslo, 2020), 151, https://www.duo.uio.no/bitstream/handle /10852/77489/PhD-Aubinet-2020.pdf?sequence=1&isAllowed=y.

Journal Prompts

- What feelings came up for you as you read this chapter? Were there any parts that made you uncomfortable? Lean in; what made you uncomfortable about those parts?

- Were there any parts of this chapter or the previous one that intrigued you? What were they?

- Do you have any traits that members of your family have said you share with an ancestor? How does that make you feel?

- How does the concept of prelife figure into your life? If you believe in prelife, how does that impact your life and death experiences?

- Do you believe in having come to earth with a mission or plan? If so, what do you think was your reason for coming to earth?

- In your worldview, where do the dead dwell? Is it a place? What does it look like?

- What feelings come up for you when thinking about the afterlife?

- In your worldview, are the dead static to who they were on earth, or are they capable of change? In what ways are they capable of change?

- Do you believe the dead can impact our lives? If you do, in what ways?

- In what ways do you believe the dead are potentially dangerous to us?

- How do you feel about being forgotten eventually?

- How do you feel about having unfinished business after you die?

- What are customs or superstitions you were taught to respect the dead? How do these customs shape how you view the dead?

Chapter Three
Who Are the
Ancestors?

In the previous chapters, we explored the question of personhood and how that relates to the dead as a category of being. We now turn our attention to the identities and roles of the ancestors, and to exploring what can constitute an ancestor.

I would like you to keep in mind some questions as we move through the following material: What differentiates an ancestor from just another dead individual? What special relationships and responsibilities define an ancestor from a non-ancestor? How do we react to ancestors over other dead or incorporeal beings? Can you treat other beings and parts of the world as ancestor? What can relationships with non-blood relatives look like, and how does that affect this sort of work? In this chapter we are going to explore the boundaries of how *ancestor* is commonly defined.

The ancestors are an interesting group to think about because they are unique to individuals while also connected to vast numbers of the living. Only siblings share the same group of blood ancestors, while individual ancestors are connected to a multitude of living people. Indeed, there are two individuals from a very long time ago (mitochondrial Eve and Y-chromosomal Adam) who are literally related to all humans currently living. That is a lot of descendants to watch over!

While it would be easy to just say, "Ancestors are our dead blood relatives," in my own ancestral journey, I've found this is too simple of an answer.

In my opinion and experience, *ancestor* is defined through the lens of relationship, but that word offers us a vast spectrum of potential relationships with an equally large spectrum of candidates. Unlike the dead, who are a whole category of being, I would contend that an ancestor has a direct connection to our development in some way. And as I grow into my own practice, I'm seeing that those connections transcend the purely biological.

Over the next two chapters, I'd like to discuss various forms of ancestor and how these forms, whether beings or concepts, can impact our spiritual lives. I would like the reader when reviewing this section to always ask themselves how they feel about each of the pieces discussed, and how their own cultural background has prepared them to see each of the following. While presenting these different points of consideration, I encourage readers to focus on types of relationship. How might a similar type of relationship with different beings impact how you define those beings in your practice? I think this becomes a very relevant way of viewing who you include in your ancestor veneration if you choose to expand the definition to include non-blood-related individuals. As always, the impetus is on the individual reader to answer for themselves what they consider ancestor to mean for them, and who or what will be included in that work.

Blood Relatives

Blood relatives are those individuals we are related to genetically through birth. This might seem like a straightforward form of ancestor, but I'd like to throw in an important question posed from veneration traditions: are blood ancestors only our direct lineage of parents, grandparents, and great-grandparents, etc., or do they also include the peripheral array of aunts and uncles, great-aunts and great-uncles, as well as cousins, etc.? When it comes to ancestor veneration, this is an important consideration.

Blood relatives are an interesting group to think about because they are both unique to individuals while also connected to vast numbers of others. Your particular group of ancestors is unique to you, because you inherit half of your biological ancestors from each of your parents. Yet, all of those individual ancestors in your pedigree are also connected to a vast amount of your distant living relatives. Indeed, there are two individuals from a very long time ago (mitochondrial Eve and Y-chromosomal Adam) who are literally related to all humans currently living. This interesting aspect of the relationships ancestors have with the living makes for both a truly intimate and expansive connection.

I think it is fair to say that when we think of the term *ancestor* we often think of our own blood relatives, but it should be noted that this is a cultural viewpoint of what constitutes familial connections. The way we see ancestors in Western terms is generally blood relatives only, but when we look around the world, we see variations on what *ancestor* means to individuals and groups. When you put a call out and start to form relationships, do you do so with the view that it will only be your ancestral parents and grandparents? Or does the whole family line include anyone you are genetically related to?

This became an interesting topic of discussion between my former god-father and me one evening after dinner. I was knee-deep in digitizing my own family's pictures, and he asked me to scan some of his own and try to edit them so he could have some decent portraits of his uncles and aunts for his ancestral work. We somehow got into the discussion of whether it was appropriate to display images of those adjacent dead in a Lukumi ancestor shrine. That is, are ancestors only those directly blood related to you in a pedigree or also those who are related to you such as aunts and uncles, cousins, etc. He said that even within Lukumi there were variable opinions on what constituted an ancestor. In our *mojuba*, the ritual prayer calling on our ancestors both individually and collectively, we would usually only name our direct lineage (as noninitiates, your blood relatives, and as initiated priests, your spiritual lineage), but I know others who include mentors and important community members. Who would you include and why? What relationships would you honor through an ancestral lens?

Adopted Relatives

A very common question comes up again and again around ancestor work, and that is: What if I'm adopted? Do I venerate my biological ancestors or the ancestors of my adoptive family? The problem of this issue, I think, is culturally based and is answerable through culture. I think one of the key pieces that can shed light on this issue is how we see our ancestors. Are they individually bound or are they communally bound? Individual lineages, as we have already discussed and which will crop up again and again throughout this book, include one's biological relatives, whereas communal ancestors are the individual identities subsumed by a collective identity that belongs to the whole extended group. If individual lineages are important, then the issue of adoption raises the central question. If the communal collective of the ancestors is more important than individual lineage, then the issue of adoption doesn't matter quite as much.

Let's take the question from the route of individual importance. I know individuals who practice ancestor worship by working with the ancestors of their adoptive families and are seemingly responded to as kin by those ancestors. I also know people who will only venerate their blood relatives and don't consider themselves connected to the ancestors of their adoptive families, though they respect them a great deal. Different sets of relationships and different sets of responsibilities.

How we view adoption and the questions that come up around whether the blood ancestry of the adoptive parent can be claimed by the adopted child is specifically nuanced per culture. Not all cultures see family ties the same way, and in many collectivist societies family members that are not biologically related are recognized both legally and spiritually. In some societies the number of aunties or uncles someone has is not limited to how many siblings a parent has. This speaks to the core concept of relationship and how those connections are built.

Over the years, there are people I've adopted as my chosen family, and the emotional connection I have with them has been so strong. The social and emotional relationships are similar to other forms of family connections, often as strong if not stronger. I feel like we all have those people who join us on our journeys and take on roles as siblings, lovers, comrades, mentors, and parental figures. The strength of these relationships makes me wonder how we relate to them if they pass before us. Do we consider these individuals our ancestors? Do we work with them in an ancestral veneration way, even if they do not quite fit the definition of an ancestor? The answer to this question, I think, really depends on what our spiritual viewpoints are, and as we work through the following chapters, what metaphysical and cosmological rules we ascribe to.

Lineage Ancestors

Lineage ancestors are those individuals who become part of a chain that an individual belongs to. While this also includes biological lineage, for the purpose of this discussion, I am focusing on those non-biologically related individuals who through initiation are added to the chain of lineage by their elders. In this case, the best example would be individuals initiated into spiritual or religious lineages of masters and students. Lineage in spiritual circles becomes very important not only to preserve teachings, which are often oral, but also to help identify, authenticate, and place an individual within the group as an insider and not an outsider.

Lineages are found all over the world, and in many traditions are worn as badges of office for the initiated. For example, my former godfather in Lukumi can trace his religious lineage back two hundred years to the first priestess in the lineage to arrive in Cuba. The authenticity of one's lineage can be verified by the elders of the community, who are tasked with keeping those oral records, and more than enough frauds have been uncovered because they concocted a fake lineage that was uncovered by such elders.

Lineage is also vital in some traditions to claim legitimacy, such as in Buddhism or Hinduism, where every monk and swami should be able to recite their lineage back to the founders of their traditions. Failure to do so calls into question one's legitimacy, and as such, the authority a position imparts to the individual. In these forms of religious and spiritual expression, self-initiation is not condoned.

Lineage does not necessarily have to be spiritual; it is any line of individuals who hold an office or share an experience, but it is always a passing down of the torch from one to another directly. The US presidential system is a good example of this, where the inauguration is the moment when the existing president hands over the reins of power to the incoming president-elect, who is initiated and installed. That act of transforming a civilian into the commander in chief through the inauguration links that individual to all predecessors in the lineage of the presidency. This is what differentiates this category from ancestor by group affinity, because group affinity does not necessarily mean a direct association.

Ancestor by Group Affinity

Affinity ancestors are connected to us through shared experiences or vocations. A widespread example of this type of ancestor would be any form of saint who presides as patron over a profession, place, or activity, with anyone engaging in that profession or activity falling under the protection of that saint. Kinship and relationship are built not by blood or direct contact but through shared experience, where the identity of the ancestor becomes tied to that common trait, experience, or even responsibility.

When asked, I think most people can find a non-blood-related individual who is meaningful to some connected part of their identity. If I were to break down my own affinity ancestors by aspects of my life, I would say: Carl Jung, Sigmund Freud, and Roberto Assagioli for my psychotherapy; Shakespeare, Katharine Briggs, Sir Walter Scott, and W. B. Yeats are all connected to my storytelling; Antinous and Hadrian, Oscar Wilde, and Alan Turing are all connected to my gay identity. The difference for me between an individual we connect with because of shared experience and an affinity ancestor is that the affinity ancestor somehow impacts who we are in a substantive way. Oscar Wilde impacts me as an affinity ancestor because he was a trailblazer who lived and loved in a time when our sexual orientation was illegal, and he personally contributed to the development of the community I exist in now.

This idea of affinity ancestors impacting us in a meaningful way can be taken up by entire groups, and often becomes symbolic of a whole community. An excellent example of this type of ancestor veneration on a society-level can be found among veterans and state-organized honors of the war dead. If you go to any small town or city in North America and Europe, there will usually be a monument to honor the fallen dead of major military conflicts. Many countries around the world have a Tomb of the Unknown Soldier, or sometimes Tomb of the Unknown Sailor. In Ottawa, the Tomb of the Unknown Soldier is guarded daily between April and November by service members. The Tomb of the Unknown Soldier usually contains an unclaimed body of a fallen soldier, entombed to embody all the unclaimed dead. The tombs and other memorial structures become places for honoring the fallen dead and veteran survivors. In this way, these individuals become connected to each other through shared experience, and the show of respect is codified in solemn ritual, protocol, and custom.

Looking to personal identity raises a point we will see in the coming chapters: group legends and heroes. Aside from my other spiritual endeavors, I am a folklore fanatic, and one aspect of folklore is that it tends to retain individuals who are important for group identity. This process begins first with historical figures whose lives begin to take on all sorts of apocryphal biographical elements. Eventually, if the individual is still relevant to the living individuals, they become legendary, and the truth of their story is a kernel in a much larger character. This is true for every group when you look at the dynamics of their stories, and so it is with every group we belong to.

Ancestor as Founder

Founder ancestors are those individuals who, either through blood relationship, adoption, or affinity, founded the group one belongs to. We see this form of ancestor as the founders of lineages, social movements, institutions, religious orders, communities, entire nations, and all manner of other social systems. The relationship you have to these founder ancestors will depend upon the nature of the group, and some relationships will be healthier than others.

In some cultures, we see the traditionally understood founders of a family line as holding a special place and over time becoming deified or turned into household spirits. In ancient Rome, the household gods named *dii familiaris* were understood to be the deified ancestral founders of the family, who became contact points for all the spirits of the family line. Household deities or spirits are a recurring feature of many European cultures, perhaps due to the influence of old Roman religion or as part of a general Indo-European trend. Particularly, we see the connection between household spirits and ancestors in Slavic traditions, such as in Russia, where the house spirits (*Domovoy*, male, and *Kikimora*, female) are understood to be the two founders of that homestead or family. By comparing many stories from across cultures, we see that house spirits are often intimately connected with the symbolic and literal core of the home: the hearth. In ancient times, most polytheistic traditions had a designated hearth or domestic deity such as the Greek Hestia or Norse Frigga.

We can expand this concept further and see how, given time, a deceased human ancestor can become larger than life and transform into any number of different spirits and even gods. As time goes on and individuals move out of living memory, facts can become distorted, and the identity of the ancestors begins to take on new aspects based on the needs of the living. Founder figures can become associated with specific places (as *genii loci*) or elevated to powerful beings like saints or gods.

A *genius loci* (pl. *genii loci*), a term coined by the Romans, is a spirit who embodies the essential nature of a place. House spirits are genii loci because they are found only within the home and perform duties that support that environment, whereas mermaids or mountain trolls are spirits of place because their essential natures embody those environments. What can often happen is that deceased humans become connected to places, whether because they died there (such as ghosts) or because the place became associated with an important moment in that individual's story (such as a pilgrimage site). When this happens, the identity of both place and the deceased individual merge to a point where simply being in that place also means you are in relationship with or under the power of that spirit.

There is an interesting and related occult concept called an *egregore*, which is not the same as a genius loci but operates very similarly. An egregore is an artificial entity that is formed through the collective thoughts and will of a group of people. Whereas a genius loci is tied to the nature of physical place, an egregore is tied to a social place, and often the two operate concurrently. According to egregore theory, whenever a group of people come together, a certain collaborative spirit forms between them all based on the shared desires or goals of the group. Often, the entity formed through such collaboration takes on a life of its own. A pop culture example of this concept is found in Neil Gaiman's *American Gods*, which tells the story of an assemblage of ancient deities struggling to survive amid the emergence of new powers such as Media, Technology, Globalization, and even Conspiracy Theories.

Occultist Mark Stavish explores the concept of egregores and their relationship to ancestral veneration. He makes the point that the concept of the family unit shared by individual members becomes an egregore, and says, "Offerings of food, drink, tobacco, and prayers to the dead, particularly to one's ancestors, strengthens and maintains the collective notion of 'family,' even if only on a psychological level."[34] Stavish goes on to explain that this collective notion of "family" can develop power that influences others, especially if the family over several generations becomes notorious in some way.

---

34. Mark Stavish, *Egregores: The Occult Entities That Watch Over Human Destiny* (Rochester, VT: Inner Traditions, 2018), 38–39.

Establishing an ancestor founder figure as the face of this collective identity both strengthens the group and empowers the individual figures themselves.

If we connect all the above concepts, it is not impossible to see why in many worldviews founding ancestors become so important. We will explore the interaction of ancestral story and personal story more a few chapters from now, but consider for yourself, are there founding figures you already relate to through your associations who impact and influence you? Who are the founders of the places you live in, and how do they relate to your life?

Precursor Species

It is understandable to associate the word *ancestor* with our human fore-bears only, and while we may culturally understand in a general sense that we evolved from previous species, I think we are missing out on potential deep ancestral work if we overlook those who came before we were human. Modern genetic research demonstrates that our species is quite young considering the timescales prehistory tends to deal with, suggesting modern humans evolved from a precursor hominid species only about as early as 300,000 years ago.[35] Individual members of this modern human species whose genetic material became common to all living humans are mitochondrial Eve, estimated to have lived between 150,000–200,000 years ago, and Y-chromosomal Adam, who is estimated to have lived 180,000–200,00 years ago.[36]

While we have the concept of these recent common human ancestors, in the past few decades mounting evidence shows that after Homo sapiens left Africa (estimated at around 100,000 years ago), these small populations bred with other human species (the Neanderthals and Denisovans) that had branched off from previous precursor species. The DNA evidence shows both Neanderthal and Denisovan DNA in the genes of many contemporary human populations.[37] DNA research is interesting because the story of the evolution of our species seems to have been a dynamic and sometimes dramatic tale of survival, encounter, connection, and relationship. Who we are

---

35. John H. Langdon, *Human Evolution: Bones, Cultures and Genes* (New York: Springer, 2022), 527.

36. Langdon, *Human Evolution*, 24–25.

37. Langdon, *Human Evolution*, 500.

now in the twenty-first century, the very physical bodies we have, are a product of evolutionary processes over immense spans of time.

To think about our ancestors from 100,000, 500,000, a million years ago and know that we exist because they survived is not only fascinating—it is humbling. How might considering our nonhuman or prehuman ancestors affect our ancestor veneration and our connection to the landscape? How might the relationship that a hunter-gatherer from 50,000 years ago had to their landscape impact our relationship to the earth now, especially knowing their relationship allowed that ancestor to survive long enough to create offspring? What lessons can we learn about ourselves by studying the development of our species?

Ancestor as Collective Force

In 1978, inside the Grotta Scaloria near the Italian town of Tavoliere delle Puglie, archeologists found a remarkable stash of human remains dating from around 7,000 years ago. The remains had been ritually de-fleshed, the evidence suggesting this took place a year after death. The bones had been placed into the cave interspersed with animal remains and shards of broken pottery.[38] What reason could there be to sort and co-mingle the bones of the dead in this way? What meaning or reason was there to de-fleshing the bones a year after the individual died?

Around the world, there are many examples of cultures that comingle bones of the dead, whether intentionally or because of an emergency such as war or plague. When done intentionally, one rationale I have heard offered is to remove the last connections to the earth for the spirit of the individual and to deliver them to the realm of the dead. In some funerary customs, there are what are called primary and secondary burials. Primary burials are for the use of the body in funerary ritual and exist only as a stage of the whole mortuary procedure. Upon completion of the mortuary ritual, the remains are buried a second and final time, often with meaningful or practical modifications such as de-fleshing.[39]

---

38. Ernestine S. Elster et al., eds., *The Archaeology of Grotta Scaloria: Ritual in Neolithic Southeast Italy* (Los Angeles: Cotsen Institute of Archaeology Press, 2016), 82.

39. Bryant and Peck, *Encyclopedia of Death*, 855.

I think we often look at ancestry in the West as being one of individual pedigrees, but in collectivist cultures, the identity of an individual is intrinsically linked with the community. Collectivism is a form of social connection where an individual's identity is interdependent on their immediate and extended family, which is in turn tied to the caste, clan, or tribe in a large extensive web of social relationships that form the fabric of the community. This network of interdependent relationships carries with it traditional roles and responsibilities, with varying degrees of rigidity and social mobility. Individual and collective actions reflect on everyone in the extended network and vice versa. Collectivism stands in stark contrast to individualistic cultures, which privilege personal achievement, goals, and success. It has been my observation that the vast majority of thriving ancestral veneration traditions tend to be connected to collectivist cultures over individualistic ones.

Collectivism seems to have been the norm for societies around the world and throughout time, and it makes sense to me that in this worldview individuality is subsumed into a collective community as we move out of living memory. When you listen to elders from various Indigenous cultures, many address the dead in blessings and prayers as "the ancestors and all our relatives." That piece about "all our relatives" speaks directly to that collective concept, as well as relatives in the nonhuman areas of the world. In many cultures, we see ancestors being led by founding figures or particularly powerful leaders who speak for or stand as spokespeople for the collective. The entire ancestral grouping acts as a collective on behalf of their descendants, regardless of the nature of the relationship, and these figures stand in as accessible personas who become touch points to all the rest.

While we have discussed collectives on a large scale, collective ancestors do also work in smaller groupings and through different types of relationships. I would like to give you a very specific but good example of how a different type of ancestral collective than some of the ones we've talked about so far can impact someone's life. My friend Thaddeus is a proud gay man in his late twenties from the southern US who has been living with HIV since 2014. We originally met and bonded over our interest in ancestral work, and one day we sat down to talk about his practice. He said that he didn't have a real connection to his biological ancestors because of family trauma, but as he began practicing, he became aware of the presence of several other spiritual guides in his life. Through working with some of these guides, it was revealed that his "Collective," as he calls them, are all connected to him through HIV. When HIV moves into a new person, it tends to, like all viruses, mutate slightly. By analyzing and comparing the differences, doctors can determine how many previous hosts the virus moved through. Thadd was told that there were eight previous people the virus had moved through.

Whereas his relationship with HIV has been a struggle and adjustment, he has found a certain level of empowerment by working with this collective of predecessors. The virus is inside his body, and he said that, just like his blood relatives are inside his body, a small part of these previous hosts are also connected to him. In taking care of himself (such as staying fit, routinely testing viral levels, and keeping up with antiviral drugs), he's doing things that his predecessors couldn't have done. He told me that he sees living his life as a form of veneration to those in his collective who passed on. We live in a generation now that benefits from the hardships of those who endured the horrors of the 1980s and 1990s. His practices around taking care of himself are an upliftment to these ancestors, and he told me he can feel nudges from them guiding him toward healthier choices in life. When he was able to access drugs that considerably lowered his viral load and contributed to his overall well-being, he told me that he could feel a wave of relief from these ancestors.

Journal Prompts

For each of the above types of ancestors, answer the following questions to explore further how you feel about them.

- How do you connect with this concept of ancestor?
- How does this concept make sense to you? How does it not make sense?
- What are you curious to explore more of in relation to this concept?

Chapter Four
Expanding the Concept of Ancestor

In the previous chapter, we discussed various kinds of ancestors who once lived, whether related by blood or through affinity.
We touched on how sometimes the spirits and identities of living ancestors
become transformed into something greater than their corporeal identities,
whether through the passage of time or because of the needs of descendants.
In this chapter, we are discussing various ways the concept of ancestor can be
expanded and what that might mean for your life and relationships.

Throughout the world, there are individuals and populations who claim
descent from fantastical nonhuman or legendary beings. Sometimes these
ancestries are created to serve political purposes, and sometimes they are
explained as random couplings, sexual assault, or accident. Whether we believe
that humans can literally be the descendants of a god, a spirit, an animal, or a
mythological or legendary human is really beside the point. The purpose of
these narratives, I think, speaks to relationships both to individuals and the
community. Ancestors that secular society might not recognize as real have as
much potency and impact on individuals and communities as the more recognizable forms explored in the previous chapter. The impact these characters
have on those who look up to them is very real.

The late Cree writer and Crown attorney Harold R. Johnson writes in
his *Firewater*, "The stories we told about ourselves and our beautiful land in
fact had real effect. The stories connected us to the land and connected the

land to us, and we became the same story."[40] As a storyteller, I understand the deep importance that story has for us and its subtle but profound influence. What Johnson writes above, I think speaks to a relationship where we become products of the stories we tell ourselves, and in a way those stories and the characters involved become animate individuals in our lives that we can have deep personal interactions with. Memory technique researcher Dr. Lynne Kelly writes about this in her work on Indigenous memory systems—how Indigenous traditions around the world work with characters and spirits who embody the teachings of the stories, which are the repositories of the shared wisdom of the collective. As Kelly notes, story is powerful because it has developed in most cultures to take advantage of our neurocognitive makeup. Our brains have evolved in such a way as to utilize symbol and sign to interpret and relate to the world around us, something that can be manipulated and utilized through the technology of storytelling. Kelly postulates, while carefully not minimizing the deep spiritual dimension of story, that the corpus of legendary, mythological, and folkloric stories found in every culture act as oral memory systems populated by characters who are easy to relate to and aid in memory practices. Sometimes these individuals are understood to be spirits with sentience and agency, and other times they are characters who dwell in other spaces accessible through ritual and story alone.[41]

In this chapter, I'd like to explore ancestors who are conceptual and allegorical. I challenge readers to be mindful of your own cultural upbringing and what your folklore, religious, and cultural narratives tell you about non-human ancestors and how they fit into identity and relationships between individuals and in groups. Then, consider how your ancestral work might include some of these following individuals or how you might relate already to some of these characters or concepts in your own spirituality.

---

40. Harold R. Johnson, *Firewater: How Alcohol Is Killing My People (And Yours)* (Saskatchewan, Canada: University of Regina Press, 2016), 4.

41. Lynne Kelly, *The Memory Code: The Traditional Aboriginal Memory Technique that Unlocks the Secrets of Stonehenge, Easter Island and Ancient Monuments the World Over* (Sydney, N.S.W.: Allen & Unwin, 2016), n.p.

Nonhuman Progenitor: Creator Deities

For most religions, the first ancestor(s) are usually divine or spiritual in nature. One could go so far as to say that religions centered on a creator being are ancestor veneration. While for many readers your cultural upbringing might teach you to see a distinction between deity and ancestor, there are many traditions where this is not so clear-cut, and ancestor figures have become gods through the process of apotheosis.

In some traditions, the creator is called father or mother, and the people are direct descendants. In other traditions, the creator is a primordial figure who, after their work is done, take very little role in cosmic events. An example of this would be the Norse primordial figure Ymir, the ancestor of the frost giants who was killed by Odin and his brothers and from whose body the physical world was created. Other times, the individual continues to be relevant and takes on the role of leader of their descendants, such as the god Brahma in Hinduism, who continued to have an honored role as the grandfather of gods, demons, and human beings.

Taking this a step further, many systems of nobility around the world derive authority and power from being descended from a divine being or important spirit. Many institutions of royal or noble families have traced back to an ancestor who was a demigod or creation of divinity. The ancient Egyptian pharaohs at various times saw themselves as the spiritual children of the gods Osiris, Ra, Amun, and other deities. Julius Caesar claimed descent from the goddess Venus. The Japanese imperial family derives descent from Prince Ninigi-no-Mikoto, who in Shinto is the son of Amaterasu, the kami of the sun. Queen Elizabeth II, if we trust the various chroniclers, was a descendant of both the Norse god Odin (through her Norman ancestors) and his Germanic counterpart Woden (through her Anglo-Saxon ancestors), as well as the French water spirit Melusine (through her Angevin ancestors) and the devil through her Plantagenet ancestors. It must be noted that sometimes these associations were held in belief, while others were ceremonial propaganda to identify the ruler with the power of the divinity or spirit…but what a pedigree she had!

While the discussion so far has been on divine ancestors, a very good example of non-divine creator ancestors is found among the Indigenous peoples of

Australia. There is a shared concept called the Dreaming or Dreamtime, referring generally to the body of laws, practices, ceremonies, traditions, stories,
and history passed down by the ancestors to the present generation about the
first ancestral creator beings who shaped the landscape. These creator beings
are not understood to be gods in the European sense; they are ancestors whose
stories both explain the origins of the people as well as the shape of the land.
The people are tied directly to these ancestral creator beings through claimed
ancestry, the living landscape, and the ceremonies connected to both.

It would be a disservice to say all Australian Indigenous peoples have the
same concept of the Dreaming, and each group has a different relationship to
this concept. The Dreaming is a reality of creative forces shaping the fabric
of the world, which beforehand was a vaguely defined plain of cloud or featureless sea or land. From this featureless space emerged the various Dreamtime spirits, some in forms like humans and others as animals. Through their
journeys across the land, the land took on identifiable forms and was carved
out and shaped. The Dreamtime spirits are not immortal and could die, and
some did, while others always exist perpetually in the space of the Dreaming,
which can be accessed through traditional ritual practices.

The Dreaming is not just a time long ago. Because Indigenous Australian
concepts of time are nonlinear, the Dreaming is always unfolding at some
level. The people see themselves as descended from the Dreamtime spirits,
and through their memory systems of ritual, song, and dance interact with
the Dreaming through their culture.[42] The Indigenous understanding of these
beings is that they were the forebears of not just humans but all living things,
and so all living things are kin. This understanding of all life as kin is found
throughout the world and speaks to a very old, interconnected relationship
between humanity and the rest of nature. For more information, the documentary *Kanyini* by respected Indigenous elder Uncle Bob Randall was suggested
to me by one of my sensitivity readers, and it explores from an insider perspective the relationship of the people and their lands.

---

42. Philip Clarke, *Where the Ancestors Walked: Australia as an Aboriginal Landscape* (Crows
Nest, N.S.W.: Allen & Unwin, 2003), 16.

Mythological and Fantastical Forebears

Nonhuman, otherworldly, and legendary ancestors are common features in most human cultures. What would a purpose be for claiming a fantastical legendary forebear? There are many reasons different cultures would derive descent from an otherworldly being, from political to social identity. Politically, individuals or regimes might boost their own legitimacy and power by association with specific legendary individuals. As allegory, the origin tales tend to stand in to explain certain relationships or features of the people connected to the legendary forebear and locate people within a greater community. On a personal level, the relationship between an individual and their mythological forebear can serve to help define that individual within a broader narrative. To echo what Harold R. Johnson said: we become the stories we tell about ourselves.

It was not just rulers who engaged in these types of stories but the regular folk as well. One widespread motif in folklore is the otherworldly partner, where a human marries a fairy or magical animal. The typical tales describe a scenario where a young farmer or fisherman comes upon a maiden of the Otherworld (a selkie, fairy, mermaid, swan, water spirit, nagini, etc.) and somehow manages to capture and marry her. They live happily for a time (as happily as a captured individual can be) until the marriage is interrupted in some form either because the man breaks certain conditions or the woman finds a way to escape and return to her own realm. Often, these maidens leave behind offspring who are said to inherit the powers of their mothers, and that power continues down the family line.[43] A notable example of this are the famous Physicians of Myddfai from Wales, a dynasty of court physicians who were taught their medical skill from an ancestor who was a fairy maiden from Llyn y Fan Fach ("little lake near the peak").[44] In other communities, the stories are told to explain particular features, abilities, or roles of the people.

---

43. A particularly in-depth study of the otherworldly consort tales is *The Serpent and the Swan* (1998) by Boria Sax.
44. W. Jenkyn Thomas, *The Welsh Fairy Book*, illus. Pogány Willy (London: Abela Pub., 2010), 1–10.

I mentioned the spirit Melusine above when describing Queen Elizabeth's mythological pedigree. Melusine is a water spirit (or demon) who is said to have married the French Count Raymond of Poitiers and bore him children. Just as other tales of this type, the marriage was a happy one, but there was a condition that the new countess needed absolute privacy at certain times. After the count invaded her privacy, Melusine was discovered to be a serpent from the waist down, and she flew away never to be seen again. The descendants of the count and Melusine reveled in this otherworldly pedigree to explain their prowess on the battlefield.[45]

Of the many reasons humans would want to claim a nonhuman ancestor, chief among them is to situate themselves as unique or define their role in a larger cosmological order. This is the same reason that groups and individuals ascribe to famous human ancestors and divine creators. By attaching oneself to these origins and perpetuating the story, families and groups define themselves against the nature of that ancestor, making sense of their current place in social order. Many ancient and modern peoples engaged in this form of narrative construction. Rulers and politicians looked to the models of demigods in ancient epics, likening themselves to the heroes of myth. These beliefs directly impacted the social view of these individuals as embodying divine qualities, marking their role in society as unique and otherworldly.

Politics almost always has a role in why certain nonhuman and legendary ancestors pop up as progenitors. One example close to my own heart is the legendary King Arthur. The history of King Arthur is a long one, but suffice to say, over the 1,500 years since he was alleged to have lived, he has become an important symbol to different groups for different purposes. Originally a figure from British tradition, King Arthur and his Knights of the Round Table were swiftly adopted by the English and Norman nobility as a way of anchoring themselves to the island (many of their own ancestors were invading Saxons or Normans).

Many Plantagenet and Tudor kings took an interest in King Arthur for his political symbolism as the last ruler of a united Britain. King Henry VII,

---

45. Carol Rose, "Melusine," in *Giants, Monsters, and Dragons: An Encyclopedia of Folklore, Legend, and Myth* (New York: W. W. Norton, 2001), 241.

founder of the Tudor dynasty, took this political interest to the next level. Henry Tudor had extremely tenuous claims to the throne he sat upon, deriving descent and thus his claim to the throne from an illegitimate son of John of Gaunt, son of King Edward III, through his mother Margaret Beaufort. John of Gaunt was Henry Tudor's great-grandfather, and so there were five generations of cousins and extended family who had much more direct claims to the throne than Henry, whose father came from a Welsh noble house of Twdr. After the tumultuous Wars of the Roses, there were very few legitimate heirs left, and Henry had many supporters. Henry did whatever he could to strengthen his claim, including marrying Elizabeth of York, the daughter of King Edward IV. He likewise imprisoned or exerted power over any other possible rival claimants. Henry also went a step further and engaged in a propaganda war that tied his Welsh roots to King Arthur, deriving political and symbolic authority both from the throne he sat upon and these links to the great King of the Britons, a figure who unified the post-Roman British. Styling his court after Camelot from the medieval romances and even naming his heir Arthur, Henry Tudor, if not outright stating he was descended from the great king, was at the very least styling himself as a natural inheritor.

Throughout the Tudor period, the House of Tudor connected themselves to the ancient monarch and took steps for that association to be cemented in popular culture, even going so far as to have a massive replica Round Table painted with the Tudor Rose insignia, which currently hangs in the Great Hall at Winchester Castle.[46]

While Henry's claims may seem bizarre to us now, it certainly isn't a unique history for the nobility. Around the world, nobility have wanted to connect themselves to powerful progenitors for the purposes of political, spiritual, or symbolic authority. It is also a way for these families to excuse their bloody role in society while also claiming strength from the otherworldly progenitor. If you were a warrior from the Middle Ages in Europe, a time when war was constant and conflict inevitable, you would want to have a certain reputation that would intimidate your enemies. It has been

46. Thomas Penn, *Winter King: Henry VII and the Dawn of Tudor England* (New York: Simon & Schuster Paperbacks, 2013), 96, 305.

my observation that a traditional way of emphasizing personal qualities both before and after the advent of Christianity was to identify with animals. For example, the ancient Romans as a people identified strongly with the wolf. Anglo-Saxons and other Germanic peoples often incorporated animal names into their personal names (Wulf and Beorn, for example), and many of the ancient British mythological figures are associated with animals: Arthur's etymological connection to the bear, Brân the Blessed to the raven). This tradition continued into the medieval period with heraldic animals, where the animal embodied a specific quality of the individual that was useful in both setting them apart from their fellow nobles and as a device. For example, the use of the boar by Richard III or his ancestor Richard I, the Lionheart.

In the quest to understand social or personal identity, in medieval Europe a cottage industry of scribes and clerics arose, eager to put forth their knowledge of genealogical protocol. They took available data to craft new descent for families whose origins may have been less than noble. While it should be noted that many writers and scribes were simply working with the data they had available at the time, attempting to make sense of sometimes contradictory data, others outright forged connections willfully for their patrons. Geoffrey of Monmouth (1095–1155), a British scribe who wrote *History of the Kings of Britain* in 1136, was regarded by one of his contemporaries, William of Newburgh (1136–1198), as a forger. Another such character was Annius of Viterbo (1432–1502) whose works liberally mixed classical and biblical figures to create fantastical lineages from Noah. In Annius's fabrications, he was a giant who lived for six hundred years and sired a progeny of giants who, eventually through successive generations, shrank to become the ancestors of the Romans and eventually the contemporary French and Italian nobility.[47] It was only a hundred years after Annius's death that the scholarship was closely examined and rooted out to be forgeries. Yet, to many of the noble families he worked for, the illustriousness of the pedigrees he concocted had very real social meaning. Even today, I think we can look to our own media and culture to see examples of people who overemphasize or claim certain ancestors to boost their status, such as the nouveau riche hanging portraits of landed British gentry in their mansions in Los Angeles as long-ago noble ancestors.

---

47. Rose, "Noah" *Encyclopedia of Giants*, 270.

Individual families reevaluating their family narrative and history is wide-spread. This same dynamic is also found at the community level, where the history and thus identity of a social group is reinterpreted or renegotiated through reclaiming or creating new narratives. A very good example of this dynamic on a community-wide level can be found in India, where a common social narrative is group descent from a legendary forebear found in the epic literature. The Indian caste system is a perfect example of the form of collectivist culture spoken about in the previous chapter. Complex networks of associations and allegiances derived from positions in society, traditional professions, and roles in society. Indian last names are often profession, descent, and caste based, and so you can usually tell what caste a person belongs to by their last name alone.

The castes by descent are interesting because they have been used as evidence for social position in society and the standards that groups hold themselves to. The name Yadav, for example, is traditionally shared by a group of subcastes of agriculturalists from northern India. While traditionally the group has been labeled as peasants by other castes and went by the name Goala, the community adopted the title Yadav and claimed descent from the ancient King Yadu and his association with the god Krishna of the epic *Mahabharata*. Since the early twentieth century, Yadav activists have been working to raise the standard of living in their community and reframe or reclaim a status of nobility.[48]

This shifting away from and outright rejection of a low caste status by the Yadavs has been an inspiration to other similar communities. As such, other castes like the Yadavs have joined and formed bonds, which have integrated those communities into that shared heritage. This form of reframing has taken on a political role and led to inroads in raising the quality of living for the community by Yadav activists. Now, members of the caste can be seen in many sectors of society not previously connected to their traditional caste roles. Similar forms of reframing and reclaiming have happened in other caste and professional communities, and as such, we see that complex dance of social identity and origins played out often in both South Asia and the diaspora.

---

48. Susan Bayly, *Caste, Society and Politics in India from the Eighteenth Century to the Modern Age*, 3rd ed., vol. 4 (Cambridge, UK: Cambridge University Press, 2001), 204.

Consider your own cultural or family background. Are there figures like the ones discussed above that stand in as ancestral-type figures? How do these figures relate to your community? How does their story inform your own?

The Land, Sea, Rivers, and Sky as Ancestor

Cross-culturally, the sky, sea, and land have been personified as deities and have been venerated as ancestors in the same ways discussed above. In many ways this can be seen as allegorical, but in a very real sense we did originate from these spaces. Our ancient precursor ancestors evolved in the sea, the food that grows in the land is consumed by us and becomes part of us, and the sky is the origin of all the elements that contributed to life on earth. We are intimately connected to these spaces, even if we sometimes forget it.

Indigenous traditions around the world understand this deep relationship to the land and sea. They know that the relationships between humans and the earth are far deeper than just symbolic, poetic language—that the relationship is one of mutual responsibility, sustenance, and a cyclical emergence from and departure back into nature. When you pick up a clump of dirt, you are holding in your hands the decayed organic material of the dead. When you eat food grown in soil, that plant matter has grown using the materials of the earth beneath it, and you are taking that material into your body. Your body is constructed from matter that originally lay in the ground, which at one time was part of another living organism. When you swim in the ocean or a lake, that water you're immersed in has been around for at least 4.5 billion years and has quite literally been part of many other living organisms. When you step into the sea, you're stepping into a place that was the origin of the precursor species that evolved into us. When you look up at the sky, you're looking at a space that sent down all the nutrients needed for life on earth to evolve, and it continues to do so. You see the sun, which has contributed energy and heat to our world since it first began emitting light. You see the galaxy around us, the community of stars and planets.

I think a lot of descendants of immigrants feel disconnected from the lands they inhabit and yearn for an ancestral homeland. Because of colonialism and migrations both forced and voluntary, so many people are living on lands that they don't have an ancestral connection to but which are home for them. As a Brit living in North America myself, I have felt this strange longing for back home, but where is that exactly? I think what can happen is that there is that ancestral understanding of origins somewhere else, but that connection to that other original homeland is so many generations back that people can find themselves caught in an in-between state. Not to mention that the very concept of a homeland is as much a narrative of relationship as it is a geopolitical reality. Coming back to what Harold R. Johnson spoke of before, the land and the people living on it become connected in a shared story.

Dr. Robin Wall Kimmerer addresses this issue of settlers and the story they tell themselves in *Braiding Sweetgrass*. As Dr. Kimmerer puts it, becoming indigenous or naturalized to place is entering into an active relationship with the place you are, regardless of where your ancestors originated from.[49] Dr. Kimmerer describes this process as waiting for the invitation to enter into an authentic dialogue with the place you inhabit, a mutual sense of responsibility for those others who inhabit and understand the unique needs of that place. We should not "just blunder in as if the whole world belonged to [us]," and we certainly shouldn't claim an identity that isn't ours.[50] Instead, understand the damage that the immigrant narrative can have on your relationship to where you currently occupy.

Settler guilt or longing for a long-lost homeland has created issues with how immigrants relate to and build relationship with the new land they come to inhabit. Becoming indigenous to place is becoming responsible for how you relate to and with the land you're on, as opposed to trying to make it into a version of where you imagine your ancestors lived.

What would it be like for you to see the world, the sky, the sea, and important rivers through the lens of ancestor veneration? How might our relationships to the world around us change if we start to see them as progenitors? While we often think of ancestors in terms of living organic beings, what about the world that is our home? How do we relate to the features of this world

---

49. Used here by Kimmerer not to suggest that non-Indigenous people can claim Indigenous identity, but that they should approach colonized lands in a way that respects and affirms both the land and the first peoples as an act of reconciliation and moving forward into healthy dynamics.

50. Kimmerer, *Braiding Sweetgrass*, 210.

and our own origins? What if we saw the earth as grandmother, the sea as great-auntie, and the sky as grandfather? What would it be like to see the land you are on now as an ancestor, or at least as a part of your extended family?

Conceptual and Fictional Ancestors

In the journey of writing this book and challenging my concept of *ancestor* for myself, I came across an interesting view I had not clued in to previously: the idea of a conceptual ancestor. This is slightly different than the ancestor types we explored above, in that blood relatives, the divinities, and legendary figures have an association with reality, even if that reality is an alternate space. Conceptual ancestors are in a way like affinity ancestors, those individuals who have contributed to who we are in some way, but different in that we know these individuals are fictional. I would say we all have relationships with fictional characters of some kind, whether they are the superheroes of our comics or the heroes and heroines of our media. Fiction is so compelling to us because it is a rare opportunity to step in and be an observer to a slice of a reality that isn't our own. It is understandable to connect with a character that we relate to, and the most compelling characters are those we learn about ourselves through. So, the question then becomes, if we are greatly impacted by a relationship with a character to the point that we grow because of that relationship, could it be said that these characters are ancestral to the different versions of ourselves that we grow into?

I had not considered seeing fictional individuals as a form of ancestor until I started diving into and exploring the craft and magic of storytelling through my Bardic studies. I explored how story and the characters that exist in it can relate to and interact with the audience, and through that relationship, powerful inner magic can be woven.

The real game changer for me was reading the work of Dr. Lynne Kelly and her study of memory systems around the world, particularly her research into the Hopi and Zuni peoples' connection with their *kachinas*. The kachinas are often portrayed as gods in white literature, and they are a pantheon of hundreds of individual figures who are believed to dwell in mountains and each embody a certain teaching. As Kelly explains, they are "ancestral characters" who appear and fade as the culture's needs change.[51] The kachinas are represented as beautiful dolls that children are given to learn the story of that kachina and as costumed dancers who embody or are possessed by the kachina spirit. They are not worshipped but are honored as ancestral character spirits whose stories contain the knowledge and embody the lifestyle of the people. Through relationship with the kachinas, children and adults learn about the world, proper relationships, and themselves.

Kelly goes on to speak about how she was inspired to approach a constructed pantheon of "ancestral characters" of her own journey by selecting 130 individuals who had some influence or impact on her. Upon compiling her list of affinity ancestors and creating a suitable memory system to assist in remembering them, she remarked, "It is very hard to explain just how powerful these 'ancestors' have become within my memory spaces. Their stories not only relay practical and historical facts, but also ethical issues that arise from the stories of these real people, some admirable, others not. I had not expected that I would so often ponder the moral implications and ethical lessons to be learnt from their lives and relate them to my own."[52]

In exploring what Kelly did, and inspired by the spiritual technology of the Puebloan peoples and their kachinas, it struck me that there may not be many differences between our relationships to the stories of "real" ancestors and the stories of fictional characters. While Kelly used 130 affinity ancestors connected to various parts of her journey, one could easily use this technique with fictional or conceptual ancestors. While we are objectively talking about two different forms of being, does that aspect negate the very real psychosocial impact both sets of relationships have on us as individuals?

I started to think about some of the characters who have been important to me and who I often reflect on along my own journey. At some time in my life, characters like Lestat, Avatar Aang, Steven Universe, Green Lantern, Morgaine le Fey, Sherlock Holmes, Raistlin Majere, Paul Muad'dib, Titus Groan, Spock, the Dragonborn, Peter Pan, and others have been deeply important to me. If I were to include this list of fictional characters with the list of affinity ancestors I have, on a purely relational level, I don't see a difference except

---

51. Kelly, *The Memory Code*, 89.
52. Kelly, *The Memory Code*, 277.

one group is "real" and the other "fictional." The impact these characters have had on my life is real; the adventures I followed them on are real to me, and ultimately who I am now is informed by them in the same way the stories of historical people have impacted me. While this might sound like a bizarre concept to some readers, it again comes down to relationship.

If any of my readers were bookworm introverts as teenagers, perhaps some of your best friends were characters like Harry Potter, Meg Murry, Frodo Baggins, Mildred Hubble, etc. I remember when I was about ten or twelve, my dad brought out a box filled with dusty old books chronicling the adventures of James "Biggles" Bigglesworth, a fictional 1930s adventurer and English RAF pilot. These yellowed, old books were some of my dad's treasures from his childhood, and he excitedly encouraged me to read them. I wasn't hugely into 1930s adventurers back then and at the time didn't understand why he was insistent I read them and why he looked so dejected when I said no. I realize now what he was saying was, "Biggles was a really important person to me when I was your age, and I want to share him with you." Part of my life's journey has been to learn how my dad says "I love you" through wanting to create opportunities to spend time together and share what he's passionate about. In many ways, Biggles is like an uncle I never knew I had because I imagine he was like an older brother to my dad growing up.

Now, you might be wondering how this might look in a veneration practice. I am not suggesting you must include these fictional characters as part of your blood relative or affinity practice, but I invite you to consider what form honoring these ancestors can take. In my own practice, I do notice a difference in that on an energetic level I am connecting with the spirit of the "real" individuals, while with these fictional characters, I am honoring the part of myself that they represent.

What fictional characters are you connected with? What did these characters teach or impart to you? What did you learn about yourself from these characters? In what ways might you honor and treat these fictional characters like ancestors? In what ways would honoring "real" ancestors and fictional ancestors be different for you? How might this form of relationship impact or inform your relationships with other forms of ancestor?

Our Other Intimate Relationships:
Our Pets, Friends, and Spirit Guides

A common question about ancestor veneration that comes up, and we have alluded to it in previous chapters, is whether there is a place for our friends and our beloved pets. In a similar vein, how about the role of spirit guides? Is it appropriate to venerate the spirits of these individuals within our ancestral practices, or do they receive different treatment through different practices?

I'll be honest, for my personal practice, I do include my pets. I don't count them as my ancestors, but I do have a little shrine set up to them, and I light candles for them. The shrine contains locks of their fur, urns of some of their ashes, and pictures. Some religions consider animals to be soulless, and other traditions see them as being subsumed into a group identity in death, but I don't subscribe to that feeling. My answer to this question is to do what feels right. This might sound wishy-washy, but I think the process of losing a pet allows us greater access to understanding the emotional connection possible for the dead, because our feelings for our pets are almost always ones of love. They may not be ancestors, but they are part of our family, and in my opinion should be honored as such.

Spirit guides, on the other hand, are something else and depending upon the tradition you follow will not be counted as ancestor. Spirit guides come in many forms throughout the world, but every religion has some concept of a nonfamilial guide or protector. Abrahamic traditions have angels; many Indigenous North American traditions have guides and entities encountered on vision quests; New Age, Spiritualism, and Spiritism have spirit guides encountered through séance; and many African-derived Caribbean traditions have the concept of a spirit court that walks with you. Whatever way you view spirit guides, in most of the traditions I have seen, they are usually not ancestrally connected to us.

The form of espiritismo I practice, which is much more like the original Kardecian Spiritism, posits that spirit guides are individuals who through affinity or similar life experiences are drawn to working with you in life so that they may work off some debt of their own or assist another through issues they themselves went through. Every individual has a court of spirit guides who work with and can affect one's life in a similar way that the ancestors can. The big difference between a spirit guide and an ancestor is that spirit guides don't have the same conflict of interest that an ancestor potentially might have, especially those ancestors closer to us. It was taught to me that ancestors, especially those closer to us, have a conflict of interest because they are linked to us through blood or familial relationship. Just like in life, our family who are dead might have agendas and thoughts about how we should live our lives. It's certainly possible an ancient ancestor from two thousand years ago might have an agenda, but I have been taught that the more distance an ancestor has from being alive, the less likely it is that they have an agenda to control or somehow experience life vicariously through the living.

Spirit guides are one of the reasons that espiritismo was incorporated into some communities of Lukumi in the first place. It is taken up by those who practice both the Lukumi ancestor practice and espiritismo concurrently in order to work with this third class of spirit. Some espiritistas incorporate working with their spirit guides in the same space as their ancestors, while others separate the practices and form different spaces. I think this is an area that readers will need to decide on their own, if they work with spirit guides at all, and come to a comfortable arrangement in. Some spirits don't play nice with each other and sometimes need to have compartmentalized corners of our lives. Some spirits also have conflicting needs or agendas that need to be responded to with healthy boundaries.

If you consider deities, ancestors, and spirit guides as being three classes of spirit potentially working directly with us in our lives, then how do we work with them? If you don't believe in spirit guides or have your own beliefs about them, then this is not as applicable to our discussion. But if you do believe in spirit guides, what do you believe they are, and how do they intersect or not intersect with your other spiritual practices? Do we work with them in the same way as ancestor veneration?

Journal Prompts

- Who do you consider to be an ancestor? Are ancestors only those related to you, or do you consider non-blood relatives ancestors?

- How are ancestors different from other spirits?

- What relationships do you have with your ancestors?

- How do your ancestors operate in your life? How do individual ancestors operate? How do they operate collectively?

- How does the concept of nonhuman ancestors make you feel? In what ways is this concept relevant or irrelevant to you?

- Do you belong to any lineages, whether spiritually or professionally? In what ways are the individuals that came before you in these lineages ancestors? In what ways are they not?

- In what ways do legendary or mythological figures impact your culture or life? Are there particular individuals that cast a long shadow in your life or culture?

- In what ways do you view deities or spirits as ancestors?

Exercise Two
EXPLORING CONCEPTUAL ANCESTORS

For each of the subheadings of ancestor we explored above: nonhuman progenitor; mythological and fantastical forebears; the land, sea, and sky; conceptual and fictional ancestors; and other intimate relationships, work through this journaling exercise and explore these figures more.

Type of ancestor: _____

1. Make a list of individual figures you connect with related to the categories of ancestor we've explored in the past two chapters. Write five to ten examples to begin with and feel free to add as you go. Try not to add too many examples to begin with so that you don't overwhelm yourself.

   • What do you notice about this list you've made? How do the figures relate to each other? Are there subgroupings within this list?

   • Are there particular individuals you connect with more strongly than others?

2. Choose a specific individual from the list above and answer the following questions. Feel free to repeat this step multiple times with everyone.

   • Who is this individual and how do you relate to them?

   • What impact has this individual had on your life?

   • How does this individual inspire or discourage you?

   • When did you encounter this individual in your life? How has your outlook on this individual changed since you first encountered them?

   • How does this individual relate to your family or cultural group?

Chapter Five

Defining Ancestor Veneration

In the previous chapters, we explored different ways that the living and the dead have been conceptualized in religious traditions, as well as discussed the various forms of ancestor. We now turn our attention to ancestral veneration as a living spiritual practice and how one can define it. In this chapter, we will discuss some of the crucial components that, in my opinion, help to differentiate ancestral veneration from other forms of spiritual practice. While it would be tempting to try to broadly define what ancestral practice is and isn't, I think it's more valuable for each tradition to define itself. One definition cannot adequately encompass ancestral work, and part of your job in creating your practice is to define it for yourself. What can be explored are some common elements that often underlie ancestor work. In this chapter, we'll discuss the difference between mourning traditions and veneration, the arguments proposed for the morality of veneration work, a note on the practical benefits of ancestral work, and what potential hazards working with the dead can pose and how to mitigate those dangers.

Mourning versus Veneration and Worship

As I developed this book, it became very clear that grief stood out as a primary reason for why we are attracted to ancestor work. Death is the ultimate change, the final mystery, and an experience we will all eventually face one day. In coming to terms with the death of a loved one, often the feelings that come up for

73

us are our own passing. Our sorrow of losing a loved one becomes mixed with the fear of loss of self, and this fear can drive many to want to connect with and be reassured that there is life after death. At the beginning of this book, I said that ancestral veneration is not about death but about continuation of relationship. In this chapter, we will explore grief, and I challenge you to consider how grief comes into your work with your ancestors and what lessons grief can hold for your relationship with yourself.

There is, however, an important distinction between mourning traditions and veneration, although they do often overlap. Mourning has connotations of seeing ourselves as separate from the dead and experiencing death as a loss. Veneration, on the other hand, has the connotation of seeing the dead as accessible agents with influence in the world. While mourning practices are centered on remembering the dead, I would suggest that veneration practices are centered on responding to the dead. For the purposes of building a veneration practice, I think it is important to understand how grief affects our relationship with the dead and at what point our veneration work transcends grief work.

The need for closure is an important one no matter the loss. I was taught once that when we grieve a loss, we are not grieving the person but the missed opportunities with that person. Part of the major sting and the process of grief is coming to terms with a new normal, as we are no longer able to interact in the same way. That feeling of absence is tinged with uncertainty about that person continuing somewhere else and our own fears of death. Ancestor veneration has an important role in how death is navigated throughout the world, because it challenges our perception that death means an end. On an intellectual level, we might strongly believe there is an afterlife, but on an emotional level, we might doubt because it is so intangible. Ancestor veneration and relationship building with those who have passed promise us not only closure on the loss but invite us to step into a new dynamic with not only our remembered loved ones but so many others whose stories flowed into ours, just as our stories will flow into the next generation. Ancestor veneration thus transcends mourning and funerary traditions, which are important but serve to facilitate a transition process into death for the individual.

As we talked about in previous chapters, I think there is a craving within Western culture to reconnect to our dead in ways that transcend mourning and grief. Whereas in most other cultures the ancestors are often present beings whose shrines are integrated parts of the social and familial landscape, the West has been divorced from the dead for many years now. The funeral industry sees to it that we never really have to deal with death. Bodies are cremated or prepared to look as lifelike as possible. When someone dies, the body is whisked away by the coroner, and in many people's experiences, that is the last time we see the person again. If we do see the body, it can be an unreal scene where the body is pumped full of formaldehyde, painted, backlit, covered in flowers, and looking like the individual is just taking a nap. People don't die in the West; they just disappear, leaving uncomfortable voids.

I don't mean to minimize or disrespect the feelings of very real grief, but I have noticed that we don't treat the dead very well culturally. In our discomfort, we treat the dead as voids to be ignored and eventually filled with something that distracts us. This is very different from other cultures, where rituals such as washing the body, wakes, public displays of grief, and even taking care of and handling the remains well after the person dies are common. It is hard to ignore the reality of death when it is in the home in front of us. Likewise, ancestor rituals and holidays devoted to celebrating the dead, such as Día de los Muertos, underline that intimate connection between all members of the family regardless of the state of being.

A concrete example of this change in approach can be seen in the tradition of the silent café or dumb supper. The dumb supper has emerged in the past few decades as a Neopagan tradition connected to Samhain, but its roots go back further in time. The concept is to create a space where both living and dead are invited to a candlelit dinner party. Attendees remain silent throughout, sitting across from empty chairs that are devoted to the dead. The focus of the ritual is to honor, communicate with, and spend time with the dead. At the end, time is allowed for all present to share their process and what came up for them in a safe environment.

I have been involved in several silent cafés now, and each one has been a transformative experience. The power of silent cafés, at least for me, has been the immediacy of the dead. One experience I had saw me sitting with my great-grandfather and then his son, my grandfather. As I sat eating a slice of delicious cake, a conversation with these men was going on in my mind. The experience was visceral, the connection felt very real, and ending the experience felt almost like waking up from an emotional dream. One moment I was there talking to my grandfather as he told me how proud he was of who I was becoming and how deeply proud of my dad he was. You see, while my dad loved my grandfather deeply, there were many times he was hard on my dad, expecting perfection.

"You have to understand," he said to me in that liminal space, "If I knew then what I know now, I'd have been different."

We talked about his relationship to his own father, and he even joked about how good the cake at the event was!

Just as quick as the experience began, I was sitting again in a quiet room filled with people, and the feeling of communion with my grandad was a memory. This feeling is very different from the sadness of mourning and more like heading home alone after parting company with friends. It is also a very different feeling than connecting to the dead through divination or a medium.

Contrast the silent café with the death café, which is an initiative to normalize the discussion of death in a relaxed environment. You are talking about death; you are not talking to the dead. Death Café (the organization that originated the idea) was developed by Jon Underwood and Sue Barsky Reid, based on the ideas of Bernard Crettaz. They organized a space to come, eat cake, and talk about death.

Death cafés are not necessarily a support group for grief but are a space to explore all the topics related to death. Whether it be grief or the funeral industry, the metaphysics or philosophy of death, death cafés create the communal environment to discuss what is often a taboo topic and expand the discussion away from just grief.[53] In many ways both the silent café and the death café serve to expand the relationship between living and dead by shifting the focus away from loss to a new kind of relationship, just in slightly different ways.

Ultimately, the major distinction between mourning practices and veneration practices is that mourning centers us on grieving the loss of our loved ones who have passed, while veneration invites us to build relationships with all of our ancestors, whether we knew them in life or not. We may start out

---

53. Jack Fong, *The Death Café Movement: Exploring the Horizons of Mortality* (Cham, Switzerland: Springer International Publishing PU, 2018), 5.

being attracted to veneration because of grief, but what veneration offers us is an avenue to a whole spectrum of relationships with a continuum of beings.

Journal Prompt

- How have you seen mourning in your life? Whether it was your own process or someone else's, what was the experience like?

The Morality of Ancestor Veneration

Ancestor veneration is not just about honoring the dead; the practice itself has wider implications and can affect greater society. The Chinese philosopher Confucius taught the essential idea of filial piety and that ancestor veneration was a moral exercise. By learning to cater to the needs of the dead we learn to serve the needs of the living better. What I believe he meant was that through the ritual care of our ancestors' needs—not just simply remembering them in the past but learning to respond to their needs as sentient beings existing in a present moment just like us—we learn to develop healthier relationships overall. There are deeper implications for Chinese culture with this statement as well, for the Chinese see a direct relationship between family life and the effective running of the universe.[54] Chinese culture is based upon a hierarchical universe with the *dao* permeating, where everything has duties, responsibilities to and expectations of everything else. In a sense, traditional Chinese cosmology could be represented via the adage "a place for everything and everything in its place." We see that ancient cultural paradigm very much at work in modern Chinese culture. Respect for one's elders is returned through the elders' responsibilities of caring for the young and vice versa. As individuals become ancestors, it is thus a duty of cosmological importance to care for one's ancestors in the same way that you would care for one's own

---

54. Bernard Formoso, "From Bones to Ashes: The Teochiu Management of Bad Death in China and Overseas," in *Buddhist Funeral Cultures of Southeast Asia and China*, ed. Paul Williams and Patrice Ladwig (Cambridge, UK: Cambridge University Press, 2012), 192–217.

children and parents. This form of selflessness is really self-catering as well as serving the needs of the whole.

In many ways the Chinese view of the universe is similar to the ancient Romans, who believed that the stability of the world was dependent upon ever-expanding circles of relationship. The prevailing view in pagan Rome was that an ordered household had direct influence on and relationship with the harmony of the town, and then the region, and ultimately the entire state. The effective functioning of each stratum of society was built upon the stability of the preceding. The foundational core of Roman religion was in the home, particularly the hearth, which was echoed on a large scale by the Temple of Vesta, the sacred hearth of Rome. This is one reason why during the imperial era, the cult of the emperor was so important because the person of the emperor was seen as both the embodiment and the father of the empire. In this way, the imperial cult and the worship of previous deified emperors mirrored traditional Roman ancestor veneration.

This aspect of ancestor veneration as a moral duty is found in most traditions, even those that seek to appease and placate rather than honor and propitiate. In Lukumi, we have a cosmological view of the world that centers humans, who are surrounded by all the important beings of our practices: ancestors below us, orisha around us, Olodumare above us. This view sets out duties and responsibilities, and places all within the grand scheme. Ancestor veneration, then, is foundational to all the other practices that come after. And as a foundational step, it is viewed as an essential building block in further spiritual development, which always factors in other beings rather than solely the self—no matter the tradition we look at. This is further reflected in the words of educator and US presidential candidate Shirley Chisholm, who said, "Service is the rent we pay for the privilege of living on this earth."[55] Service is often a form of sacrifice, and sacrifice leads to returns of some kind.

---

55. (This quote is also commonly attributed to Marian Wright Edelman); Henry Louis Gates Jr. and Evelyn Brooks Higginbotham, eds, "Chisholm, Shirley" in *African American Lives* (New York: Oxford University Press, 2004) 167.

Journal Prompts

- How does duty factor into your life? What does duty mean, and what duties do you owe and to who?

- In what ways could your ancestors rely on you, and in what ways could you rely on them?

- What does service mean to you? What does service mean in your spiritual practices?

Practical Benefits of Ancestral Work

While we talk a lot about relationships in this book, this is only one part of why you would want to engage in ancestor work. Propitiating and venerating the ancestors so that you can develop a strong relationship with them often has the benefit and goal that they become spiritual allies. If we believe that they have power to positively impact us through their blessings and wisdom, then a goal in developing a strong relationship is to allow them to positively intervene in our lives.

As spiritual beings, their access to the unseen forces of reality gives them a special ability to act as intermediaries to effect change in areas that we cannot. This line of thinking is the exact reason why spirits, gods, and other unseen forces are revered and worked with—to gain their favor for practical reasons. When our ancient ancestors needed rain, they propitiated the spirits of water and storm; when they needed advice on life, they sought out the oracles and diviners with special relationships to gods. The reality of our world is that in everyday life, spiritual enlightenment really needs to take a back seat to the material necessities and security of a safe roof and full belly. So, who better to ask for assistance with those lower levels of the hierarchy of needs? When young people are challenged in their life, they go to their parental figures for support. To the dead, those of us who are living are probably like young people, and they are there to help us. I have noticed that when people talk about their ancestors, it can often be this vague and nebulous concept, but for me it really is that simple: they are our grandparents, literally. Some of them are not going to be people we'll want to know, but most of them we can build both personal and collective relationships with.

In terms of the practical, there are various reasons why you would approach ancestors for their blessings and intercession in your life. The way one goes about gaining the favor of the ancestors is similar in many traditions to how you propitiate deities and spirits. Sacrifice and offerings are the most widespread, but contractual magic and agreements are other major forms I have noticed. Offerings can include prayer, food, material goods, symbolic offerings, and even dedications offered in the hope of reciprocity, whereas contractual agreements and magic take the form of "If you [help me with my exams], I will [offer chickens in your honor]."

An important point to realize with the ancestors is that they are there to be worked with, and one builds a relationship with them to access. Where veneration practices come into play is that, like any relationship, there is a certain responsibility on each party to support that relationship. Some relationships are built through listening, some are built by spending time together and going on adventures, while some relationships are developed for specific purposes. Each kind of relationship and what we gain from it is entirely dependent on reciprocity and respect. The type of blessings and intercession the ancestors give will be determined by how much respect we show, which will in turn determine what we can reasonably ask for.

Journal Prompts

- What is it you want from your ancestor veneration? Apart from the psychosocial benefits, what are the tangible benefits you perceive for engaging in this work?

- What areas of your life would you want the ancestors to bless? What areas would you want them to stay out of?

- What wisdom, strengths, knowledge, or influence do you hope to access within your ancestral collective? How would you want these things to appear for you?

- How comfortable are you approaching your family for help in general?

- When is propitiation healthy, and when is it unhealthy?

- What is your ability to receive blessings in your life? What prevents you from receiving help?

Potential Hazards of Working with the Dead

While we approach ancestors for their blessings and intercession, we must also understand that not all ancestors are healthy beings and can sometimes cause us harm, whether intentionally or unintentionally. The reason seemingly all spiritual traditions have established practices of decorum in interacting with the spiritual world, including initiation and the development of spiritual specialists, is to keep everyone involved safe. The spiritual world can be a dangerous space for those who are unprepared to engage with it. The best way I can describe this danger is to use the analogy of driving a car or other large vehicle. Generally, many societies don't allow just anyone to drive cars because the act of driving is a specialized skill that comes with specialized knowledge. When you learn how to drive, you are taught the rules of the road, how to use the vehicle, and how to communicate with others while driving. Many readers might have taken a driving education program or learned with parents sitting next to them. When the time comes, you take a test that certifies you understand how to drive safely and can be allowed to independently operate a car by yourself on the road system without crashing.

In many ways, interacting with the spiritual world is like entering a road system. If you are not careful or do not understand what you are doing, you have a chance of harming yourself or others by crashing. The purpose of initiation is like learning how to drive a car, whereby initiates of a practice or tradition are properly shown how to interact with the spiritual. In many traditions, initiates are then certified or responsible for assisting noninitiates in utilizing that practice or tradition. This is one major reason why so many initiated individuals from closed practices balk at the idea of self-initiation. The safety element here is basically that the training prepares you to engage with a sphere of reality that you were unprepared for previously.

Often, spiritual traditions develop organically in partnership with specific groups of spiritual entities, like gods or ancestors, who utilize specific forms of communication, symbol, ritual, and other elements. These developed partnerships have been built over many generations and include mutually agreed upon roles and responsibilities, which support the receiving of those benefits. As part of the process of initiation where an individual gains access to the benefits or knowledge from the established relationship, there is also the commitment to take on the roles and responsibilities of that relationship. This is, again, why closed systems insist that only initiated or insiders of that system practice, because the system has within it those roles and responsibilities. In the initiation process, an individual is given the tools to best take up those roles and responsibilities and start to engage with the spiritual partnership. These safety measures include ways to communicate with as well as verify the identity of specific spiritual entities and, simultaneously, exclude or prevent spirits or gods that are not part of the system. This is a very important safety measure because not all spirits have good intentions, and so using a system that is mutually designed to only call out to specific spiritual partners prevents someone from connecting to a spirit that is not a part of that partnership.

In the case of this book and for you who are building your own practice centered on your ancestors, this is essentially what the whole second half of the book is about, developing the mechanisms of relationship with your ancestors. But you are tying into a lineage of relationships going back into the mists of time. Developing relationships with the ancestral spirits is different from developing relationships with deities or other types of spirits because the relationship is already there. The job is to reacquaint yourself with your ancestors and plug into their relationships with each other. You might utilize tradition, which is already a part of your heritage, to connect with the ancestral partners who are familiar with it, or you may introduce your ancestors to spiritual systems that you are part of. Either way, most of the ritual work later in the book is about forging those layers of practice to develop spiritual relationships.

Now, while you are plugging into relationships with the dead, that does not necessarily mean that all of the dead ancestors are healthy or good. There are ancestors we may not wish to engage with because they are unhealthy in death like they were in life. Most traditions around the world understand that the state of death does not necessarily make someone healthy, which is why there is an abundance of protection charms and rituals of appeasement. What makes an ancestor healthy or unhealthy is really determined by who they were in life and sometimes the manner of their deaths. This understanding brings with it a certain level of risk, mitigated by deepening our relationship with the dead and discernment about who one can approach. While we might strive to think about the dead as spiritually enlightened and expansive beings after they shed their mortal shells, the reality is that in most traditions I am aware of, this is not the case. Death is a traumatic experience both for the living and the dead, and often individuals find themselves or parts of themselves remaining in this world as ghosts because they cannot grapple with the reality of their new state. Trauma can often manifest in living individuals as defense mechanisms such as lashing out, and so it is a logical extension to think that the dead existing with trauma and pain can lash out or cause harm from beyond the grave. I have noticed this is particularly connected to strong emotions.

Years ago, I had a booth vending in the regional psychic fair circuits, spending weekends selling all sorts of crystals, tools, and gifts. Although I have mediumship skills, I was not there to read anyone and so focused on my sales and blocked out the noise of the room. Inevitably though, I would pick up on things as people drifted by and sometimes was privy to uncomfortable awareness. I remember on one of these occasions, a woman came to my table on a Friday evening. She looked around my table, not focused at all on what I was selling, and we got chatting. She asked me which psychic in the room was a good one, and I explained it wouldn't be fair to single out one over the others. She said she'd come to speak with her husband who had died a few years before, and she pointed to one of the mediums and said she was booked to go see them.

I had a sinking feeling in my stomach as she spoke more about the husband. What came to me was that the husband had been a very controlling man in life, and this woman was lost without him. What I perceived was happening was that this man could not accept that he'd died before her and was trying to control her and his son from beyond the grave. She was physically aged beyond her years, was obviously a heavy smoker, and had a slight flightiness suggesting anxiety. As she picked up a crystal or two from my table, I could tell that she was grasping for something to ground herself with. The dead husband could not control his son the same way he was controlling her, and this woman was unwilling to claim her own identity again because of his interference. She said she routinely came to these events to get what amounted to marching orders from him on what he wanted her to do. Sadly, he was leading her to join him in the grave. As she walked away, I could see the trail of negativity floating behind her. I still see her face clearly in my mind from that day, and I hope that one of the spiritual workers she has come across has sorted the situation.

In the above case, the violation of the rules of life and death was a boundary violation of roles—the idea that in some traditions the dead are potentially envious of life or distraught about being dead and want to relive through their descendants. The dead are dead; we as the living get to decide how we live our lives. The role of the dead is often meant to be supportive, and in turn, the living support the dead in whatever cosmological worldview you believe in. In cases like the example above, where individual spirits are violating the rules, offerings are made as a supplication for the dead to behave and sometimes as an appeasement to go away and not come too close. Veneration practices in this sense also serve to seek the intercession of the healthy elders in the family line, and for the potentially dangerous individual to be appeased so as not to cause further harm. If great-great-grandfather is causing disruption across the family line, go to his elders for support. This is where the concept of the collective becomes important because the negative agendas of individuals can be suppressed under the weight of the ancestors as a collective. Family protects family, even if it's protecting from one of their own.

Boundary violations of cosmic rules and order may not necessarily come from unhealthy ancestors but from those who are still deeply connected to their agendas for us. In Lukumi practice, we regularly receive spiritual readings from our elders that give voice to our ancestors and the orisha. The ancestors have a broader view of reality than we do and can speak that wisdom to us, but they are sometimes not without an agenda. The orisha are understood to have the broadest view of all under God, and so their messages usually trump the messages of the ancestors. This is because of the understanding that even ancestors can get lost in their agendas for us.

Often, the agendas of ancestors are simply wanting only the best for us, but in so doing, their closeness to us (especially the recent dead who know us more personally) can go from empowering us to manipulating us with their wisdom. Part of that overstep could be disrupting healthy routines and patterns we've established in our lives or forcing us to change too quickly, which is unsustainable and detrimental to our development. I think of the classic movie *National Lampoon's Christmas Vacation*, where several generations of the Griswold family come together, many unannounced, and all havoc breaks loose in the household. While this movie is, of course, a parody, the same familial upheaval often takes place in life. Boundaries and routines that were established by the core group are challenged or ignored, and especially in the case of elders coming into the home, old familial patterns of hierarchy might be reimposed. The stress caused by this kind of upheaval can lead hosts to want to appease their guests for the sake of social harmony.

To illustrate this point, when we consider ancestor traditions in several of the major Asian countries like Japan, Korea, and China, we see the necessity of living descendants catering to and taking care of their ancestors in the same way we would take care of living relatives. Providing the ancestors with all their needs in the spirit world is linked directly with the prosperity of the family in the temporal world. Failure to support and provide brings down the ancestors' wrath and condemnation. Social controls in these cultures are strongly linked to the family and hierarchy, and while the head of the household might rule domestic affairs, they are usually always subordinate to the elders among the ancestors, especially the founding head. To reclaim power and right to sovereignty in life, offerings of appeasement are placed to distract or make happy the deceased elders in the spirit world.

Another example of this is the Hindu tradition of *pitru paksha*, the festival where the dead are believed to come and dwell in the homes of the living during a half-month-long period after the harvest season determined by the lunar calendar.[56] Special care is given to feed the dead and perform other honors so that they don't cause havoc while dwelling temporarily in the home. In this worldview of the dead only coming back and dwelling in the home for a time, imagine having not only your in-laws and living family with you, but all of your deceased relatives as well going back three generations. The potential for long-standing family drama to be rehashed both in the temporal and spiritual planes poses a very real danger to domestic tranquility.

Ultimately, this question comes down to this for me: they are your ancestors, but you don't need to put up with any shit. Some teachers out there will say to banish these ancestors from your life, and if that is part of your tradition, then do it. But I have always been taught that it is the ancestors who self-police themselves. If you have an ancestor who is a potential danger to you, call on your other ancestors to use their weight to prevent that individual from doing harm. Banishing an ancestor who is unwell will not help them; it will only entrench the issue deeper, and that ancestor will then come

---

56. Denise Cush, Catherine Robinson, and Michael York, *Encyclopedia of Hinduism* (London: Routledge, 2010), 598–599.

back again and again for your descendants. Part of our work on healing is to assist the ancestors with coming into healthy states, and just like with life, that means establishing clear and healthy boundaries and assisting when we can.

If you wish to explore this issue of unhealthy ancestors more, especially as you develop your own practice, I highly recommend the work of Dr. Daniel Foor, psychologist and spiritual practitioner of several lineages. His *Ancestral Medicine* modality explores this issue in much greater depth with concrete systems of healing that he has developed utilizing the multiple lineages he is initiated into.

Journal Prompts

- Are there ancestors that you had strong boundaries with in life? How might those boundaries translate to your veneration practices?

- In what ways might your veneration be affected by family or cultural norms and drama?

- What practical boundaries do you need for your own sake with specific ancestors? How about ancestors as a whole group?

Chapter Six

Ancestor Veneration and Personal Story

One of the dynamic aspects of ancestral work is how ancestral story often connects us with our own personal stories. There is something intrinsic to the human experience about trying to locate ourselves in broader contexts as a way of exploring our origins and forming visions of our future. As evidenced by the popularity of genealogy research, there is an unmistakable draw for us to learn about those who came before and to also see if we recognize our own selves in those lives.

It has been my experience that individuals interested in ancestral work often begin with the stories of their ancestors as touch points, and this makes sense, as these inform us about these people now passed. But those stories are not situated in a vacuum, nor are they just curious anecdotes that are removed from our own lives. In a very real sense, the ancestors in their times formed the context that we exist in now. By understanding more deeply and forming relationships to the lives of our ancestors, we form deeper understandings of our own lived experiences.

In this chapter, we will discuss various elements of the intersection of personal story and ancestral story. We will discuss what uncovering your ancestors' stories can look like, some of the issues that might arise, and the repercussions of choosing whose story to focus on. This section will not teach you how to research ancestral story, but I have included resources to assist you in this aspect of the work. This chapter focuses more on your relationship to the stories you uncover as opposed to finding those stories.

Uncovering Your Ancestral Story

The intersection of personal story and ancestral story should come as no surprise to many readers of this book, as one of the key reasons so many people are interested in genealogy is the seeking out of roots. Popular television shows centered on family history research in recent years, such as *Who Do You Think You Are?* and *Finding Your Roots*, speak to this deep connection between living individuals and the history of their family lines.

The connection transcends mere history and goes deeper; there is a longing to understand these people who contributed to creating us, and in that longing we inevitably reflect on our own journeys. Consider the stories of your family of origin or group affiliation: What do they tell you about that group? How do those stories inform your sense of identity and the identity of the group? Every group has its narratives that are used to conceptualize and reinforce values and norms, as well as create the container for individuals to relate to one another.

When I was starting my family research, many of the individuals on my family tree had only a name and some dates. To me, they were not people but vague ideas. When I really dove in and learned about them, the individuals who had previously only been names took shape and form. We often, I think, tend to see ancestors as foreign entities living in strange lands we've never visited. Learning the stories humanized these individuals; I could start to relate to their lives in a slightly different way.

While it might be easy for me to encourage you to speak to your family about the stories of your ancestors, I am conscious that not all readers will have strong connections to family to facilitate this. I also realize that for some readers, your family might not even have these details because for any number of reasons you lost that data or were not allowed to keep it. We have access to so much information on the internet now, but I have found family history is a giant puzzle, and everyone I've met who has this as a major hobby has spent years collecting little pieces of evidence to add to the puzzle. You sometimes must play detective and tease information from context or general social history. I have provided some resources to help with this process, one of the best being a family history links database called Cyndi's List, started originally by Cyndi Ingle which she shared with members of the Tacoma-Pierce County Genealogical Society in 1996.[57]

Relating to the Ancestors—A Systemic Lens

As much as we are biologically the descendants of our ancestors, so, too, are we socially descended from them. We live surrounded by remnants of the perceptions, beliefs, biases, and traumas of our ancestors in the way we ourselves show up in the world. A key moment in my ancestral work was having to do an assignment during my psychotherapy program on family history as it related to family dynamic and culture. The assignment used a psychotherapeutic lens called "family systems theory," an approach to analyzing and understanding family dynamics that was developed by Dr. Murray Bowen in the 1950s. The theory seeks to understand familial conflict from a systemic point of view rather than a moralistic one. Instead of seeing individuals or families as morally flawed and bad, individuals and families are understood as products of their upbringing within the contexts of core and extended family cultures.

Bowen suggested that families are essentially complex emotional systems that develop and are transmitted generationally, and which influence and are influenced by the individuals making up that system. The family system evolves in such a way as to create unwritten rules, specific types of relationships, and roles within the family to serve the needs of that system's continued existence. Bowen highlighted that families often fall into healthy or unhealthy dynamics depending on how the leaders of the system (parents, grandparents) were equipped to deal with stress by their own families of origin. The way someone deals with conflict, for example, is often directly related to how conflict was dealt with in the family they originate from.

Now, Bowen's theory often looks at unhealthy issues in families, but all the positive and healthy developments can also be accounted for through

---

57. Cyndi Ingle, "About Cyndi Ingle," Cyndi's List of Genealogy Sites on the Internet, accessed November 26, 2022, https://www.cyndislist.com/aboutus/.

this theory. Healthy dynamics are passed down within the family in the same way as unhealthy ones and are also present.[58]

The assignment I worked on for my course was called a genogram, a specialized family tree that tracked information back through the generations. The number of lenses you could use to overlay onto a genogram makes this a dynamic tool for reflection and analysis. Often, when I looked at the family history as provided by my mum, the genealogical evidence, and the culture of my family, I could begin to make interesting deductions. For example, I grew up in a family where both my parents were self-employed and driven to succeed in business, sometimes at the expense of their own health and stress levels.

Anyone who has grown up in a family business will know that often the business takes up a lot of room in the family, and that is what happened with my family. When I explored the historical evolution of both sides of my family's story, I found spookily similar correlations between the stories of my maternal and paternal great-grandfathers. On both sides of the family the emphasis on success and being a self-made person was strong, and I could trace that family ethos down the generations to me. I applied the same method to other stories and dynamics—not all of them positive—and began to get a much fuller sense of how things happening five generations ago show up in my life now.

The process was powerful, and around that same time, I was also exploring ancestral veneration. I took an opportunity to speak with some of my paternal ancestors at a silent café, who gave me greater context to how this core belief of the family had impacted them, and I was able to bond with them. The whole process shifted my relationship with my parents as well because I realized how the pressures of the family belief had potentially impacted them too, and my grandparents and great-grandparents.

Now, while the Bowen system is a good tool to look at the immediate and extended family, the dynamics explored in this system can be helpful to think about society in general. The contexts of our ancestors create our world, just as our social context now is creating the world of our descendants. Culture in general is a dynamic system and has within it both emerging trends and older

---

58. Ona Cohn Bregman and Charles M. White, eds. *Bringing Systems Thinking to Life: Expanding the Horizons for Bowen Family Systems Theory* (New York: Brunner-Routledge, 2011), n.p.

traditions. Ancestral work requires us to look at the context our ancestors were present in, and this can be a powerful technique for teasing out information about our family stories. Learning more about history in general can give us clues about how our ancestors lived and understand how our world now connects to them. Visit living history museums, eat historical foods, learn about those contexts so that even if you don't know your ancestors' names you can relate to them through the contextual and peripheral data.

Curating the Perfect Ancestral Tree

In digging deeper into our family stories, it is inevitable we will connect with our ancestors' lives and relate to some individuals more than others. We start to see our experiences reflected in the lives of ancestors, and their stories can act to reinforce our own. This is a very normal human social trait; we gravitate toward those we feel we have a sense of affinity or belonging with. Your entire list of affinity ancestors from several chapters ago speaks to that connection. Now, this form of relationship alone can tell us a lot about ourselves, but I think it also presents several issues that I'd like to discuss.

I will give a very good and personal example of this work. In Neopaganism, I notice it is common for many individuals when first starting on their new path to emphasize ancient pagan ancestors while ignoring or degrading Christian ancestors. This often seems to be among individuals who exhibit signs of religious trauma or who are strengthening a connection to their newfound Neopagan beliefs. Part of this, I think, can be understood as a process of conversion where rejection of Christianity, often because of trauma, also requires the rejection of any cultural components or symbols connecting to that which is being rejected. In looking to an ancient pagan past and finding kinship with the ancestors who are perceived to have originated or followed the beliefs being taken up, there is also, I think, a sense of validation and affirmation.

It is not my place to comment on how individuals relate to their ancestral story, but I would challenge readers to consider how the ancestors might be relating to you while you are trying to relate to them. For example, I used to be one of those individuals who wholesale rejected my Christian ancestors because as a gay kid growing up in a tiny town, I did not see much love directed at me from my Christian neighbors. The turning point for me was when I started to understand that my story and who I am intersect with my ancestors in so many different ways that we are bound to have things in common and not in common.

When I was exploring myself as a teenager, I needed to connect with groups of ancestors who affirmed me because of being in a vulnerable place. When I no longer had that need, I was able to look to the whole family story as being more complex, and likewise, it allowed me to understand myself as more complex. Take stock of what ancestors you look to and what their characteristics are that you connect with. Then strive to consider if that connection is built from a place of security or if it comes from a place of insecurity.

The Uncomfortable Faces of Ancestral History

As you delve deep into your ancestral story, uncovering your ancestors' lives and how you relate to that history, you will become aware of uncomfortable truths. The uncovering of history and stories that bring up unease, regret, disappointment, discomfort, and shame is very normal and to be expected. Our society tends to put a lot of effort into covering up uncomfortable truths, but I believe it is vital to focus not only on the positive and inspiring in our ancestral background but also the ugly. I understand my readership will probably be of a very diverse background, and I hope that this section will apply to you as you work with your personal and ancestral story. Many of the examples given below involve North America and the United Kingdom, two areas that form my story, but I hope that they point you toward thinking about your own context.

Often when diving into ancestral story, we come across history that we don't like or that has been hidden by the family. That history can be connected to individuals or be a chapter in the history of society that is now looked on with embarrassment. Family systems are very good at covering up and sweeping under the rug uncomfortable history or those individuals who the family system deems threatening. All families have secrets that they don't wish to let out, certain private details or information that they fear will tarnish the reputation of the family.

As you read this, I am sure you can think of some uncomfortable realities of your family of origin that hold with them shame or embarrassment. If you are having a difficult time coming up with any, then it proves that your family system of origin did a good job at shielding you from that undesired reality. Perhaps you yourself are that undesired truth that your family of origin find embarrassing or shameful, the black sheep of the family or the outlier who had to choose between living your life or succumbing to the expectations to conform.

We talked previously about unhealthy individuals in your ancestral line and the potential dangers connected to these individuals, but what I'm speaking about here is how the living family relate to the story of these individuals or chapters. This is often where the narrative put forward by the family system can be very different from the reality. As we discussed above, family systems are cultures that are handed down in whole or in part to the next generation. Part of that family culture are various narratives that support the family's values, beliefs, and outlooks. We are often trained from birth to know what the rules of the family are and what subjects are taboo. Often, scandalous members of the family system can be scapegoated and become black sheep for not following or affirming the unwritten rules or family narrative. This scapegoating is perpetuated by the family system as a way of control and to safeguard the family from what is perceived as an existential threat.

Let us look at a very specific but good example of how this might look. Take for example a common scenario for white families in the southern United States who, upon researching into their history, discover that they have black slave ancestry. For many generations, there was social stigma about a heritage like this, and so for some families that history becomes hidden. The information is kept secret because of the perceived shame and loss of social privilege. Meanwhile, those ancestors remain intentionally ignored by the family and forgotten, and as a result, individuals can become even more vehemently racist as a way of coping with the cognitive dissonance of suddenly finding themselves as the direct products of a complex and terrible history.

The above example is specific to a percentage of readers, but it raises powerful questions: How do we work with ancestors or their stories when we are trained by our family to be uncomfortable with them? How do we work with ancestors who we personally don't agree with or are uncomfortable about? I don't have a good answer for this, and the answer will very much depend on your specific context. I understand what being oppressed is because I am queer, but I also know that I hold privilege in society. I know that I am a product of the complex social history of the UK, and that history becomes personal for me because I have ancestors within the past five generations who originated from England, Scotland, Wales, and Ireland. At various times and continuing to this day, there is an uneasiness between these four countries around this history. What do I do with all this history and the ancestors who were part of or directed some of these events? I can only say that the darker and uncomfortable aspects of our stories cannot and should not be ostracized, and part of our work must be in understanding and taking responsibility for the world we were handed. We cannot take responsibility for the world we live in if we don't understand how we got here. We all have a role in tearing down barriers and working toward reconciliation between each other. Likewise, it is my belief that we cannot do that work without the partnership of the ancestors, even the ones who are unhealthy. In working toward ancestral healing, we work toward holding accountable our ancestors while also forming healthier relationships with them and between one another.

The Problem of "Founders"

This topic came about because of a discussion with one of my editors, and I think it's important to point that out to show how culture tends to blind those of us with privilege. I had originally placed into this book a piece about celebrating the founders of communities as ancestral to place, related to what we discussed in an earlier chapter around founding figures.

I remember when I was younger and had just moved to Canada. The education system then spoke a lot about the settlement of Canada from the perspective of the settlers. I used to think what a weird term "founder" was, and it made me think of someone wandering through the woods and then suddenly finding a fully built town or village and claiming it for themselves. Of course, the reality is that for most places touched by colonialism, what happened was conquest and claiming territory regardless of who lived there.

While I have grown up in Ontario, I'm from the United Kingdom where most towns were founded hundreds if not thousands of years ago. Many of these settlements were created by now-mythological figures, and so they become more like affinity ancestors than direct ancestors. However, coming to Canada, I grew up in a town that was settled by mostly German settlers in the 1850s and was founded by a single settler. The streets were all named after the town's founder, and there was a mural of his face on one of the main buildings. For those who grew up in the town and whose ancestors helped to establish the community, this is their lineage and the context of their relationship to that land. But that history comes at the expense of Ontario's Indigenous communities whose own ancestors hunted and farmed that same land for thousands of years before European settlers came. Their relationship to that place was submerged in favor of the settlers who came in and took that land.

This is not unique to Ontario; it is a common story across so many colonized lands. Part of the struggle as it relates to ancestral work is how do settlers reconcile their personal relationships to the land they were born in, while also acknowledging that the context of that relationship comes from disenfranchisement and colonialism? How does one relate to ancestors who were settlers, understanding now the harm that colonialism did and continues to do to Indigenous people? How do descendants of settlers relate to the ancestors of Indigenous peoples who are in the land they are occupying if their own sense of identity sees those ancestors in that land as other?

I know the answers to the above questions for me, but the answers may be different for you. Certainly, for many communities, moves have been made to uncover hidden history and celebrate healthy aspects of both sets of history as a way of building relationship between Indigenous and settler. Specific examples of reconciliation include changing town and place names back to Indigenous language names and removing statues celebrating colonizers. This is done not to shame settlers for existing, but as an outward paradigm shift to state that the settler story is not the only one worthy of being front and center.

Becoming aware of and teaching hidden history is another key factor in this work, though not without controversy. Reconciliation can be initiatives to support the sovereignty of groups we don't belong to but who are our neighbors. A major part of that work is to understand our own privilege so that we are able to build equitable and respectful relationships with those who don't share that privilege. This is to say, understand the limits of your privilege in society, the limits your privilege creates for others, and strive to dismantle that privilege by understanding how that privilege was created in the first place. As we currently see with the backlash against teaching critical race theory in schools in the United States and teaching truthful Indigenous history in Canada, not all members of society are ready or prepared to face these histories of oppression. Neither are they willing to see the way that history has created the current state of the world.

This, I think, has created crises of identity for many communities in colonized lands, and I think it helps to explain the deep longing for ancestral homelands we've discussed previously in chapter four. In my opinion, the way forward is the process of reconciliation, the intentional work of deprogramming and challenging the systems of oppression that all of us were handed and working toward a society of inclusion for all. Marginalized communities who bear the brunt of that oppression are already doing that work; it falls on the rest of us to join in and build a better context for all of our descendants. Part of that work also includes settler descendants becoming, as Dr. Kimmerer puts it, indigenized to an area; that is, learning to build an authentic and long-lasting relationship with the land. Building relationships with Indigenous neighbors means approaching them with integrity. I believe doing so will go a long way to solving many issues of identity crisis that settler communities find themselves facing, and to begin to heal ancestral trauma.

Many of these issues are at the core of the work of Ontario author and artist Pegi Eyers, whose own ancestors originated from England and Scotland. In her tome, *Ancient Spirit Rising,* Eyers explores how disconnection from an authentic relationship to land has caused many white individuals in alternative spirituality communities to adopt or appropriate Indigenous traditions. This is done as a way of minimizing the feeling of being adrift from ancestral traditions and relationships based in homelands they do not live in, while also rejecting what is perceived to be oppressive dominant forces such as Christianity. This appropriation of Indigenous traditions and co-opting of Indigenous relationship to this land does nothing to build authentic relationship. Eyers discusses in depth many specific ways settlers can reconnect with ancestral story and connect to the land they inhabit, while also respecting and celebrating Indigenous relationships to the same land. This building of a new type of relationship, which both acknowledges the incredible harm already done and removes settlers from the center of the social story, offers the opportunity to write a new story with new parts for all of us.[59]

Standing on the Threshold of Personal and Ancestral Story

In considering the points raised above relating to uncovering our shared history, I hope that I've illustrated some of the many ways that ancestral and personal story can interact. Just as we talked about the influence affinity and conceptual ancestors can have in a previous chapter, I hope you have started to question and wonder about the influence your ancestors and the unhealthy and healthy aspects of their story have had on you.

Journal Prompts

- Who do you count among your ancestors? Who do you not count among your ancestors?

- In what ways do you identify with your ancestors; are there particular labels you share with them? (For example, "My Scots ancestors," "My Pagan ancestors.")

- In what ways does your identification with your ancestors foster healthy relationships to them? In what ways does it foster unhealthy relationships?

- Are there groups of your ancestors that you feel uncomfortable with? In what ways do you suppress or hide these ancestors? What about these ancestors makes you uncomfortable?

- What role do you believe you have in creating the context for future generations?

---

59. Pegi Eyers, *Ancient Spirit Rising: Reclaiming Your Roots & Restoring Earth Community* (Otonabee, Ontario, Canada: Stone Circle Press, 2016), n.p.

Exercise Three
EXPLORING ANCESTOR STORY

Consider for yourself a story of a particular ancestor (of whatever kind we've talked about so far) and use the following questions to dig deeper into the narrative. Begin with positive stories and challenge yourself to explore the darker stories. Feel free to work with any ancestral story whether lineage, affinity, or conceptual.

1. In your own words, recount a story of your ancestor that informs you a little about who they are.

2. Consider the following prompts in connecting with this story:

   • What about this story do you connect with?

   • What does this story tell you about the ancestor?

   • How has this story impacted your life and the world you live in?

   • How did you first hear this story? (In the case of family history, who told you? In the case of affinity or conceptual, how did you first learn about this story?)

   • What emotions come up for you in relation to this story?

   • How do you see your own story in this individual?

   • How has your relationship to this story changed as you've grown older?

   • Is this a story you want to pass down to your descendants? Why or why not?

Chapter Seven
Ancestor Veneration and the Community

As a private practice, ancestor veneration can be powerful for us to use to work through our own grief, gain blessings for our own lives, and explore our personal story more, but ancestor veneration around the world has social dimensions. While it is true we each have a unique set of ancestors, it is also true that many of our ancestors are shared with multitudes of community members to the point that family trees look more like vast family webs. Walking down the street, you probably pass by people you are related to on a daily basis, and those relationships are from ancestors many generations back. Our story and ancestral lineage connect with everyone's eventually until we can't see this as only a private practice anymore.

This reality of ancestral work creates some wonderful opportunities to connect to community through honoring the dead. Likewise, the community dimension of ancestor veneration transcends lineage ancestors and can be expanded to include affinity and conceptual ancestors. Whether that community is defined geographically, socially, familiarly, or spiritually in scope, ancestral veneration can serve as an important linchpin in building relationships with others in the community. In this chapter, we will discuss some ways that ancestor veneration can and does show up in a communal form, and what possibilities this has for your practice.

The first major aspect of ancestral work as it relates to the community is its potential role as a container for cultural expression and exploration.

This extends from personal practice and moves into communal practice with family or your community. Any of the various ancestor festivals of the dead around the world speak to this community face of what would otherwise be a personal or individual family affair. The community comes together to celebrate and honor the dead, whether it be specific individuals or the dead in general. What often happens in these events is you see the interrelationship between the needs of the individual and the needs of the community, as the event often incorporates communal tradition with individual experience.

In the case of ancestral work, there can often be found within such events a continuity of cultural expression that embraces old traditions while reinvigorating them for the current time. The traditions become a liminal space of contact between all members of the entire community, both living and dead. One could argue that culture in general acts this way, as a meeting ground between what came before and what is emerging. Even if the practices change and shift, a teaching I have received in my own traditions and that seems reflected in those other traditions I have viewed, is that the ancestors recognize the practice and maintain their place in the community process because they understand the changes through the lineage of bearers. An ancestor from five hundred years ago, whose lived experience was very different than our own, is connected to us through every subsequent individual leading up to us. Through that lineage, that individual ancestor connects to us and understands what is being done.

Below are some specific examples of ways tradition broadly and ancestor work specifically can be utilized in the community. These are just starting-off points to have you consider ways your ancestral practice will or could engage with the community. This is not an expansive list, but consider for yourself as you read through these examples how this approach to your work will intersect with others and in what ways some of the dynamics below have already shown up in your community. In particular, consider how your ancestors' stories and lives may have been impacted by some of the elements spoken of below.

Dancing with the Ancestors: Engaging with Tradition

Culture connects us to the past and to the future, and while aspects often change to suit the needs of different generations, there is usually enough retained to form a continuity. There are many aspects of culture we could look at, but let's look at folk tradition. Folk tradition often looks like specific cultural or ethnic markers that identify individuals as belonging to specific groups. It can appear through arts and crafts, songs and music, dance, foods, drama, storytelling, and certain forms of oral communication. Folk tradition is often shared throughout a community (with variation) and includes all members of the group. When someone engages in folk tradition, they are taking a role in a ritual or a series of actions that have been done before and will hopefully be done again.

Consider for yourself some of the family or cultural traditions you engage in and how you came to engage with them. Were you taught dances or songs by beloved family members? Were you told certain folktales about certain places in the community by wise and cherished storytellers? This is a powerful dimension of culture in that we engage with material that we didn't originate but have responsibility for. Often, folk tradition is a monolith that serves to weave the various generations of a community together. Take, for example, folk dance, where there are particular traditional costumes, and these costumes have stayed more or less the same for decades. Individuals separated by time suddenly find common ground through that tradition, inviting the generations to connect on equal footing. This is a powerful form of bonding that takes place.

The nature of culture is to change and evolve, and unfortunately sometimes older traditions get lost, forgotten, or suppressed along the way. Once gone, folk traditions take with them an aspect of culture difficult to revive. However, a culture can revive and recreate older traditions, which will take on new meaning and often also take on different forms. Revitalization is the act of bringing back to life older traditions, which through whatever social process became victim to neglect, and through being revitalized, they are recreated and take on new dimensions for the current generation. We see this in the various folk movements, which take up old traditions and bring them into the modern day for the benefit, entertainment, and education of the modern community. What essentially takes place is a co-creative process where at first a small group takes interest and revives the tradition, and as it is presented back to the larger community, an interest builds until the culture reestablishes the tradition as a living shared space. Sometimes the tradition is close to what was originally practiced; more often the practice is inspired by the original but has an identity and form of its own.

An example of the resurrection of folk practices is the Welsh hobbyhorse tradition, the *mari lwyd* ("grey mare"). Mari lwyd is a New Year's tradition where a horse's skull is decorated and paraded around the town on a pole by an actor covered by a white sheet visiting home to home and engaging in wassailing. The tradition originates in South Wales and began to die out around the beginning of the last century. In recent years, the tradition has been revitalized by enthusiasts in the folk movement, and an annual gathering of mari lwyds takes place in Chepstow, Monmouthshire. The tradition has been taken up by different groups for different reasons, one such group being the Urdd Derwyddon Môn (Anglesey Druid Order) headed by order founder Kristoffer Hughes. The UDM has equated the figure of the mari lwyd with the Welsh otherworldly figure Rhiannon, envisioning the mari lwyd as the winter form of the goddess.[60] While this is not an interpretation shared by other groups, this is exactly the sort of reimagining that often occurs with revitalization. The older tradition is revitalized and a new form is developed that is deeply meaningful for the present community. The community's own ancestors may have practiced the original tradition, and the new revitalized version is both grounded in the present while connected to the past. In the case of the Druid order's use of mari lwyd in their spiritual relationship with Rhiannon, the new version of the tradition invites outsiders to become part of the community.

How does this above example affect ancestral work? The mari lwyd was a tradition going back many hundreds of years, and though with slightly different meaning ascribed, was an experience that those ancestors who took part in it enjoyed. By reinvigorating the experience and bringing it back from the brink of extinction, the experience is saved for new generations to take part in. The importance, then, of revitalizing traditions is both to make them relevant and meaningful to the present while also experiencing something your own ancestors partook in, connecting to them through that experience. I think experiencing shared traditions has a massive impact on building relationship

---

60. Kristoffer Hughes, *The Book of Celtic Magic: Transformative Teachings from the Cauldron of Awen* (Woodbury, MN: Llewellyn Publications, 2014), 103.

with your ancestors. The experience becomes a gateway for individuals into a shared reality with the ancestors through a shared communal experience.

Community Building and External Education: Creating New Traditions

So far, we have spoken about traditions as shared experiences between you and the ancestors. Another key dynamic of engaging with tradition is community building. While previously we explored the relationship between individuals engaging with traditions that the ancestors also took part in themselves, let us explore the opportunities for meaningful community building by creating new traditions. In particular, let's explore the opportunities that ancestral work as a community activity can provide. Art and cultural festivals, media, and cuisine have all been used as spaces for cultural and community gathering and bonding, but they've also been used as spaces for activism and education directed externally.

Ancestor veneration spaces have also been part of this process, especially in diasporic communities. As a form of social activism, community organizing has been centered on the enacting of the public rituals of the tradition. A very good example is one of the Day of the Dead celebrations in Los Angeles, which was founded in the El Movimiento (a.k.a. the Chicano Movement), a political movement for Chicano rights that occurred concurrently with the civil rights, women's rights, and queer rights movements.

The organization at the heart of this LA Day of the Dead celebration is East Los Angeles–based Self Help Graphics & Art, a community arts center originally founded in 1970 by a small group of artists and printmakers from the local area, many belonging to the Chicano community. One of the founders, Sister Karen Boccalero, approached her religious Order of the Sisters of St. Francis and gained a grant to move into a bigger building, which could accommodate more community activities. Working together, they began offering workshops, outreach, and arts projects to express, reclaim, and explore Chicano heritage and identity. One of these early community events was the Day of the Dead, an event that many members of the Los Angeles Chicano community were not familiar with because it did not factor into their lives in the United States. Starting small, but growing considerably, the Day of the Dead celebrations have over the years taken on different meanings for all who have taken part in it. At Self Help Graphics, the imagery of the Day of the Dead has been linked with exploring other themes, and in other communities the festivities have included imagery that expresses political viewpoints and raises awareness of issues that affect those local communities, such as violence, war, and the homogenization of Chicano identity with Mexican American identity.[61]

The celebration of LA's Day of the Dead has shifted at times to embrace new traditions that developed in the southwest United States, such as the use of paper marigold flowers. Likewise, the embracing of adaptations that have spread across both Mexico and the US such as face painting.[62] At its core, though, aside from the community celebration, is the ritual act of commemorating the dead, and this has been taken up in the yearly ofrenda at Self Help Graphics & Art itself, each ofrenda being dedicated to a particular theme or story deeply relevant to the community.[63]

With the example of the Day of the Dead by the Chicano community, we see this tradition touching on and being the vehicle for various community and personal needs. We see how an ancient celebration has become the container for community activism, expression, communication, and exploration. The old customs have been modified to fit with a new environment, and in so doing, the new forms become deeply meaningful to the living community while still being accessible and devoted to the dead.

Sometimes, traditions can be formed in reaction to crises and the need to educate others to fight against disaster. In the 1980s, as the HIV/AIDS pandemic descended on the world and so many people were dying of the mystery disease, many LGBT victims were abandoned by their families of origin, and their bodies were unclaimed for burial. The pandemic was particularly ravaging to young gay men, and as they died and left holes in their communities, different organizations sought ways to honor them and put pressure on authorities to take the pandemic seriously.

---

61. Regina M. Marchi, *Day of the Dead in the USA: The Migration and Transformation of a Cultural Phenomenon*, 2nd ed. (New Brunswick, NJ: Rutgers University Press, 2022), 48.

62. Artbound, season 10, episode 3, "Día de Los Muertos/Day of the Dead." 2019, KCET, 56:17, https://www.kcet.org/shows/artbound/episodes/dia-de-los-muertos-day-of-the -dead.

63. Marchi, *Day of the Dead in the USA*, 49.

In 1985, gay rights activist Cleve Jones, who had been organizing a yearly candlelit march in honor of Harvey Milk, who had been murdered about seven years before, saw that over one thousand people had died of AIDS in San Francisco alone. During the 1985 march, he asked that attendees write the names of those who had been lost to AIDS on placards, and they were taped onto the San Francisco Federal Building. Onlookers were struck at how the placards resembled a patchwork quilt. Community members were encouraged to sew large memorial panels with the names of loved ones who had been lost so that they would not be neglected and forgotten.

The first gathering of community members materialized into the NAMES Project AIDS Memorial Quilt, which seeks to bring awareness to the pandemic and to memorialize those who were lost. In 1987, the National Mall in Washington, D.C. served as the first unveiling of the quilt with a whopping 1,920 panels filling the size of a football field. By 1988, when the quilt returned to Washington to be displayed in front of the White House, it had grown to more than 8,288 panels sent in from people across the United States. As of 2020, the quilt is composed of 48,000 panels memorializing more than 100,000 individuals, and the extended collection of artifacts housed now at the American Folklife Center numbers more than 200,000 cards, letters, and photographs.

The quilt galvanized the community and became a potent symbol of honoring the dead and supporting the survivors. While members of the LGBT community would have preferred a disease like AIDS had never existed, the use of a tradition like the quilt to both honor the dead and send a clear message that this is a real issue needing to be addressed is powerful. The quilt has become a living symbol for the community to rally around, as well as a way to teach younger members of the community about a history so easily shamed and forgotten by society.

Organic Fusion of Diverse Traditions

Another side of perpetuating community identity is to encourage cohesive community formation when there are disparate parts or new community members. As colonialism hit the world and we had unparalleled numbers of people migrating or being displaced from different regions over a relatively short period in human history, we suddenly had large populations with mixed heritages. Ancestor veneration practices and spiritual traditions have been used in these regions to stitch different communities together and help foster a unity among groups who have very different origins.

South America and the Caribbean are both areas where a vast majority of people have heritages from disparate groups, and these shared heritages have formed new syncretic traditions. The Venezuelan religion of María Lionza is typical of this sort of syncretism. The tradition centers on three major individuals, understood to be the three prime manifestations of God: Negro Felipe, Queen María Lionza, and Chief Guaicaipuro. These three individuals (called *Tres Potencias*, "Three Powers") are worshipped in a trinity not unlike the trinity of Catholicism. Surrounding the Three Powers are a host of ancestral spirits organized into various courts, such as the Africans, Indigenous, Doctors, Holy Criminals, and Vikings. The leaders of these spirit courts are particularly revered historical figures important to the history of Venezuela.[64] While incorporating elements of Indigenous, African, and European traditions and figures, the tradition is grounded solely in the landscape of Venezuela with various sacred sites around the region.

This tradition is so interesting because it quite literally represents and includes the various peoples who are part of Venezuela's diverse ethnic makeup, as well as all those who are of mixed heritage. When a practitioner works with their spirits and engages in public ritual, they can see themselves represented perfectly in the plethora of spiritual beings and ancestors of the tradition. Similar traditions such as Haitian Vodou, Sanse, espiritismo, and the various Brazilian spirit religions all represent mostly equally the various people of these regions in defiance of the white hierarchies of colonialism.

What can this look like for you and your community? Depending on what your community is defined by, look to see who isn't included in your plans. If you are honoring the ancestors of a particular geographic community, invite Indigenous community members and embrace the ancestors who share a relationship with that place. If you are honoring affinity ancestors such as fictional characters, include diverse voices and expressions around that character. If you are creating a practice for yourself and invite others into that practice, create space for their traditions to be present, even if just temporarily.

---

64. Barbara Placido, "'It's All to Do with Words': An Analysis of Spirit Possession in the Venezuelan Cult of María Lionza." *The Journal of the Royal Anthropological Institute* 7, no. 2 (June 2001): 207–24. https://doi.org/10.1111/1467-9655.00059.

Uncovering Hidden History

We spoke about this in the previous chapter, and so I'd like to bridge what we discussed around uncovering hidden narratives and what that can look like in a community setting. Jumping off the example of the AIDS quilt, group ancestral veneration and remembering the dead can often serve to ensure history is never forgotten or repeated. History is often recorded to put dominant cultures in the best light or to sweep under the rug any history that challenges positive social identity. Marginalized groups often become victims of this sort of erasure, and so I would suggest that folklore and veneration traditions that are not directly controlled by institutional powers are where you will find expression of community needs around the remembering of history the dominant society finds uncomfortable or a threat. Sometimes practices and projects are formed to uncover previously hidden history and put it into the spotlight.

Sitting at the mouth of the East River, east of the Bronx, in New York City lies the infamous Hart Island. Hart Island is around a mile long and is used by the city as an internment ground for any unclaimed body in the city's morgues. Throughout history, the island has been used as a cemetery and quite a few times as a mass burial ground. During the recent COVID-19 pandemic, the unclaimed bodies of people who died because of COVID were buried on Hart Island.[65] This is not an uncommon use of the island, as it has been a public cemetery for decades. It is estimated that over a million people's remains are buried on Hart Island; among them are AIDS victims whose bodies could not be buried anywhere else because either funeral homes or cemeteries would not accept them. A project has been established to methodically search out and name the individuals buried there. Called the Hart Island Project, the project seeks to identify remains in the unmarked plots and reunite the remains with their families and loved ones. Many of the new interments on Hart Island are now rigorously documented, and the Hart Island Project seeks to uncover the identities of those still-unmarked graves.

---

65. Elyse Samuels and Adriana Usero, "'New York City's Family Tomb': The Sad History of Hart Island," *The Washington Post*, WP Company, April 27, 2020, https://www.washington post.com/history/2020/04/27/hart-island-mass-grave-coronavirus-burials/.

The nature of memorial projects like this is to be relevant to the needs of the living community while also remembering the dead. Very successful projects are adaptive to the shifting needs of the community and are expanded to incorporate other issues while not losing the focus of the original intent. This is where the use of symbols as a form of communication becomes very relevant, and those symbols go on to inspire other forms of community expression.

For example, in June 2016, a lone gunman entered the Pulse nightclub in Orlando, Florida, and opened fire on the crowd. In total, forty-nine patrons were killed and over fifty others wounded. To date, this is the second largest mass shooting in US history, and it was perpetrated against the LGBT community. This incident reverberated around the globe and impacted even remote queer communities; friends of mine from all over were shaken by this, and I must admit, so was I. I remember standing in my kitchen and just bursting into tears for weeks after the shooting, even though I didn't know any of the victims directly. But I did know those victims…when I looked at their faces I saw the faces of my friends, my lovers, my little ones that I've taken under my wing over the years, and I saw myself. Within days, memorials were staged around the country, and a shrine was built outside the night club. The feelings of outrage continued for months and still continue to be felt. At one North Carolina university, Wake Forest, the local LGBTQ+ Center recognized that students would be returning in the fall with the massacre still fresh in their minds and so began a project to assist students in processing the incident and memorializing the dead. Taking inspiration from the AIDS quilt, the center invited students to contribute to a memorial quilt commemorating the forty-nine lives taken. That symbol of the quilt is a potent one: it covers, it warms, it protects, and it comforts.

The NAMES Aids Memorial Quilt and other memorials like it have had an impact by giving identity back to the victims, who would otherwise be condemned to a faceless statistic. They create space for the community to come together to process the trauma of the loss and take stock of the crisis as it unfolds. There are many other examples found in many other communities—especially the marginalized—where that interplay between symbol, individual, community, and problem forms the connections for activism.

Public memorials, no matter how large or small, have impact, and they invite the community to engage. Consider your communities, in whatever form you want to focus on, and consider what purpose public memorials have served. Were there any memorials to community ancestors or honored dead? How did the memorial impact your community? What relationship do you have to that memorial?

Memorial projects are just one form that communities employ to tell the histories that are often suppressed. Think of any marginalized group and you will find attempts to tell the story of the group and the early pioneers of that community. As we discussed in the previous chapter about confronting uncomfortable history, we now see in many colonized countries movements to bring to light the history of the marginalized through reclaiming Indigenous names of places, telling the stories of important heroes from these peoples, and placing the colonial encounter into proper perspective that is inclusive of all people in the community.

Another face to this sort of work is how the needs of the ancestors can also double as a vehicle for education on contemporary issues. For example, in recent years there has been a movement in multiple regions to repatriate remains and return artifacts stolen by the scientific and anthropological communities as specimens of study. Many of those "specimens" are the remains of individuals whose burial places were discovered, disturbed, excavated, and put on display for the entertainment of a public who have no connection to said remains. Sometimes these remains were displayed as curios or held in library basements as anthropological specimens. This issue is a potent one, for it involves deep-seated human connections to the remains of our dead and their spirits, and points directly to how one set of beliefs is often systemically privileged over others in multiple societies.

A well-known example of this is the case of the Kennewick Man, an individual who lived approximately nine thousand years ago and whose skeletal remains were discovered in 1996 in Kennewick, Washington, in the United States. Local Indigenous governments, especially the Umatilla people, demanded the remains be turned over for reburial under NAGPRA (the Native American Graves Protection and Repatriation Act, 1990). NAGPRA had originally been written as a way of protecting Indigenous sites and as a reparation for how Indigenous burial grounds had been treated historically (a.k.a. looted by scholars in academia).

The gravesite of Kennewick Man fell within a stretch of land along the Columbia River that was held sacred and claimed by five Indigenous peoples, but which was managed by the US Army Corps of Engineers. The government seized the remains from the archaeologists, who promptly sued for sole custodianship of the remains. The law as written stated that any archeological finds can be claimed by an Indigenous group as cultural property if that group can establish cultural affiliation with the item. The anthropologists argued that the Kennewick Man, being almost nine thousand years old, could not possibly be traced to living Indigenous peoples in the area due to the amount of time that had passed, and they refused to give over the remains. What ensued was a nine-year legal battle for custody of the remains, and the Kennewick Man became emblematic of the systemic issue of laws controlling the Indigenous communities and their affairs.

Eventually, through DNA analysis of two modern residents of the Colville community, a link between the Kennewick Man and the tribes of the local area was established and the remains were repatriated to the Umatilla, Wanapum, Nimíipuu (Nez Perce), Mamachatpam (Yakama), and Colville communities.[66] In February 2017, twenty years after the remains were found, the ancestor was buried in a secret location in a private ceremony attended by over two hundred members of the five communities. In a statement, JoDe Goudy, the chairman of the Yakama Nation Tribal Council, said, "The Ancient One, may now finally find peace, and we, his relatives, will equally feel content knowing that this work has been completed on his behalf."[67]

Reframing and Rejecting Oppressive Narratives

As we've discussed so far, the family system is very good at stifling what it has deemed to be a threat or an embarrassment. In a smaller family, the disagreement and estrangement between two siblings can manifest in family narra-

---

66. Morten Rasmussen et al., "The Ancestry and Affiliations of Kennewick Man," *Nature* 523 (2015): 455–458, https://doi.org/10.1038/nature14625.

67. Amy Klinkhammer, "Kennewick Man's Bones Reburied, Settling a Decades-Long Debate," *Discover Magazine*. February 21, 2017, https://www.discovermagazine.com/planet-earth /kennewick-mans-bones-reburied-settling-a-decades-long-debate.

tives vilifying the other, causing a rift between two branches that is taken up by future generations. Part of ancestor work is to uncover for yourself what the truth of these stories is and make up your own mind about how they will impact your relationships. Not all reactions from the family system to perceived threats are meritless, and many times they do come from healthy boundaries.

Society at large acts in many similar ways to smaller family systems, but on a much broader scale. Consider for yourself right now, in the society you live in, who are the heroes and who are the villains? If you put on the news or listen to your politicians, who or what are considered desirable or a danger? What are some of the stories told about these individuals or groups? Are these stories justified, or are they used as tools by a dominant society to pigeonhole others?

For example, the reclaiming of vilified or intentionally forgotten figures and honoring and celebrating them as a way of shifting and subverting a narrative imposed by dominant forces is a powerful act of ancestral work. If you belong to a marginalized group, chances are this is not a new thing for you, and you might be thinking about an individual that your community has worked with in this way. Who a society or culture vilifies or makes a hero is always telling about that culture's self-narrative.

Often, one culture's revolutionary will be another culture's rebel. In terms of dominant cultures actively oppressing minority groups, often it is a mechanism of controlling the narrative to demonize the leaders of that group or eliminate any mention of them altogether. The goal of this process is always to control the narrative and gain power over the target group by imposing a narrative that serves the dominant power's agenda. Where ancestor veneration comes in is that often the struggle against that dominant power becomes an important part of the culture and a narrative that begins to interact with other cultural narratives.

For example, in Canada, the Canadian government and the Métis people's narratives of Métis leader Louis Riel were very different at one point. To the government, Riel was a treasonous rebel who posed a threat to social order and stability; to the Métis, Riel was a charismatic leader fighting a just cause against a government who sought to supplant them from their land. Nearly 140 years after his death, Louis Riel is still a potent figure and symbol in the

Métis community, often looked to as a source of inspiration and strength for Métis leaders. Louis Riel has become a symbol for Métis struggle for justice and right to exist. It is telling that the power of reclaiming a vilified hero in the face of oppression does have impact, as in Manitoba where there is a publicly recognized holiday for Louis Riel.

Journal Prompts

- What does community mean to you? What kinds of communities do you belong to?

- How does your community honor the dead or ancestors of other kinds? What relationship do those ancestors have to your community? What do the stories of those ancestors tell you about your community?

- In what ways does your community respect or disrespect the ancestors?

- Are there folk or historical heroes in your community who were vilified by overarching powers?

- Do these villains or heroes deserve the treatment they received? What narrative did you grow up with? How has that narrative been affirmed or challenged?

- What lessons do these heroes (or villains) teach? What is your community's relationship to them? What does that relationship teach you about your community?

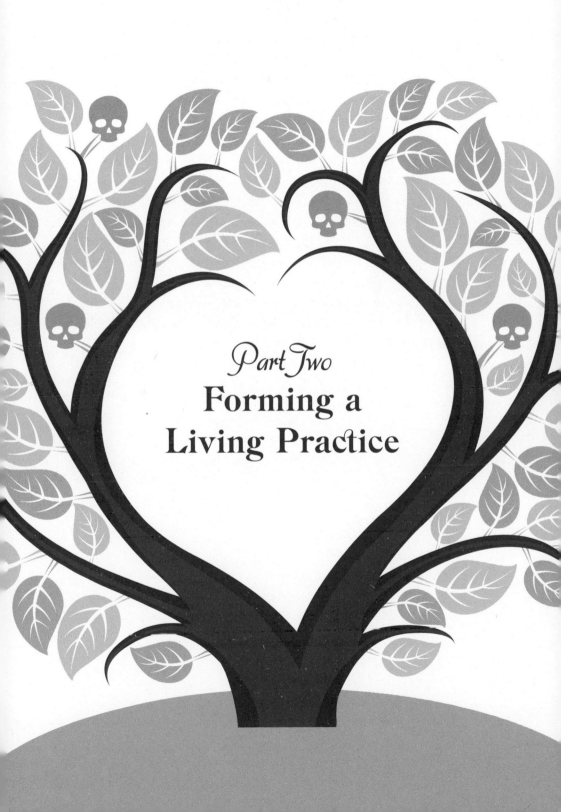

Part Two
Forming a
Living Practice

Section Introduction

In the previous section, we explored conceptualizing ancestors and what venerating them can mean. We discussed how ancestor veneration can impact various parts of our lives and what the practical applications might be for building a practice centered on them. This theory was presented with the intention that you reflect deeply on your own beliefs and how your practice might organically emerge from your insights about your worldview.

In this section, we will be applying the insights gained in part one to a veneration practice by exploring various aspects of a living spiritual practice. We will explore elements such as the building and meaning of a sacred space, the use of instruments or props in your work, and the various ways we can connect with and honor the spirits through what we do. Some parts explored here may not be as applicable to you, while others might already be part of how you relate to and work with your ancestors. Whatever the case might be, as we move through this material, there will be journal questions to assist you in digesting and relating to each part.

Chapter Eight
Conceptualizing
Lived Practice

Lived practice is anything you do that applies your spiritual beliefs to action. In this chapter, we are going to focus on some key practical pieces that I believe are important to consider while engaging in spiritual work to maintain an optimum, safe, and healthy practice. As I developed my own relationships to spirits and the ritual practice with my ancestors, I found the following pieces were especially important to consider. They challenged and invited me to step into an authentic and responsible practice, while also being safe.

Interdependency

In the Western world, we're used to living individualistic lifestyles, where our value comes from our own individual success and merit, and we judge others on these same scales. Most of the world, though, tends to live collectively, where individual success is tied to the success of the family and community. *Interdependency* is the understanding that as individuals we rely on each other to live healthy, successful, content lives. This reliance is organized around an almost symbiotic relationship, where the needs of all are taken care of without privileging one individual over another. Interdependence is about anticipating individual needs while also serving the needs of others; it is not about unhealthy compromise. Neither is interdependence about relying solely on one another for the need to be met; instead, there is a level of resiliency that prevents unhealthy codependent or even parasitic relationships from forming.

In this worldview, when individual needs are pedestaled, the system becomes unbalanced and unhealthy. The natural world is the best example of an interdependent system developed through evolution and the establishment of relationships that carry on generation after generation. While members of the system might not be fully aware of the role they take in an interdependent system, they do understand their personal responsibilities and rely on the contributions of their fellow community members.

When it comes to spirituality, many of the traditions I know of understand that a nature of reality is the interdependence of all beings on one another. In a metaphysical sense, we are all connected in multiple overt and covert ways, and our relationships reflect this in their multidimensionality. When considering ancestor work, I have found it useful to consider how even the structure of blood relatives becomes a vast web of various relationships and responsibilities all predicated on trust. Likewise, if we consider death as a transition to another form of existence and not an end, we understand that relationship and responsibility continues, albeit in perhaps a different form.

Journal Prompts

- In what ways does interdependence show up in your life? In what ways do unhealthy codependency or parasitic relationships show up in your life?

- What are your needs, and how does spiritual practice fulfill them?

- What are the needs of the spirits or deities in your life, and where does your relationship to these beings fall? Are these relationships interdependent, codependent, or parasitic?

- In what ways can you foster greater interdependence in your relationships and life?

Sacrifice versus Martyrdom

Jumping from the above discussion, though, I think it's also worth talking about healthy boundaries around sacrifice. Like any spiritual practice, working with the ancestors demands a certain degree of sacrifice. What do I mean when I say *sacrifice*? I am not talking about mindlessly making a small offering out of habit, but really being considerate in building your relationship with these individuals. I am talking about earning the blessings, wisdom, and insight that the ancestors can provide by being an equal partner in the work and showing up.

Maya Angelou said, "Whatever you want to do, if you want to be great at it, you have to love it and be able to make sacrifices for it."[68] Working with ancestors is all about reciprocity and priority. We must learn to be able to prioritize our practice so that we can better receive the blessings of the ancestors. Prioritizing practice is about sacrificing those more selfish elements in our personalities and learning to develop relationships with others, seeing ourselves as interconnected and interdependent. Like other forms of spiritual work, there are no half measures.

Sacrifice is often misunderstood because there can be a fear of being forced to give something up, when sacrifice is more about letting go of selfishness and self-centered approaches to life. Sacrifice is about faith and trust, giving something valuable up in hopes of a return. However, please do not misunderstand me; sacrifice is not martyrdom. Martyrdom originally meant sacrificing oneself entirely for the greater good or a cause, but now martyrdom can often look like prioritizing others over one's own self because it gives the martyr a sense of self. Martyrdom is essentially self-centeredness projected onto the needs of others. When we really think about it, we are the fruits of the labor of our ancestors, who, I think, want us to thrive and go forward to continue bearing fruit. As a living person, I hope my descendants grow up in a world that is better than the one I dwell in, and so I imagine the healthy ancestors feel much the same way. We serve the world by being responsible community members, but responsibility is also to oneself, and

---

68. Maya Angelou (@DrMayaAngelou), "Whatever you want to do, if you want to be great at it, you have to love it and be able to make sacrifices for it." Twitter, July 23, 2015, 3:50 p.m., https://twitter.com/drmayaangelou/status/624305657898930176.

so there is a balancing act between our priorities and the priorities of the community. Both sets of priorities are important, and finding a healthy balance between the two sets us up for a healthy existence. Martyrdom, however, especially when it is a subpersonality that feeds our unhealthy aspects, doesn't serve anyone.

We must shift from a selfish view of the world to a self-first view of the world. The first is narcissistic, egotistical, and opens us up to viewing everyone around us as accessories to our story and goals. A self-first view of the world is about healthy boundaries, interconnections, and understanding our place in a much greater whole. Martyrdom is about distrust; service is about trust.

Sacrifice in the realms of ancestral work is about showing the ancestors that you're dedicated to building a reciprocal relationship, that you will not take them for granted, and that you will live in authenticity. Sacrifice is sometimes putting their needs over your own, within reason. When we make offerings to ancestors, when we develop relationships with them and learn how to communicate with them, we're sacrificing our time and focus on that process. The deeper we go into the work, the richer the blessings and fuller the relationship and connection are.

Journal Prompts

- What does sacrifice mean to you? In what ways is sacrifice healthy, and in what ways is it unhealthy?

- What does dedication look like to you?

- How do you balance your personal priorities with those of your community or family?

- What does responsibility to oneself look like for you?

- What is being a responsible community member?

The Issue of Mixing Practices

An issue that has come up in my work with clients and students is whether it is appropriate to mix practices that originate from vastly different sources. I am not talking here about practicing traditions in parallel; I practice multiple traditions side by side in my own spiritual life. I am speaking of whether you can take an element of one practice and use it in the context of another, and whether this is appropriate. For example, if you decide to include a particular prayer or way of approaching spirits learned in one tradition and use that same approach in a different tradition, is this appropriate? Is this respectful? There is no easy answer to this, and I think one way of exploring this is that central word: relationship. What is the relationship between the spirit or beings you are working with? What are the dynamics between the practices you wish to mix?

If you belong to a spiritual tradition already, ask your elders what form of ancestral practices already exist. If it does have ancestral practices, then this is a deeper conversation with your elders about how to integrate other practices into your personal approach. By "other practices," I mean incorporating traditions that relate to your specific ancestors, especially if you were not born in this spiritual path. I'll give a concrete example of this: When I joined my Lukumi house, I was taught about ancestor practices that are standard and expected as part of the traditional ways of the religion. When attending events such as drums or work weekends, these elements are what you will see: a chalk-drawn semicircle with nine intersecting lines on the floor, a platter containing a cup of coffee, a glass of sugar water, a glass of white alcohol, a bowl containing a sample of all food served in the meal, and a lit candle. Now, there are variations and alternative practices in the religion, but that is essentially what I was taught. Each of these elements have great symbolic and metaphysical significance, and they are required because they are expected by the ancestors themselves through the lens of this system.

As someone whose blood ancestry is not Cuban or Yoruba, I practice the parts of the tradition as they have been handed to me. It took time to understand what was essential for the practice in Lukumi and what elements I could and could not apply to my own personal practice. In conversation with my former godfather and my ancestors, my personal practice has evolved to the point where it is a comfortable balance between serving the ancestors in the Lukumi way and serving my British ancestors in ways that are culturally and spiritually relevant to them and myself. I have photos of the ancestors up because visuals are important for me, and I include the use of tools and objects because they assist me in bonding. Every part of my shrine and practice is relevant, with intention. There is nothing in my personal shrine that doesn't have a reason to be there; even if it is just decorative, that decoration serves a purpose.

This brings us to the second piece of this issue, and that is eclecticism. If you don't belong to a tradition and you are building your own from an eclectic approach, then there can be a tendency when first starting out to emulate what others are doing out of a sheer desire to do something. For this, I think we need to approach this issue logically and with a bit of care. This whole book is about developing relationships with *your* ancestors, not the ancestors of someone else. When you emulate a tradition because it looks cool or it's what you think you must do to "do it right," it can be confusing not only for you but your ancestors as well. If you haven't been inducted into a tradition and the ritual is not meaningful to you apart from it looking aesthetically cool, what are the chances that great-grandma is going to understand? I have been taught that ancestors will come to understand a ritual from a tradition they don't practice through you, but if you don't even belong to that tradition either, then it will just be static.

Traditional approaches always bring with them metaphysical worldviews and specific logic as to why, how, where, when, and what. Specific collections of practices evolve around each other because they align with and support a base set of assumptions, and this is why it's sometimes dangerous to misappropriate a practice without understanding the baseline logic behind it. It would be like trying to place a PlayStation video game on a Mac computer: at the very least, the game won't work; at the very worst, it may cause damage to your computer.

Now, this does not mean that we cannot take inspiration from others, but I would recommend that you understand the practice and how it might be applicable to your life before emulating it. I myself do not burn sage as either a smudge or a cleansing for two reasons: it isn't a practice I have been given by an Indigenous person, and it isn't applicable to my practices. My ancestors didn't burn white sage, it doesn't grow in the UK, and there is no connection between it and my identity. The traditions I belong to have their own forms of cleansing, which have organically been adopted by or evolved within the shared culture.

Now, if smoke cleansing feels like it does the job and your ancestors are part of that ritual process, look to see what smoke tradition might exist for your background. My Scottish ancestors did burn juniper and cleansed through holy waters and practices such as *saining*. My English and Welsh ancestors did much the same thing. My Irish ancestors cleansed through the gorgeous smell of burning peat. So, while I don't smudge with white sage, I might incorporate these traditional ways of my background into my life sometimes. Likewise, there are other forms of cleansings connected to the spiritual traditions I do belong to.

Sometimes, however, we do come across or experience something that becomes special to us, and it does affect our relationships with our own ancestors. A friend of mine has experienced Día de los Muertos on multiple occasions while visiting Mexico. Experiencing the celebration and taking part in both public and more private displays of the holiday struck something in her, and she has since incorporated some of the practices into her own ancestor work. Being invited into the practices by her Mexican friends in a way initiated her into the ritual elements.

The reality is that as a human community, we are bound to be inspired by each other, but we must be mindful of the decisions we make for ourselves and how they will impact our relationships. My friend was invited in by the people and their ancestors to celebrate this cultural festival, and by being invited in, her own ancestors were invited in to the extent that they resonate with this festival as well. In this way, it is not cultural appropriation but a limited initiation into that community's rituals. This is a very different dynamic than choosing something we are not connected to and emulating it, which confuses both our own ancestors and the ancestors of the people whose tradition it belongs to.

A third part of this issue of mixing practices is about performing practices that we personally do not follow but may have been important to our own ancestors. I'll give you a concrete example of this dilemma: a student I once had spoke about how she left the Catholic Church because she could not reconcile the church and herself. Although she understood the place the church held in her community and culture, she no longer considered herself a believer.

As far as she knew, her ancestors had been Catholic going back into the mists of time, but she struggled with taking part in Masses for the Dead, and in some ways this struggle led her to want to develop her own practice. In hopes of connecting to her dead ancestors through other means, she visited mediums and psychics who gave her a connection to her loved ones. It was at one of these meetings that a message came through asking her to go and light a candle in a church for her ancestors. She told me she didn't feel comfortable with the request and didn't do it.

Years after denouncing the church, she was on a trip to Italy and visited the village where her grandmother had been born. While sightseeing, she came across a small church and felt a draw to go inside. The church was not very large, and it wasn't the main church in the village, but something pulled her to go and have a look. The church was empty, but there was a rack of votive candles arranged, and she wandered over to look. From seemingly out of nowhere emerged an old woman who greeted her with a dignified smile. My student and the older woman spoke a little (my student didn't speak very good Italian), and sensing this, the older woman resorted to some broken English. The older woman gave my student a candle and pointed to the display, encouraging her to light it. My student said that something just felt right, and her feelings about the church fell away, and she lit the candle and said a prayer. It was only after the fact that she discovered through her relatives that the small church was where her grandmother as well as other ancestors had been baptized.

So, there are several issues to speak about in the scenario above. On the one hand, how do we reconcile performing a practice that originates in a belief system we don't agree with or are not comfortable with? Whose needs in the above scenario were being served when my student was asked to light the votive candle by her ancestors? What kind of relationship can we have with practices that we can't get behind but were important to our ancestors? I feel like in many places, folk tradition will usually solve this issue for us if the culture dramatically changes. I think about British folk traditions holding onto ancient pagan, Anglo-Saxon, and then Catholic traditions, sometimes in different forms. In lieu of a religious practice, there may be a folk practice that serves the same purpose. Likewise, there may be practices in the tradition you follow that honor the dead and serve the same purpose as those which were practiced by your ancestors.

There isn't an easy answer to this, but what I can suggest is that there are rewards in practicing something for the dead that you yourself wouldn't normally do. In my espiritismo practice, I practice the Puerto Rican *mesa blanca* form taught to me by my godfather, which was taught to him by his elders. This form of espiritismo contains many Catholic prayers, which are important to the system and how it functionally operates. Many of the spirits connected to the system were themselves Catholic in life, and so part of the mechanics of the system is to appeal to these spirits' own spiritual points of view and the rituals that were important to them in life.

For me, I recognize that while these prayers are not important to me religiously, they are important to the spirits I work with and the traditions I practice. In my personal espiritismo practice, one of my spirit guides was an Italian American in life and grew up with Catholic prayers. While I don't see my spirit guides as ancestors, my practice with them takes on many similar forms as my ancestral practices, and I treat them much the same way. As a sign of respect and to service the needs of my spirit guides, I have adopted certain practices that I perform for them. For example, another one of my spirit guides was Jewish in life. Out of respect, I learned the *El Malei Rachamim* prayer to say for her and her evolution, understanding that while I am not Jewish myself, I am saying it for a spirit who was Jewish. Learning this prayer for her deepened the relationship we have, and although not an ancestor for me, she is still an important spirit in my life. This same approach is true for ancestors, as they are part of us in many ways, and so building your relationship with them might look like saying prayers that were important for them in life even if you don't practice them yourself.

Ultimately, when blending practices of any kind, you have to be mindful, considerate, and respectful of them. I follow multiple traditions in parallel, but the traditions do not mix. They complement each other, but for my own reasons, and with respect in mind, I do not blend them. I practice them each as paradigms in and of themselves, and I am quite comfortable with that arrangement in my life.

Journal Prompts

- What practices already exist in your life, and how do they relate to each other?
- How do the primary key words *intention* and *relationship* apply to this issue?

Culturally Specific Practices versus Taking Inspiration

The issue of cultural appropriation is an important one, and it is one that unfortunately causes a great deal of debate and offense in spiritual communities, especially Paganism and New Age. I have noticed that the offense is usually from those on the receiving end of criticism, who use the excuse that no one owns traditions and thus people should be free to do what they want. For the purposes of this book, I want to make a point about being mindful of culturally specific practice and connect this to the discussions above around respect and relationship. It is my opinion that those who do not see cultural appropriation as existing generally don't understand what it is.

Cultural appropriation is when members of a dominant or privileged group take on the practices of marginalized groups without there being an organic process of fusion or fair exchange. If we look at places in the world such as South America and the Caribbean, what we have are cultures that formed from the interactions and exchanges of many cultural groups, each of whom benefited from or are still represented in the traditions that formed. These places, I would argue, offer us examples of an organic process of cultural exchange between those who considered themselves equal. I am not speaking about the dominant Catholic cultures, but the various folk traditions and minority religions that formed through such contact. Cultural appropriation, however, is neither organic nor a process between equals, but always has an element of a dominant power taking and reusing whether the marginalized like it or not.

It's a large subject for discussion, but how this applies to ancestral practices and spirituality is this: there are many traditions that belong solely to a group of people and their ancestors, and outsiders have no business emulating or practicing them, full stop. It is up to that group to decide what is and is not appropriate for outsiders to do with their cultural rituals. I have seen the argument used in Neopaganism that no one owns the spirits or rituals and that everything is up for grabs. While it is true the spirits have agency to do as they please, on a logical level, why would they go out of their established traditions? Humans are, as we've talked about, social and ritual creatures that co-create shared signs and symbols. Cultural rituals are shared forms of communication, and spiritual traditions are forms of communication with the spirit world.

If we see deities and spirits as being ancestral, as they are understood in many cultures, then the living descendants of those spirits have a certain relationship to their shared rituals and beliefs. It is through the process of initiation that individuals are taught the safe and correct way to communicate with these spirits. You are taught the social protocols that these spirits rely on and expect when engaging with them, and knowing these cues signals to the spirits that you are an insider to the tradition and not an interloper.

To put it another way, consider the following two scenarios: Imagine going to a party you're not invited to, where you don't know anyone, and you don't know the social rules. However, you go because it seems like a cool place and feel entitled to enter because you're used to having access. So, you wander around, eat food that doesn't belong to you, and see a group conversing. They obviously all know each other, and they are laughing because of an inside joke, which you don't understand. You go over and try to emulate that inside joke, and it fails miserably. Everyone probably feels very awkward.

Now, imagine being invited to that same party, even if you don't know anyone except one or two friends. Your friends introduce you to the rest of the assembled, you learn the social dynamics of the party, and make a few jokes. At the end, you are invited back to another party in the future. Eventually, this group of strangers become your friends, and you are an insider. You might plan your own parties with elements from the first and invite some of the guests from the original over. This is the dynamic of cultural appropriation versus cultural diffusion, where outsiders become insiders even if they did not originate in that group.

On a purely practical level, consider the logic of practicing rituals that your own ancestors wouldn't recognize, that you have no meaningful relationship with, or which as an outsider you don't understand to begin with. It doesn't make much sense to practice things that you don't understand, and only through relationship and interaction with the stewards of those practices can you understand them, if they are open to that.

I speak from personal experience here, as I practice several brown and black traditions. Hinduism, espiritismo, and Lukumi are all cultural religions as well as spiritual; indeed, the difference between culture and spirituality is sometimes impossible to separate. There are certain cultural pieces that I as a white person cannot engage with, and that is okay. Even now, there are cultural aspects that are at odds with other parts of my cultural upbringing, and it requires a great deal of conscious awareness to know what is appropriate in each culture I find myself in. I am not saying one needs to initiate entirely to be given the opportunity to understand a practice, but you need to understand that many practices are only for the insiders to the tradition and so emulating the outer trappings is inappropriate and disrespectful, not only to those people but to your own ancestors as well.

That piece around initiation also brings with it certain metaphysical realities as well. Initiation is not just being given a club tie; all forms of initiation I have been taught are energetic rebirths. The process of initiation is a form of death and rebirth into the tradition or practice you're being initiated into. The ritual is the outward form of a deeper energetic transformation that prepares an individual to work with the energies contained within the tradition. Tradition itself is a container, an agreement, a protocol of parlance between initiates and the spirits or gods the tradition works with. Real danger comes from working with things one doesn't understand, and ritual initiation is part of the process of preparation. This is why so many oathbound or initiatory traditions insist that outsiders must not, should not, cannot emulate or copy their practices. Outsiders risk the consequences if they do. This is no different from ancestral practices.

While this might seem like finger wagging, it's really about opportunity. I invite you, the reader, to dive into your own roots and traditions deeper, to connect with your ancestors and their ways, and through that process gain a much deeper connection. Along the way, you might find yourself inspired by the practices of others, and there is nothing wrong with that, because as human beings we all share a deep reverence for our dead. It has been my experience that, when approached with respect and appropriate boundaries of privacy, most people I have met are happy to talk about their practices and their ancestors. They are equally very happy to hear about mine as well. I think, as with anything, we need to respect one another; part of that respect is knowing when to share and when not to, and not becoming defensive if someone is not interested in explaining or cannot speak about their practices.

Journal Prompts

- Are there cultures whose practices fascinate you? If so, what about those practices interests you?

- Are there cultures to which your ancestors belonged but you yourself do not? What about those cultures fascinates you?

- How important is it for you to practice authentically?

Authenticity and Controlling the Process

In building an ancestral practice, one must think about the process and how it will affect all the other pieces. When we see what others are doing, there can be a certain amount of projection that takes place, and from that can come wanting to emulate them. This is very true in alternative spirituality circles where the drive to be seen as authentic can often lead practitioners to stray from personal integrity. While emulation isn't a negative thing in and of itself, the consequence of this is losing the sense of one's own goals. We might begin to fixate on what others are doing, comparing ourselves to them and judging what they are doing as more correct than what can be organically and authentically developed by ourselves.

Those who come from traditions that are already predefined and have set arrangements within the tradition benefit from a certain structure. Those structures are tried, tested, and true and help to facilitate the communication between ancestors who shared those practices in life. Those who are rediscovering or developing their own practice don't necessarily have that benefit and can fall victim to the above issues. Don't run out and buy all sorts of tools, decorations, or crystals if you feel that your practice is not authentic enough. It has been my experience that through building a relationship with the ancestors, my practice has been co-creative, and the tools I use in my practice have emerged over time and organically. This has helped me to build a practice grounded in authenticity, rather than a practice striving to look authentic.

While I utilize the ancestral traditions taught to me in my experiences with Lukumi, I have expanded my practice to be relevant to and appropriate for the relationships of my own ancestors. In the Caribbean traditions, there are practitioners who have but a single glass of water and a single cigar, and that is their ancestral shrine. There are also people who have large and elaborate *bovedas* with images, accoutrements, symbols, and all manner of different spiritual aids. What will work for one person may not work for another. What is crucial here is that the process grows organically for the practitioner and changes as the relationship with the ancestors deepens. As we will explore in following sections, ritual is a form of communication, and eventually relationships will become intimate enough that an understanding develops, which doesn't need the same overt signals that you may have begun with. When trust and intimacy are built, an authentic practice of co-sharing will develop.

Consistency of Practice

Once you start a practice, it must remain consistent. Building a routine that is sustainable and that will feel less like a chore and more like a responsibility is key. Consistency is the cornerstone of a relationship. These are people— dead people—but people, and as we know, relationships in life can wither and die if we don't stay consistent. The dead, as is seen in many traditions around the planet, become accustomed to certain practices. If you suddenly stop, they may become restless or decide that you are not ready or grateful for their intercessions in your life.

I believe that consistency must form a foundation to anyone's spiritual practice. Without consistency, you will not develop and you will not truly deepen your practice. Spiritual practice has often been likened to bodybuilding, and bodybuilders will always tell you that without the hard work, you will not develop your body. That means going and exercising regularly, eating a healthy and balanced diet, understanding how your unique body functions, staying hydrated, and being mindful of the stress in your life.

Journal Prompts

- In what ways are you consistent in your life? In what areas are you inconsistent?

- When forming a spiritual routine, what has worked for you in the past? What has failed or been a hurdle for continuing the practice?

- What is the relationship between your mental, physical, emotional, and spiritual health when it comes to being consistent in your life?

Physicality of Sacred Space

One of the most recognizable—and I would argue important—features of spirituality are the spaces we build to connect with the spiritual realms. Sacred space as a foundation for spiritual practice is any place set apart from the mundane world, whether permanent or temporary. These are spaces that help to separate the sacred and the mundane so that you can access unseen and cosmological forces. In developing your relationships with your ancestors, it is well worth thinking about creating a space devoted to the purpose of veneration, a focal point for your own internal work as well as a connection point between yourself and the ancestors. In this chapter we will explore several major points of consideration for what an ancestral space could be for you. Many of the following chapters are built from these foundational points.

What Is Sacred Space?

Sacred space is any space set aside or demarcated for sacred purpose. What that sacred purpose looks like and its relationship to the created space depends upon each tradition's needs and uses. They are experiential gathering spots where you encounter others and engage in some form of relationship. The most important piece to a sacred space is the understanding that they are multidimensional spaces, and many purposes are served simultaneously. They are not like other human spaces, such as our homes, where different parts serve singular purposes. For ancestor veneration, I would propose they serve the following key purposes:

- Spaces to encounter the ancestors
- Spaces to house the relics or ritual tools connected to the ancestors
- Spaces to perform ritual or conduct prayer
- Spaces for meditation and reflection
- Spaces to safely incorporate the dead into your everyday life

The Cosmological Significance of Space

Sacred architecture always has deeper cosmological or meaningful spiritual significance. Aspects such as the orientation of the space, the placement of objects within and near it, the relationship to specific cardinal directions, the level of privacy built in, and even how the space is constructed and with what are all significant. These elements often correspond to greater cosmological beliefs and are often an attempt to replicate the macrocosm in micro. Whether we are talking about small shrines or large buildings you enter into, the principles are often the same. Because the relationship between us and the sacred space is more often than not interactional, the rules governing conduct within these spaces are often also grounded in social and cosmological laws.

The Features of a Sacred Space

When it comes to sacred spaces that you may construct, it is useful to consider the following specific features of a space in relation to your underlying worldview, relationships, practices, and beliefs. Considering the use of space in this way will assist you in deepening relationships with ancestors you relate to through other parts of your practice. Likewise, as I learned to become more intentional with my practice, these points were questions that came up for me.

Orientation

In many traditions, sacred spaces are oriented in particular ways to follow cosmological significance. The orientation of space, or the objects within, serve both practical and symbolic purposes. The orientation of major parts of the space plug both the individual and the space itself into the larger macrocosm.

For example, in traditional Lukumi homes, the ancestral shrine is often found near the back exit, which is both symbolic of death and energetically the natural flow of the residence. Diametrically opposite in the home, at the front entrance, is where the set of five orisha spirits called the Warriors are often placed, ready to guard against any enemies that may come knocking. The kitchen, as the space where we prepare food for ourselves, is not located anywhere near the ancestor shrine so that the boundary between life and death is affirmed. Similarly, the orisha shrine holding the resident orisha spirits is not located close to the ancestor shrine so that the two different forces of life and death do not interact. The home is thus in alignment with notions of a cosmological scheme.

In many traditions, compass point orientation is very important to link up the sacred space with notions of greater cosmological order. In many world traditions, the universe is ordered so that different parts of the compass points constitute different portions of the world. The purpose of aligning your local space with this greater worldview is to enhance the qualities of the microcosm by aligning it to macrocosmic forces, recreating the universe on a smaller scale.

In Hinduism, for example, home temple spaces for the gods are usually located in the northeast of a room or building. In Hindu cosmology, north and east are both ruled by deities connected with prosperity and life, whereas south and southwest are connected to deities of death. While there is variance among Hindu traditions, there are many aspects that are common to the majority of sects. Many Hindu spaces have similar features: a defined entrance, a boundary of some kind between the temple space and the mundane world, and a central sanctum hosting the main icon of a deity. Immediately above the cult icon shrine is a structure symbolizing the sacred mountain peak that acts as the axis mundi of the Hindu universe. In a temple building, these elements will be present as part of the building, whereas in home shrines the elements will be present on a smaller scale and may be part of the room or the shrine itself.

Cosmological significance varies from tradition to tradition, but there is always logical and intentional reasoning dictating placement. For example, if you live near an older Catholic or Protestant church, have you ever noticed that many of them face east? Traditional Latin churches are often oriented east-west, with the altar located in the eastern arm of the building. Most older churches are constructed in the shape of a cross, and the altar thus sits in the space corresponding to Jesus's head on the cross. Likewise, east is the general direction of Jerusalem in the European context, and so by entering a church, you are oriented toward Jerusalem when facing the altar. . In traditional churchyards, bodies are usually positioned on an east-west axis, matching the focus direction of the church architecture. Every religion I have come across has some relationship to spatial orientation, even if the space is a natural setting.

How might orientation considerations come into your practice? Would they align with cosmology connected to your spiritual beliefs? Will your ancestral space be interior or exterior? What meaning do you ascribe to the cardinal directions? What impact might this have on your relationship with spirits and ancestors?

Placement of Objects

Placement of objects in the sacred space and their relationship to each other is a second major point of consideration. Perhaps the placement might be connected to cosmological understanding, or it might be more related to the relationship between those items and their symbolic role in the space. To speak candidly here, an ancestor altar can be as robust or as frugal as you want it to be, but I would stress that when including objects into your practice consider the role that object will play, even if it is only as decoration. The intentional placement of objects in a space can open up some interesting possibilities and add layers to your practice.

For example, the many-tiered ancestral altars of the Mexican Día de los Muertos (called *ofrendas*) conform to a traditional layout developed from the fusion of traditional Aztec culture and Catholic imagery. Viewers of Pixar's *Coco* will be familiar with the ofrenda constructed by the Rivera family. A typical ofrenda is constructed with multiple tiers, each tier containing pictures or objects connected to the ancestors following a generational pattern.

Above or around the ofrenda is an archway, often constructed of marigold flowers, representing a doorway to the spiritual world that the dead travel through to join the living. Marigolds are a flower traditionally connected with the dead in Aztec culture. Offerings and sometimes belongings of the dead will be placed around the ofrenda, creating a welcoming space for the spirits to return to.[69] An important aspect of the shrine is that each element is instantly recognizable and familiar to both the living and the dead, even if there are variances or innovations. The shrine constitutes a space of contact that is a continuity across the generations. The traditional symbols were used by the dead themselves when they were alive, creating a space that is not defined solely by one time period.

In thinking about objects and their placement within a space, it is good to consider the space like a document. The layout, constituent parts, and even how you interact with the space can be read by anyone with the specialized cultural knowledge, the audience in this case being your ancestors. Even if your ancestors did not belong to the same culture as you—say, your ancestors from a thousand years ago—they are linked to you through association. This relationship between meaningful placement and the objects themselves facilitates a form of communication between all involved. This meaningful placement reinforces cosmological and aesthetic attributes to create a space that is both functional and symbolic. Consider the objects and their placement within your sacred space, and contemplate the following questions:

Journal Prompts

- What purpose do these objects serve? Are they tools, offerings, decorations?

- What is the meaning of the placement of objects within the space?

- How might you or your ancestors read the entirety of the space with the placement?

- What overt and covert meaning is signaled?

---

69. Marchi, *Day of the Dead*, 12.

The Energies of Space

Have you ever entered a space and instinctively felt the need to whisper? Have you ever entered a place and felt completely at ease or completely on edge and don't know why? Around the world, there are concepts of innate universal energy such as *mana, prana, chi,* and so on; these concepts of energy explain the above phenomenon of feeling a space. It is no surprise that sacred sites tend to be ancient, and most show signs of reuse by different cultures and different traditions.

In an animistic worldview, space takes on an identity the longer it exists in a consistent form. As we develop a relationship with a place, it begins to take on an unmistakable presence, which is only deepened as time goes on. Animism explains this as innate energy taking on identity and, in many ways, becoming alive with the qualities that we can then pick up on. When you intentionally construct a space, whether it be sacred or domestic, that space will begin to develop an identity, and you will feel it as much as experience it in other senses.

Privacy or Level of Visibility

How visible might your space be to a casual observer? In many traditions, holy places are set apart from the mundane in some way, and often within public sacred spaces, there are more private spaces nestled within. There are many reasons for this; one of the largest is the ability to protect the uninitiated from the overwhelming power of the enshrined and at the same time respect the privacy or power of that which is enshrined inside. Will your space be more public and able to be seen by guests, or will it be in a more discrete location? I have found that being conscious of where my shrines are has deepened my relationship to them.

This is something I have struggled with over the years and only really came to a place of peace and understanding with recently. For a very long time, I lived with my parents or with roommates, and I lacked the space necessary to indulge in partitioning off an area for spiritual work. When I finally moved into my own place, I erected my ancestral shrine in my living room, viewable by anyone who came. I am usually very open about my spirituality and have always had my shrines or altars in and around my main living spaces, not to mention not having space to do otherwise.

I finally invited a guy I had gone on a few coffee dates with over, and we sat in the living room chatting. His reaction to my shrine was veiled discomfort, as he wasn't sure what it was and why it was there. He asked me about the shrine and what it was, and so I explained. The conversation led in the direction of me having to justify my way of living. It was at that moment I had an epiphany: I didn't need to explain everything. In my personal therapy work, one of the biggest lessons was to learn the difference between secrecy and privacy. Privacy is coming from a place of discernment, whereas secrecy is coming from a place of shame. I admit, I became ashamed about the shrine and its placement in my living room.

When that understanding about secrecy versus privacy came to me, I realized that displaying the shrine in a very public space like my living room was really an attempt for me to gain approval from others. I understood that I was disrespecting both myself and my ancestors. I felt empowered to reorganize my apartment so that my office space would be in the living room and my various spiritual stages would be in a back room. I've been in my apartment for two years now, and my shrines are out in the living room again. In my opinion, they are relationships that matter, and I don't want to invite people into my space if they do not respect what matters to me. The lesson and dialogue with my spirits and ancestors here was to be more discerning of who I let into my life in the first place.

Journal Prompts

- How comfortable are you in the public display of your spirituality?
- What is the difference between secrecy and privacy?
- What aspects of your practice do you feel should be kept private? What parts of your practice are you comfortable with sharing?
- What are the roles of secrecy and privacy in your family life?

How Space Reflects Underlying Belief

While practice and ritual are powerful in and of themselves, I strongly believe that ritual must not be divorced from worldview. Being intentional with sacred space means you can read the symbolic messages of objects, decor, colors, and other elements, and these messages must align with your underlying worldview. This becomes even more important when you consider this space is not entirely about you; it is also for the ancestors to interact with. If you think of this in terms of language, creating a space where the symbolic language is unintelligible either to you or your ancestors doesn't make a lot of sense. Likewise, engaging in meaningful ritual action with that space has to also be intelligible to those you are engaging with. This mutual intelligibility must be grounded in underlying worldview, otherwise it can become confusing very quickly. Belief and ritual practice must inform one another, even if the focus during a ritual is on the doing rather than the believing, the belief aspect is what is going to allow for understanding what you're doing.

I'll give you a concrete example of how this works out: in Lukumi practice, we place food offerings down onto the ground because we see the dead as dwelling in the earth. While I practice several traditions, each one with different cosmologies, when performing Lukumi ancestral practice, I place food on the ground. I also, as an extension, don't eat food that has fallen and touched the ground out of the belief that it now belongs to the dead. The interplay here between belief and ritual thus work off each other. So how does that reflect my use of space, then? When constructing a traditional Lukumi ancestral shrine, we draw the chalk *cascarilla* or *efun* outline down on the ground, we address our prayers downward, we place the food on the ground, and we select a space away from the kitchen to reinforce boundaries between life and death.[70]

In my own personal home shrine, which is informed by Lukumi and espiritismo with elements that speak to my British cultural background, I have portraits of my ancestors arranged with my most recent ancestors closest to the ground ascending upward. Use of images is not a traditional aspect of Lukumi practice, but it is one gaining traction, especially in North America. As someone not initiated into and bound by the constricts of Lukumi tradition, I take liberties with my personal shrine while also striving to understand the reasons for why that tradition practices the way it does. An

---

70. Cascarilla and efun: Ritual chalk used in both traditional and diaspora African religions. *Efun* is dried white clay, while *cascarilla* is a chalk made from powdered eggshells.

outsider seeing my shrine for the first time may not understand at all why it is set up the way it is, but it's important that I know the reason for every element in that shrine.

Journal Prompts

- How might your beliefs about the dead translate into your practice?
- What elements of your space (layout, objects, decorations) serve you as practitioner?
- How will the physical space reflect and affirm your worldview?

Chapter Ten
The Use of Color

The symbolic, metaphysical, and even psychological importance of color cannot be overstated. As we saw in the previous chapter, just as the use of space and placement can have important cosmological significance, so too does color. Color as a visual component to most aspects of our lives is a great conveyor of meaning, and its presence and impact is often so covert we don't realize the role it is playing in our day-to-day lives. So, it stands to reason that it should be an important consideration for anyone's personal practice. In this section, we will discuss how color has been utilized throughout the world in different traditions.

While we discuss color, keep in mind, as always, the preexisting biases, understandings, and assumptions you already have about color and what it means in your world. Being mindful of these preexisting beliefs and biases can be useful in developing a practice and deepening or modifying a preexisting relationship with a color. For example, some cultural color associations of the Western world include green: vegetation or nature; pink: love and femininity; blue: sky, ocean, masculinity; yellow: spring, greed, sickness; purple: royalty, mystery, magic; red: fire, passion, violence; white: purity, cleanliness; and black: death, night, mourning. These are just a few examples of many associations.

The key piece to understand here is that the meanings we ascribe to colors are grounded in a deeply held symbolic relationship and have logic behind them, even if the color association changes over time or the reason is not entirely clear. Understanding the potential logic behind color association empowers us to utilize color as a tool in an ever more intentional way. When this aspect is applied to building your practice, some preliminary questions for consideration are:

Journal Prompts

- What is the underlying reason associated with the use of this color, and what is its purpose?
- How does that meaning relate to the execution?
- What are you communicating or invoking by the color choice?

Traditional Colors of the Landscape

One way to begin this discussion is to think about which colors have been traditionally plentiful in different landscapes and the cultures that inhabit them. There are two ways to approach this topic: the colors already in the landscape and the types of colors created by pigments found in the landscape used for art and clothing. Depending upon region, certain pigments were readily available, while others needed to be traded for. As a result of these constraints, certain colors are tied to traditional artwork and cosmology, even if the local landscape had many other colors present. Likewise, the ability to obtain materials to reproduce a color affected the color's value and often it's symbolic relationship in artwork.

In Britain and other European countries, certain colors throughout history were widely available or were so rare that they were reserved specifically for the nobility. For example, during the medieval age in Europe, the average person wore woolen or leather clothing, with the colors dictated by status or availability of dyes. Certain colors, like blue and yellow, were plentiful, whereas red was a luxury good due to scarcity of products that created it. Eventually, red became more widely available as other products were found. Laws in some countries, such as the Kingdom of England, dictated what colors and materials certain classes of people could wear to uphold divisions within society.

Scarcity of color determined what colors were used in artwork such as stained glass or the paint used in illuminated manuscripts. Anglo-Saxon stained glass tends to be duller and plainer than the later stained glass of the High Middle Ages, when Britain was firmly plugged into the European trade networks. Some colors, such as the deep rich blues of manuscripts, were achieved by trading for expensive minerals like lapis lazuli, which traditionally originated in Afghanistan and was transported over the Silk Road to Europe. The vibrant reds of manuscripts were achieved by burning lead, which created a deep red pigment—a costly process that lended to the overall expense and prestige of owning such a manuscript.

In North America, the types of colors available for artwork depended upon the region. On the northern plains, the available materials created red, white, black, yellow, green, and blue, while the southern plains were restricted to red, yellow, and green. Other colors were usually traded for. As natural pigments available in the landscape, each of these colors took on both decorative and also symbolic significance.[71] Among the Indigenous Australians, materials to naturally produce pigmented paint often limited color selections to shades and tints of reds, yellows, whites, and blacks. In some Indigenous Australian art traditions, nuanced meaning was additionally created by producing shiny or dull effects in the art. The ability for a substance, such as white pipe clay, to produce an effect like shininess suggested metaphysical properties that connected the color to the power of ancestral spirits.[72]

In reflecting on your own relationship with color, it is well worth exploring the color choices that served the areas your blood ancestors came from in order to understand how color connected those ancestors to that land, what meaning they may have ascribed to those colors, and how those colors might be used by you in relating to those ancestors now. Likewise, utilizing colors as representational of ancestors (or groups of ancestors) who you know very few details about can be a powerful technique. For example, with my own practice I know that in the past four hundred years my ancestry includes

---

71. Crawford and Kelley, *American Indian Religious Traditions*, 106.

72. Clarke, *Where the Ancestors Walked*, 92.

Irish, Scottish, English, and Welsh. If I were putting together a simple ances-tor shrine for my lineages, I might include green, red, white, and blue to rep-resent these four lands and encapsulate all of the ancestors who lived within them.

Cosmological Considerations

Jumping off what we discussed in the last chapter, color has been associated symbolically with the cosmos in almost every culture. In a real way, this makes sense: the sky is colored blue, and the earth in most locations is often colored various shades of yellow or brown. Speaking symbolically, associa-tion of a color with a place often speaks to beliefs of the nature of said space and the properties of said color. Some examples include the association of color to the cardinal directions; areas of this world such as blue/ocean, green/forest, brown/mountains, yellow/desert; different tribes or peoples associated within the cosmological worldview; and the different strata of society such as clan, class, or caste being represented by specific colors, such as on flags.

How might this look for a specific culture? As Dr. Cynthia Lindquist Mala explains, in Dakota spirituality the world is divided into four cardinal direc-tions with associated colors that all animals and entities fit into: west/black, south/white, east/yellow, and north/red. West is the direction symbolizing doctoring, spiritual strength, and the Thunder Beings. South is the direction of death, wisdom, the elders, spotted eagles, and the nation of owls. East is the direction of emotional health, new beginnings and life, black-tail deer and elk, and is the color of White Buffalo Calf Woman. North is the direction of truth, common sense, the physical, natural law, and the buffalo.[73] These symbolic associations assist the people in ordering and making sense of the relationships between the various parts of the cosmological whole, under-standing one's own place in this grander scheme.

Landscapes

Color becomes an important symbol when conceptualizing the landscape or universe. In multiple cosmologies, color designates certain spaces or territo-ries, usually with metaphysical implications. So, in an ancestral shrine, might

---

73. Crawford and Kelley, *American Indian Religious Traditions*, 288.

color be utilized to underline the space as an extension of the great universal space? As written about in the chapter on physicality, many traditions treat shrines as representations of the world in miniature, and we can see this practice also expressed through art and decor.

For example, the cosmology of the Diné (Navajo) people of the southwestern United States speaks of human beings traveling through several underworlds, eventually emerging into this one. The First Man and First Woman, along with other important ancestors, traveled through four underworlds designated by color: black, blue, yellow, and white. The colors of these underworlds are significant to the Diné cosmological cycle and show up on their medicine wheel, and are also attributed to the cardinal directions. As medicine, these colors represent and embody specific attributes and resources available to humankind.[74]

Associated States of Being

Perhaps obvious to this discussion of color is how different colors have become emblematic of different states of being and are instantly recognizable within cultures. For example, in Western cultures the widespread color of death is black, evoking that image of the Grim Reaper clothed in their black cloak. In the ancient Egyptian context, however, black is a rich color of fertility and life in its symbolic relationship to the fertilizing mud that comes from the Nile. Same color, two very different interpretations based upon cultural associations and relationships. In this example, the colors take on different meaning and carry different symbolic associations of states of being. It's worth noting that black in the Egyptian context also represented death, for it was also related to the night and the underworld, which Egyptians saw as being a similar place to the land of the living. In your cultural contexts, what colors are associated with states of being? Are there certain color associations to the dead, living, and other types of beings?

Metaphysical Properties

We will discuss metaphysical properties in other sections, but it is well worth mentioning that color does have metaphysical associations, as we have seen

---

74. Crawford and Kelley, *American Indian Religious Traditions*, 138.

in the above discussions of cosmology. Divorced from any particular land-scape, color is ascribed symbolic qualities that are useful or desirable. Red in Chinese culture is the color of prosperity, in Europe pink is a color of love, in America green is a color of money, and among metaphysical crowds purple is a color of psychic enhancements. This is in part why crystals and stones of particular colors are associated with different attributes in crystal healing or magic. Every tradition has underlying ideas about the metaphysical or mag-ical properties of colors, and those colors often translate or lend their magic to other items that are colored that way. This is useful to think about for your own practice: what qualities do you associate with colors, and how might they enhance your ancestral work?

Life Stages or Rites of Passage

The connection between different colors and life stages is a powerful one and is found in most traditions around the world. Different stages of existence are symbolized by color due to the color's properties or moods evoked, and often this association stems from much deeper cultural connections. For exam-ple, pastel tones of red and blue might evoke youthfulness, whereas bolder shades might evoke prime. We metaphorically say that someone who is aging is "going gray" or someone who is inexperienced is "green."

It is well worth mentioning that the use of color for ceremony of some kind is associated with what some scholars believe to be the first intentional burials among *Homo sapiens*. Dated to between 120,000 to 80,000 years ago, they were found in a group of caves in northern and central Israel. The skel-etal remains of adults and children were surrounded by red ochre–stained rocks and alongside shell beads. The red ochre smears on rocks and tools in the gravesite suggest some ritualistic meaning, though it would be impossi-ble 100,000 years later to tell exactly what meaning the red ochre had.[75]

These people represent some of the earliest migrants found outside of Africa, certainly before the migration of the ancestors of the Indigenous Aus-tralians and those who eventually made their way to the Americas. What could the red ochre mean? Could it have been used to represent the blood covering a baby as it emerges from the womb, and so being buried back into

---

75. Bryant and Peck, eds. *Encyclopedia of Death*, xxxiii.

a womblike structure the body should be covered with that red again? Could it have been to protect the body or spirit from other forces? Really, there is no way to know, but it does say something that human beings have incorporated color in their practices for potentially over 100,000 years.

Psychological Impacts of Color

Our perception of color is proving to be determined as much by culture as it is cognition. Did you know that the vast majority of the world's ancient languages, for example, lack a word for the color blue? This startling realization has been the focus of researchers for a while, who wondered whether blue was a color ancient people could even perceive. According to studies, while the color blue has been seen for hundreds of thousands of years, the perception of color is determined by cultural relationship—specifically the ability to replicate and control said color. For example, in ancient Greek literature, the sky was referred to as "wine dark" even though it is obviously blue. Ancient cultures that had access to natural pigments or minerals that produced blue often had words for the color, whereas cultures that did not perceived blue as a shade of other colors they had access to.[76]

The ability to detect different shades of a color is the result of a combination of cultural and cognitive processes, and this is true even today. Case in point, that infamous scene in *The Devil Wears Prada* where Miranda (Meryl Streep) reams out Andy (Anne Hathaway) for not detecting the color difference between two belts.

Why is this important for our work? Understanding that color and many other aspects of ritual carry with them cognitive as well as metaphorical and spiritual dimensions, we can become even more nuanced in our practice. For while spirits do not have physical minds like ours anymore, ancestors that were once human developed originally in their cultural contexts, and in my experience often respond through those lenses, as do we.

Modern psychology teaches us that color is deeply impactful on our mood. Under the name *chromotherapy*, color therapy demonstrates that color affects both our mood and outlook. Who among us hasn't entered a space

---

76. Rune Pettersson, "Cultural Differences in the Perception of Image and Color in Pictures," *Educational Technology Research and Development* 30, no. 1 (March 1982): 43–53. https://doi.org/10.1007/BF02766547.

and felt an immediate attraction because the room feels cozy and inviting, or felt revulsion because the space feels cold and uninviting? During certain types of weather, individuals will respond differently to the level of light and the colors surrounding them. (A dreary day may evoke gloom, while a sunny day may be energizing.) We see this association with color even in popular idioms expressing mood or psychological states—for example, "being green with envy," "seeing the world through rose-tinted lenses," or "seeing red."

The research suggests that responses to color are deeply entwined with cultural conceptions of the meaning or assumptions, which in turn trigger associated memories, mental images, and our moods. This impact on us by our environment is not a new concept and is certainly something we all experience in some form or another.[77]

It is the triggering of memories or mood that I want to narrow in on when it comes to ancestor veneration and spirituality in general. When building a shrine and thinking about color, please consider the following questions:

How will certain colors represented in the space affect your relationships? In some cultures, particular colors have particular meaning that, when represented, will affect the mood of the space and can be a launching point for relationships. For example, the dominant color scheme for Chinese ancestor shrines is red because red is the color of prosperity, and so representing red so heavily in the shrine makes a statement that this is a place where prosperity can be cultivated. The relationship between dead and living is thus underpinned by the concept of prosperity.

How might a particular color affect the mood of the dead? Just as certain colors affect the living, there are teachings that they also affect the mood of the dead. In some forms of espiritismo, one of the main reasons that I have been taught that bovedas are set upon white linen with white flowers is that white is the color of purity and spiritual elevation. The goal of espiritismo is the elevation of spirits through prayer and light, and white creates that ambience of purity and elevation. In ancient Egyptian tradition, one of the reasons that so many tombs of important individuals contained an overabundance of gold, including their sarcophagi, was that gold was associated

77. Andrew J. Elliot and Markus A. Maier, "Color and Psychological Functioning," *Current Directions in Psychological Science* 16, no. 5 (October 2007): 250–54. https://psycnet.apa .org/doi/10.1111/j.1467-8721.2007.00514.x.

with divinity. Divinities in Egypt were believed to have golden skin and silver bones. Coloring the sarcophagi or the funeral mask in gold had the rationale of transforming the flesh of the deceased from mortal to immortal.

How might color affect your own mood? As was said above, color does have a way of affecting mood based on our cultural associations and personal preferences. Do colors brighten your day or bring you down? Do colors evoke moods that would be useful in your spiritual work, and if so, what are they? For me, nothing gets me energized quite like an overcast, rainy day when the greens of vegetation seem to pop in comparison to the gray shades in the sky. Just thinking about it makes me feel cozy, at peace, and ready to have a quiet day by the fire. In thinking about your own mood, how might color in your sacred spaces affect your relationships with the beings housed or connected with there? If you have an aversion to the color green because of a trauma association, would it make sense to have green prominent in a sacred space?

Associations with Individuals and Organizations

Color is often associated with individuals and organizations or groups, and as a visual cue stands in for other forms of representation. We can easily apply this same idea to the secular and look at how sports teams, political parties, or the retinues of important dignitaries are organized and represented at events. In the spiritual sphere, it is easy to find examples of this in action.

A very robust example of color correspondence to individuals comes to us from orisha traditions. Each of the orisha have a defining color, which varies between traditions and lineages but is mutually intelligible: Obatala (white), Eleggua (red/black), Oshun (yellow), Yemaya (blue), Shango (red/white), Olokun (blue), Oya (brown/orange), Nana Buruku (purple), Ochosi (green), Ogun (green/black). During ceremonies, the orisha who come down in possession, whose mounts are dressed in their colors before or after they are possessed, mingle with the non-possessed white-clad attendees. Each of the orisha are represented by these colors in the decor and objects housed in their shrines, while devotees wear the colorful *eleke* beads associated with these orisha. The elekes are a powerful, consecrated, spiritual technology that marks the wearer as either a priest of or under the protection of the orisha associated with each necklace. The elekes themselves are a sophisticated color coding system, and each orisha has a specific pattern easily recognizable to those who are privy to the private knowledge of the system. When meeting another aborisha or olorisha, color is a visual form of communication identifying the level of initiation and thus appropriate rules governing interaction.

The above example of the elekes' use of color as a form of compartmentalization of different groups of beings is not unique to orisha tradition. Indeed, the majority of the world's traditions use color as emblematic of different groups. In *espiritismo Cruzado*, the Cuban form of espiritismo, the various courts of spirits are sometimes represented by differently colored flags, or I have also seen colored ribbons tied around each boveda glass. In Haitian Vodou, the different courts of Lwa spirits (who are an amalgam of both ancestor and nonhuman spirits) are also represented by flags of solid colors, as are individual Lwa themselves.

This use of color extends to representing the individual characteristics of beings. Hinduism and Buddhism both have a robust color coding system: their deities, bodhisattvas, and Buddhas are all visualized in vivid color to represent aspects or pieces of their personality, attributes, or natures. Shiva the Destroyer is colored white or teal to represent the ash he covers his body with, and his throat is a bright blue to represent the poison he drank at the beginning of time. Shiva as Destroyer is the aspect of the trifold understanding of the universe, and the ash he wears is symbolic of the inevitability of change. Kali, a form of Shiva's consort, is blackened or dark purple to represent eternity and the color of the expanse, and her mood of destruction and change. The Vajrayana Medicine Buddha, Bhaiṣajyaguru, is colored azure blue representing the limitless sky and the power of healing.

Journal Prompts

- How does color show up in the world you live in?
- What relationships do you or your culture have to specific colors?
- How do you think color impacted the worlds of your ancestors?
- What opportunities in relation to your ancestral practice did you think of as you read this chapter?

Chapter Eleven
Physical
Representations

It is common for humans to depict the spiritual in tangible forms we can look at, hold, and interact with. Statues or icons of gods, spirits, and saints are common throughout the world and serve the important function of assisting to build relationship between humans and the spiritual being depicted. This expression of a human need for tangibility is a vital one, and something that manifests in many spiritual and secular forms. Visit someone's home, and often, unless their culture forbids it, you'll find pictures or art representing family relationships. While this is often to remember and honor these individuals, I would like to address how representation in your ancestral veneration practice could be important and offer rationale as to why.

In this chapter, I wish to explore the use of physical depictions, both figurative and abstract, in connecting to the spiritual world generally and ancestors specifically. When I say physical depiction, I mean both pictures and other forms of representation, including plaques, statues, relics, or any other object that stands in for that ancestor or spirit. Some of the questions I wish to explore are: How might image or representation enter your practice? What role can representation play in your relationships? What are some of the arguments for and against such representation? As always, I challenge you to reflect on your own deeply held worldview and how this section might support or be questioned by that worldview.

As we move from this chapter into the following chapters around use of objects, you will see many crossovers and items that could be used in multiple ways. While objects spoken of in this chapter might be used representationally, other chapters will sugest that the exact same objects or those similar to them be used differently. This is where I want to underline the word *intention* when approaching your lived practice. Many aspects of lived spiritual practice blur boundaries and cross categories. A tool in one instance becomes representational the next. What is important is that you are mindful of how, for example, an object is being used and how that same object may take on several roles in your practice.

The Psychology of Iconism

Iconism is the creation of an image that represents another figure whether physically or abstractly. When we draw a picture of, speak a word associated with, or mimic the behavior of something, we are engaging in iconism. This is a crucially important and foundational aspect of our minds and how we interact with the world around us, because we are beings highly connected to symbol on a fundamental cognitive level. The process by which our minds perceive the world is not as straightforward as simply experiencing with our five senses. While it is true that through our five senses we pick up on sensory data, we don't respond directly to that data. Our minds process and create a coherent and filtered understanding of our external environments in order to formulate an appropriate response. In essence, our brains construct myriad lenses to interpret and understand the external world.

In this process, our minds rely heavily on the databank of past experience and knowledge accumulated over our lifetime to interpret the external reality. That information is stored and recalled in our minds through the use of what is called *mental representation*. These images are the mental figures that our brains associate information with, and they take the form of images in our minds as well as the experiential components and contexts in which we encountered them.[78] There are multiple theories of how, exactly, this process plays out in our brains, but for the most part, most theories agree that we

---

78. Vesna Mildner, *The Cognitive Neuroscience of Human Communication* (New York: Psychology Press, 2015), 25.

construct symbolic representations in our minds to store information, and this information is recalled through external stimuli.[79]

Humans think abstractly, which sets us apart from many other animals, and our basic cognitive function almost always creates sign and symbol to facilitate that. Have you ever tried to think about infinity? It's not comfortable, is it? When we create representations, we're creating tangible and definable symbols that we can associate with and relate to—and in that process, respond to. In the previous chapters, we talked about character and story, and these are perfect examples of why iconism is such an important subject to explore. Our brains naturally relate through symbol, and our memory structure is associative in nature. This is the bulk of Dr. Lynne Kelly's work in memory techniques, by using external stimuli to generate new neural associations that can be recalled using physical stimuli and story.

It is in this that representation can become a powerful tool in your ancestral or general spiritual work. By using objects and representations as tools for memory or contextual recall, you can make the intangible tangible on some level. By finding an object or some physical representation, we give ourselves a clear symbol that we can use to create a mental image and thus jump-start the process of association. When we can associate to something via our mental images, we can build relationship with that subject. In truth, this relationship between our brains and symbols can be applied to any of the following chapters. It is not the only reason why one would want to utilize representation in a spiritual practice, but for me it is a foundational reason.

Uses Of Representational Objects

Apart from what we discussed previously around iconism, what are other reasons you might want objects depicting spirits and deities? Is it to communicate with the spirits? Is it to represent the spirit and ground it to this world in some way? Does depicting the spirit in physical form make it more relatable? Is it to teach the deeper mysteries of that spirit and what they represent to the younger members of the community? I think the answer is all of these, depending upon the tradition we're talking about. In my opinion, these are the four most important reasons why depiction or representation is so important.

---

79. Mildner, *The Cognitive Neuroscience of Human Communication*, 82.

Communication

If we look at traditions, namely animistic traditions, we tend to see mediums interacting with the spirits and gods, often through divination or direct spirit possession. If we look at other traditions that heavily utilize statuary and icons (Roman Catholicism, Orthodox Christianity, ancient Greece and Rome, Hinduism, Buddhism, etc.), we can see embedded within them this same need for communication but via the medium of a representation. Whereas in more animistic traditions the bodies of humans become the vessels for communication through spirit possession or the spirits reside in sacred spaces in nature, other traditions develop forms of communication through a representational medium.

In his 2011 documentary *Treasures of Heaven*, art historian Andrew Graham-Dixon commented that his understanding of icons in Orthodox Christianity is that, "You don't look at the icon; the icon looks at you."[80] Through a relationship with the image, communion between figure depicted and human onlooker is achieved. This same sentiment can be found in Hinduism, where the gorgeous *murtis* enshrined in temples are enlivened with the spirit of that deity, and the ritual of *puja* is to attain *Darśana*, literally to look at and be looked at by the deity.

Anchoring and Embodying the Spirit

Hinted at above is the reality known to many spirit workers, and that is anchoring a spirit or god to this world in a vessel of some kind. One way of seeing this is that originally the deities were embodiments of nature or place, and humans traveled to those places to commune with those spirits. As peoples changed from a nomadic to settled lifestyle, and emerging cultures began to merge different deities into one another, the spirits or deities became divorced from embodiment in the natural setting, and enshrinement in temples arose.

Objects of cult focus such as statues, images, or personal items were imbued with the essence of the deity or spirit and thus became objects of power and veneration. As time went on, looking at various cultures, we see the rise of individuated forms of deities or spirits with complimenting reli-

---

80. Andrew Graham-Dixon, *Treasures of Heaven*, directed by Paul Tilzey; London: BBC, 2011.

gious centers. While the understanding of these objects and their relationship to the Divine differed from culture to culture, the fact that a majority of human cultures both presently and historically have created similar physical representations suggests the universality of this approach.

If we look throughout the past several thousand years, we can see rituals and procedures for turning a statue or cult image into the living embodiment of a spirit or deity, and thus an object that can be worked with as well as moved around and defended. The number of deities that were captured through war and brought into enemy pantheons is evidence of a general understanding of the nature of deities. For example, the number of deities from surrounding cultures that were assimilated into the Egyptian pantheon such as Qedesh and Bes, and the general approach to deities of the Romans, who often brought the cult status of important deities back to be enshrined in temples in Rome, such as the cult stone of the goddess Cybele.

Likewise, this way of anchoring a god to a moveable object means that the deity is mobile and can be used throughout regions they may not have originally been connected with as well as represent the needs of specific locations. A very good example of this is the Ark of the Covenant, which the Israelites carried with them in their forty years of wandering the desert, and which was believed to contain within it the living embodiment of the God of Israel. Interestingly, we can see this same understanding in modern Catholic, Hindu, Buddhist, and other religious traditions that use icons or statuary with an understanding of individual spirits reflecting localized aspects of the universal persona.

Relatability

As a species, we tend to respond very sympathetically to things that look like us. One reason why horror movies involving creatures that are blobs or tentacled monstrosities frighten us is our inability to relate to such creatures. This helps to explain why deities and spirits come to be depicted in forms we can associate with and relate to. Even in traditions that don't use statuary, art will often depict the spirit or god in human forms. At the very least, many of the stories told about them attribute human characteristics and personality to the spirits and thus create that relatability. If we look at the evolution of deity iconography, we can often track how representation morphs from abstract to figurative. This is not merely an occurrence that took place in a few regions like Europe or the Middle East, but around the planet. Often within living traditions now, we see remnants of earlier abstract traditions coexisting alongside the later anthropomorphic ones.

Relatability does not just stop at depicting the incorporeal in a form that we can empathize with; often, it extends to depicting the being like our own people. It is a widespread cultural predisposition that when an element (such as a story, character, or experience) comes from the outside of a population, some of the elements are adapted so that the culture can take ownership of and in many ways indigenize it. Jesus Christ and Buddha are two such examples of religious figures where the representation of them varies from culture to culture regardless of any historical reality.

If you visit China, you will see images of the Buddha with typical Han Chinese features, same as if you visit Cambodia and take in the massive Buddha heads present at Angkor Wat, which all have typically Khmer features. The stories of Buddha's past incarnations are collected in the works called the Jatakas, and many Buddhist cultures tend to locate the Jatakas locally to their own landscapes. The same trend can be seen in every religious tradition that has grown, either through adoption or conversion by conquest, outside the bounds of the area it originated in.

This same experience of the Buddha is also shared by Jesus Christ. The first depictions of Jesus started to emerge two hundred years after his death, and Europeans depicted him with typically European features despite him originating in the Middle East. If you visit South America, Ethiopia, or Korea, you will find examples of depictions of Jesus Christ that mirror the looks of the local populations. Jesus and Mary are depicted with dark skin in the Ethiopian church, while in China and Korea he is sometimes depicted with typically Asian features. This assimilation and redefining of the representation of the spirit or god is an important step in a population identifying and associating with the figure.

Many ancient cultures adopted and assimilated gods from their neighbors, and in so doing, the figure was absorbed to fit in with the rest of the pantheon, whether through iconography or depiction. Each example has nuanced history, but an argument can be made that depicting the spiritual in a recognizable form serves a psychological purpose that allows us to relate.

Teaching Tool

Considering the cognitive mechanism of association, iconography stands in as a powerful visual tool to succinctly and easily convey data through memorable and meaningful symbol and sign. Depictions of deities and spirits throughout the world almost always follow specific cultural rules and expectations regarding what needs to be included and depicted in order for the subject to be identifiable and relatable. It doesn't matter which culture we are talking about; differentiation of figures is achieved using specific elements, which become associated with that figure alone and are recognizable. For example, the Christian tradition of icons and reliquaries has developed so that every saint or martyr is identifiable through key symbolic elements associated with them. Even if a saint in icon or statue form isn't labeled with their name, you can understand who they are based on the objects they hold, their posture, the color of their clothing, or other elements. All these elements become specific to that saint. This is an understandable approach in depicting figures of importance through art because the symbols are each memorable in and of themselves. The late art historian Sister Wendy Beckett noted that icons and reliquaries of saints in the Christian tradition become visual stories to be viewed, and in so doing, we enter the stories of those figures ourselves.[81]

Often, the iconographic symbology of these figures becomes the way by which we teach our young about the subjects, setting up the foundations for their relationships to these figures. We previously discussed the kachinas of the Hopi people. The Hopi gift beautiful kachina dolls to children to learn the iconography of each kachina. That iconography creates a vivid image of the spirit that makes the intangible tangible. Each kachina's story, purpose, and attributes are taught and associated with the iconography represented in the doll. When a child encounters the masked and costumed dancers who embody each kachina at group festivities, they will already be aware of the kachinas' role in the culture because of their intimate connection with their doll. In this way, it could be understood that the doll is not a plaything but a physical document whose symbols are read and studied.

We can relate to this idea in many ways outside of dolls or figurines, such as in depictions of our spirits or ancestors. How many of us grew up with

---

81. Graham-Dixon, *Treasures of Heaven*.

portraits of an ancestor on the walls and were taught the stories connected to the person? We may have begun to create iconographic associations already by what we were viewing in the picture. In my case, I grew up with a photo of my grandmother Poplar wearing a red polka dot dress, and from then on, I've always seen red with white polka dots as a symbol of my grandmother. I was taught about the occasion the photograph was taken, which is when my grandparents came to Chicago in the US to visit my half-uncle in the mid-eighties. An association has formed that allows me to not only remember the image but also relate to my grandmother.

Modern Forms of Representation

Let us explore some concrete examples of what physical representation of your ancestors could look like in a modern context. As always, consider how these forms of representation might be useful to you in your practice or how they might honor your ancestors' ways of understanding themselves. Some key questions to keep in mind: What significance does this type of representation have? What might be the ritualistic steps in creating said object? What role does representation play in your culture?

I would suggest there are three basic categories of depiction based upon use: containers, bridges, and art. Container objects or depictions are believed to house a spiritual being in an earthly vessel; bridges are objects that act as temporary points for the spirit to act through; while art is the depiction of a subject, but not necessarily embodying the subject. I see these three categories as a continuum rather than set categories, and so you may come across objects in some traditions that have multiple purposes.

Anthropomorphic Figures

Nowadays we tend to see many spiritual beings depicted in recognizable human form. This depicting of the spiritual in humanlike form is called *anthropomorphism*. On a sacred level, the inclination to depict spiritual beings in physical form through a figure that looks like us is understandable; it is to make the intangible spiritual into tangible material.

There is a specific delineation between art and sacred form. Art is widespread and can have a broad range of styles and forms while being understood as the intended subject. Sacred form, however, is a unique category and is usually governed by specific rules and relationships. Traditions around the correct creation of these sacred objects, rituals to consecrate said statuary or images, rules of engagement with these now-sacred objects, and even specific ritual displays of respect are employed with sacred form as opposed to mere artwork. For example, in ancient Egypt, the cult statues in temples were constructed with an inner core of silver and a skin of gold. Gold was the divine flesh of gods while silver was what their bones were made from. This is one reason why so many funerary masks of pharaohs were either painted with or made of solid gold. An interesting and intentional contradiction to this approach was the deity Anti, whose cult statue was silver, representing his nature as a flayed deity.[82]

In Hinduism, the construction of the statues you find in temples (called murtis) follow strict guidelines dictating both proportion and the most auspicious time to create as well as proper materials and dress, as laid out in ancient sacred text. Once a statue or image is deemed to have been created correctly, the ritual of *prāṇa pratiṣṭhā* is performed, which imbues or activates the physical objects with the living spirit of the deity.[83] Upon completion, the spirit is understood to reside within.

Sometimes in ancestral traditions, a statue or carving becomes a medium for communication or a proxy for the dead to utilize temporarily. Among the Torajan people of South Sulawesi, after a funeral, the preserved corpse of the deceased is taken to a necropolis area, which sometimes is a miniature village and other times a structure carved into a cliff utilizing niches and caves. Here the corpse is placed into a niche while an almost life-size effigy carving called a *tau tau* is placed exterior to the niche. The tau taus of all the individuals in the burial area are arranged in overlooking niches or inside small buildings and act as guardian effigies protecting both the burial place as a whole and the living in the community close by. Every so often, the tau tau and the preserved corpse of the individual will be cleaned and redressed so that the spirit of the deceased can continue to utilize the form as a place to inhabit

---

82. George Hart, "Anti," in *A Dictionary of Egyptian Gods and Goddesses* (New York: Routledge, 2005), 24.

83. Cush, Robinson, and York, *Encyclopedia of Hinduism*, 363.

temporarily.[84] The relationship between the corpse and the tau tau varies from region to region. Sometimes the tau tau is more important than the physical remains, while in other regions the corpse and the tau tau perform different functions for the individual.

Portraits and Pictures

Two-dimensional images are a second major form of representation, and many of us have them prominently in our homes without spiritual ritual attached. In some traditions, portraits are essential elements to have in home shrines. Prior to the invention of photography, two-dimensional images could be a laborious process that always created unique objects. The painted or sketched image might be the only one in existence, and so that uniqueness added to its specialness. When photography was invented, the process for having a photo taken was still as unique as having a painting done, and so photographs became treasured heirlooms. Indeed, part of Victorian mortuary custom was the so called "death portrait," a photograph taken of the corpse, which may or may not have been the only photograph ever taken of that individual. While we live in a digital age when photos are snapped every second, consider those rare treasures of physical photos you or your parents have stashed away.

It was during the writing of this book that I got a surprise from my mum. She forwarded me a message from a relative in Australia, a second cousin of my grandfather, who had in her collection a picture of my great-great-great grandfather Charles Poplar. Charles was someone whom I had heard many stories about, but to suddenly have a picture of him was indescribably sweet. The picture allowed me to see his face, and he became a little more real for me. To be experiencing that feeling over a hundred years after he had died was powerful. I think this is why pictures become important for traditions that utilize them; they are not like statues but a lot more like icons.

We can see how, in some ancestral traditions, a photo is an element of power. Take for example the Pixar movie *Coco*, where Miguel's great-great-grandfather Hector begs him to take a portrait back to be added to the family ofrenda. Doing so will allow Hector to visit the land of the living during Día

---

84. Hetty Nooy-Palm, *The Sa'dan-Toraja: A Study of Their Social Life and Religion*, vol 1: Organization, Symbols and Beliefs (Dordrecht, Netherlands: Springer Science & Business Media, 1979), 259.

de los Muertos, as well as become stronger in death and be remembered by the living, staving off the danger of being forgotten. In my own ancestral shrine, I have portraits of my ancestors up on the wall, and I was very pleased to be able to add my grandad, Charles.

Masks and Costume

Representation of deities or spirits via masks or costumes is found throughout the world, and seemingly for similar purposes. The use of mask and costume as a way for the human wearer to embody the character represented is a very potent one. In some traditions, the wearer might become possessed by the spirit that the mask depicts, while in other traditions, the interplay between the audience and the masked figure allows for an interactional encounter. Seemingly all cultures have utilized masks or costumes to some degree. Some notable examples include Tibetan mask dances of Bon spirits; the Yoruba Egungun cult of costumed figures representing the ancestors; the Puebloan kachina dancers; the masked dancers of the Haida and other Pacific Northwestern peoples; and the various European costumed figures, such as the hobbyhorse tradition of mari lwyd, the Burryman, Gog and Magog (whose likenesses are made from willow), the Schnabelperchten, and others. Dance is an incredibly important ritual in many cultures, and it is through mass dances and masquerade that contact with the spirit world is believed to be achieved.

Icons

Icons are part of a very specific art form utilized in Christianity that represent a saint or spiritual figure, with similar art forms in other traditions. The icon is painted using specific dimensions and traditional means, developed as a mobile way of venerating the individuals depicted. The icon is not just a picture of a saint; it is a consecrated device to communicate or commune with that saint. In Orthodox churches, we see frescoed icons decorating the interior of a church to create the interior space, while panel icons are smaller objects that are usually kept in shrines and niches. Both frescoes and panel icons direct attention toward the figure depicted, but each have slightly different relationships and roles.

In his series *The Art of Russia*, art historian Andrew Graham-Dixon noted that frescoed icons on the screens and walls of churches allow for worshippers to enter into an interactional physical and spiritual space. Eastern Orthodox churches are designed a little differently than Latin rite, and the congregation surround the priest, who in turn is surrounded by all the painted icons on the walls and ceiling. In effect, the living congregation are surrounded by the icons of the deceased saints and martyrs, forming a community of believers both living and dead.[85]

Panel icons, on the other hand, are venerated and housed differently, becoming singular points of veneration of the depicted. They are devices, not just inanimate pictures, and are like other holy devices such as *thangkas* of Tibetan Buddhism. It also strikes me that the most ancient of cave paintings may have acted in a similar way to icons: two-dimensional images that a tribe might relate to the spirit of the animal they were depicting. This is certainly not a new idea, but instead a long interpretation of rock art from around the world by both anthropologists and Indigenous people themselves.

Relics and Reliquaries

Relics and the reliquaries they are housed within are a potent physical representation of the individuals they are believed to have originated from. Relics might be a physical remain (bone, hair, tooth, etc.) or an object that is known to have been in use by or intimately connected to the individual. Reliquaries are the housing that a relic is contained within and often are a beautiful container that adds to the context of the relic. In Western Christianity, reliquaries take the shape of small figurines, gilded boxes, or reproductions of the body part that the relic belongs to.

What relics provide is a tangible spiritual connection to the individual glorified in the reliquary; whether the relic is from that individual or not is beside the point. Reliquaries, like icons and figurative statuary, seek to inform the worshipper of the story of the individual the relic belonged to while also providing a direct connection.

---

85. Andrew Graham-Dixon, *The Art of Russia*, season 1, episode 1, "Out of the Forest," 2009, BBC, 2009.

The Christian tradition has an elaborate system around and relationship to relics, and during the medieval ages, relics were a hot commodity. The authenticity of these relics was believed to be true, but with so many often-fake examples floating about, logically not all these relics could be authentic. However, as the late art historian Sister Wendy Beckett stated in an interview about the likelihood of the historical authenticity of a particular relic: "those little pieces of wood…they are holy in their meaning if not in their actuality."[86] Her meaning here is that the point of a relic is to facilitate an emotional relationship and connection to the Divine regardless of the historical actuality of the piece.

Now, this is one view from a particular individual within one faith, and as my editor was quick to point out, not everyone will believe or be open to the idea that it doesn't really matter if a particular relic is real or not. I would argue, however, that it all depends on how you look at it. Applying the idea of relics to our own ancestors, if we don't have access to a particular ancestor's remains but collect something from somewhere we know they were, such as a pebble from their home area or graveyard dirt, then is that proxy object not still connected to them because we associate it with them? This, of course, all comes down to your own beliefs and the threshold of what is true for you.

There arose within Christianity, and simultaneously in other traditions like Buddhism, the concept of a "touch relic." These are objects that are either identical to an original or are designed as having connection to an original. In the great age of the pilgrimages, it was believed that if these touch relics—often special badges depicting a saint—physically touched the shrine or actual relic of a saint the spiritual power of the original relic would rub off on the touch relic. These fabulous items were then taken home after pilgrimage for use in personal worship. In medieval Western Europe, touch relics often came in the form of badges bought at pilgrimage centers that depicted the saint and could be worn proudly as a sign you had successfully completed a pilgrimage.

For our purposes, ancestral relics could be anything from objects that once belonged to your ancestors to soil samples from sites connected to individuals or groups, such as grave dirt or soil from lands they lived on. Among my personal collection I have my great-grandfather's cane, my grandmother's handbag, stones from North Wales, a ring my father gave me, my great-grandfather's war

---

86. Graham-Dixon, *Treasures of Heaven*.

medals, and other items. What objects or relics do you have of your ancestors in your possession? What connection do these objects give you to these individuals? How might relics of other types of ancestors look?

Aniconism

Aniconism is the representation or embodying of spirits through non-anthropomorphic means. Aniconism is often found within traditions that also have anthropomorphic figures, and constitutes a region on a spectrum. While it would be tempting to say that anthropomorphic depictions are an evolution from aniconism, the reality is that many traditions contain both iconistic and aniconistic attitudes. For those traditions that espouse aniconism, often the arguments presented are to prevent the narrowing of the spiritual to imperfect form.

I think the most well-known example to readers of aniconism is Islam, which strictly prohibits the depiction of God or His prophets in order to prevent idolatry. While it is true that at times some Muslim cultures have allowed depictions of spiritual beings, including very rare examples of the Prophet Muhammad, there is no depiction of God in Islam. Instead, the Kaaba in Mecca acts as a focus point for Muslims worldwide for prayers.

Even traditions that would seem to be filled to the brim with depictions of deities in every conceivable color, such as Hinduism, contain traditions of aniconism. The Virakta sect of Virashaivism centered on the god Shiva differs from many other Saiva groups in that they vehemently oppose temple worship and depicting Shiva in fixed form. They practice a form of devotion that is centered on individual inner experience of the god, rather than fixing devotion onto exterior forms in temples. Their major religious accoutrement is a small lingam stone worn on the body near the heart.[87]

How does aniconism come into ancestor veneration? One argument from Lukumi is that by maintaining a simple aniconistic ancestor space, the living maintains the boundaries between life and death and treats the dead as a collective rather than focusing on individuals. Another potential reason why you would employ aniconism in your practice is if you are venerating

---

87. R. Blake Michael, "Foundation Myths of the Two Denominations of Vīraśaivism: *Viraktas* and *Gurusthalins*," *The Journal of Asian Studies* 42, no. 2 (February 1983): 309–22. https:// doi.org/10.2307/2055116.

nonhuman ancestors or ancestors you do not know but who are connected through a rock or soil from a particular place. There may not be a good reason to depict these ancestors in any way other than aniconism.

Associated Items

We have touched on the power of associated items already. Sometimes you don't have pictures or even the identity of your ancestors, except their location of origin. This is especially true for adopted persons or families who lost information due to war, emigration, or another dramatic move. In some ancestral traditions, the ancestors are represented by associated objects or heirlooms, and sometimes even by trinkets. These are different than relics, in that the objects never directly belonged to or came from the spirits or ancestors, but stand in for concepts, places, people, or even history.

A friend of mine who is of Scottish ancestry but whose family has been in North America for centuries, discovered that part of her family probably originated from a particular castle seat of the Macleod clan on the Isle of Skye. She placed upon her ancestral altar a picture of Dunvegan Castle and a small miniature statue of a Highlander she picked up while on pilgrimage to Skye a few years before. For her, these two objects stood in for and helped her connect with those ancestors she did not know the names of.

If you do not have images or other forms of representation of ancestors, this is where associated items may come in handy. We will talk more about pilgrimage in a later chapter, but as representation is as much about deepening that emotional connection as it is about representing individuals and groups, an item that can create that connection is a good item.

Consecration of Representational Objects

Consecration is when spiritual authorities perform necessary and tradition-bound ritual preparations to create legitimate and safe spiritual tools or invest spiritual power into something or someone. More broadly, consecration is an act of transforming and processing a subject from illegitimacy to legitimacy.

The various forms of rites of passage, initiation, and even funerary rites could all be seen as a form of consecration. When a priest is initiated, they are transformed from a non-initiate into an initiate, with access to sacred wisdom. When a young person reaches their rite of passage into adulthood, they are transformed from child to adult through a sacred act. Consecration as transformation into something sacred is preparing that person or thing to be in contact with the different spaces of reality they did not have access to before. I bring this point up because depending upon how you intend to use figurative or representational objects in your shrine or the shrine itself, you may need to think about consecration of items or space.

Ritual preparation, activation, and even programming of the mundane object are about transforming the mundane into the spiritual. In most of the world traditions that I have seen, there is a baseline understanding of the importance of this spiritual mechanism. The process for sanctifying an icon in Christianity is that the object or painting be blessed by God through a prayer, a recounting of the story connected to the figure depicted, several other prayers specific to the type of icon, and a final sprinkling with holy water to mark the icon as fully consecrated. When an icon is consecrated, it is thus understood to be a bridge between the viewer and the figure depicted. The difference between a mundane picture and sacred icon is the icon's ability to be a channel for the spiritual realms.[88]

What might this look like in your ancestor practice? If you choose to depict certain ancestors, how might those depictions be made special through consecration of some kind? What might that consecration even look like?

Prohibitions Against Depicting the Spiritual

Just as depicting spiritual beings is an integral component in many traditions, there are also many traditions with strict prohibitions against, or strict guidelines around, visually depicting spiritual beings. For those who espouse these prohibitions, these rules usually govern appropriate relationships with spiritual beings and are informed by beliefs of the nature of the spiritual. Rarely are prohibitions or controls around how we depict the spiritual without a sense of logic.

Abrahamic tradition offers us a very direct and culturally understandable prohibition against the use of statuary or depiction of any kind, particularly Islam and Judaism. In the Bible, there are prohibitions against "idolatry" and

---

88. Margaret E. Kenna, "Icons in Theory and Practice: An Orthodox Christian Example," *History of Religions* 24, no. 4 (May 1985): 345–68, https://www.jstor.org/stable/1062307.

the creation of graven images. In the Torah is the famous story of Moses and the God of Israel punishing the Israelites for losing faith in him after they constructed the golden calf. Throughout the history of Christianity, there have been movements for and against the use of statues or icons, each movement based upon a different interpretation of the biblical prohibition against idols. In modern Catholic and Eastern Orthodox understanding, the role of statues and icons is as a focus for devotion and not as a subject of worship; whereas, in many Protestant denominations, statuary and iconography is decorative only and has no spiritual or ritual use.

Of the three Abrahamic traditions, Islam has a general and absolute prohibition against depicting spiritual beings, especially God. You will find no mosque with images depicting humans or spiritual figures. While there have been examples through history of some spiritual figures being depicted, especially in the illuminated manuscripts of the Ottomans, Persians, and Mughals, there is a general understanding among modern Muslims that it is taboo. The reason for this is the prohibition against idolatry and limiting the vast perfection of God through imperfect mediums.

While monotheism tends to carry many of the examples of prohibitions against depicting the spiritual, there are many examples of animistic and polytheistic traditions that have rules or guidelines as well.

Among Australian Indigenous people and Torres Strait Islanders, there is a general prohibition against or aversion to seeing depictions or saying the names of the dead. Australian television routinely places warnings before content that might include depictions or recordings of deceased Indigenous persons to allow the viewer to decide whether to engage with the content or not. This prohibition seems to vary from person to person, but ultimately it comes down to a sensitivity for the dead individual and not tying them to the present.

One of the pieces in Lukumi that I was taught was that while working with ancestors, it is grossly inappropriate to try to create permanent embodying vessels in our world for the dead to inhabit. Depicting them through photographs is okay and has even become popular in recent decades, but this is understood not to be an embodying vessel that removes the dead from their afterlife to re-embody them in this world. The shrine and the various other parts of it are a space to commune, but there's an understanding that the barrier needs to be maintained between life and death.

When we speak the deceased person's name, we say "ibae," and we are careful not to speak ill of the dead in general. One of the customs among Lukumi practitioners is for any pregnant woman to keep her back to the ancestor shrine when feeding the dead so that a dead spirit does not try to possess her unborn baby and be reborn into the world. This form of reincarnation would pervert the natural order of life and death and cause great misfortune.

Bringing It All Together

The discussions above borrowed heavily from spirituality in general rather than just those practices devoted to the ancestors. Depending upon tradition, how one works with and represents the spirits or gods will be different from how one represents the ancestors, while in some traditions there is no difference in how one relates to the dead versus deities or other spirits.

The concept of iconism and the cognitive reality of how we relate to sign, symbol, and representation was a powerful key in unlocking my own relationship to my ancestral and spiritual practices. Understanding our brain's mechanism for how we relate to ourselves and others created opportunities for me to develop and deepen my practice. This mechanism can be utilized in ways that don't include pictures or statuary, and you may come from a culture that already has some options for you.

Another important consideration of how representational objects relate to your practice is how you intend to use sacred space. My ancestor shrine is a multipurpose space; I honor the dead there and commune with them, but it's also a three-dimensional memory space, allowing me to organize and lay out my personal history in front of me. It is for the dead, but it is also for me to remember the dead and reflect on how their lives, gifts, and foibles show up in my own life. Some of the objects within are representational of individuals, and some are representational of the story of my family.

The last and most important piece to this area of representation is how your ancestors themselves relate to the representations you want to explore. If you decide you'd like a little figurine, how would your grandparents feel about that? I already know in my family, my grandparents (both working-class northern English) would be uncomfortable with little statues representing them individually but wouldn't be uncomfortable with items that represent aspects of their personalities or images of them in their prime. For items representing them in the sacred space you're building, what conversation will you have with your ancestors to gain their insight on how they want to be represented? It has been my experience with my family that when choosing items or representations, a lot of opinions start coming through. I was standing in the shower one morning and got a distinctive image of my grandmother standing on a balcony in a beautiful great house garden. I knew exactly which picture it was. Okay, Gran, I'll print that one instead!

The chief piece around representation is that it must fit into your worldview. If certain forms of representation are not a part of your worldview or feel uncomfortable, then why have them? If you come from a culture that places emphasis on story and name over physicality and remains, then your practice may be less physical than it is ritual.

Journal Prompts

- How do you relate to representational art? What do you notice when you relate to something through representation versus more abstract forms?

- In what ways might different forms of representation affect your relationship with the ancestors?

- Do you prefer certain types of representation over others? What draws you to this form of representation?

- What feelings and thoughts come up for you when you see images of your ancestors?

Chapter Twelve

Objects of Power

Humans have an undeniable, nostalgic connection to items we know once belonged to our dead. This emotional connection is the very reason why relics of any kind are so important both individually and culturally. It is likely that you have some trinket or heirloom connected to an ancestor somewhere, and while we work through this chapter, I ask that you keep those objects in mind and the relationship you have with them. I previously wrote about the small collection of heirlooms gifted to me, each one a relic of my ancestors, and how important they are in my practice. There is something about the tangibility of physical objects that connect us to the past in ways words cannot, the fact that these objects span the distance between people separated by time.

In this chapter, we will discuss the power of heirlooms and physical objects in ancestral work not as representations for the ancestors but as tools to connect to them. We will first discuss heirlooms, how we can view them, and how they can be used as a form of communication and used for connection with our ancestors. We will discuss how nostalgic emotional connection can be useful for us in our practice and how objects can be used to imbue a sacred space with the personality of the ancestors. We're going to be talking about two sets of objects here: the first are those objects that belonged to our ancestors, and the second are those objects that relate to the ancestors but may have never actually belonged to them. For example, there is a difference between a wrench that belonged to my grandfather who used it in his work as a plumber, and a wrench that can stand in as a symbol of plumbing. The object that belonged to my grandfather has a certain power, while the object that didn't still relates to him because it is symbolic to me of his work. Finally, I'd like to make a point that the focus in this chapter is not on offerings or representation, though all of the items we talk about here could easily fall under those aspects of practice. The focus here is on objects that are powerful in their own right and are tools for you to connect with the ancestors through, and for the ancestors to use in their own way of connecting with you. These objects have greater meaning ascribed to them and are thus made powerful, whether that be because they are symbolic of other things or they are associative to power. As we work through this chapter and the following chapters, be mindful of the different ways objects are utilized.

Nature of Heirlooms

The word *heirloom* has a rich and layered meaning that I believe is crucial to ancestral work. Heirlooms are traditionally defined as those objects we pass down through multiple generations, and the passing down of the object becomes a tradition in itself. When we consider the two words that make up the word, *heir* and *loom*, we start to get a sense of the interconnections. *Heir* usually means inheritance or the beneficiary of an inheritance, whether that be of an estate, title, or power. The word *heir* shares the same root as *heritage*, and in some ways, we might look at that as taking on responsibility to legacy.

When we look at our literature and the cultural understanding of being an heir, we see in the cultures of the nobility and upper echelons this idea that heirs are taking on responsibility for the family legacy. Becoming the heir to the throne, for example, brings with it responsibility, duty, and certain ways of behaving so that the legacy of the position is not sullied. Likewise, when we look at business moguls and their children who inherit the family businesses, the expectation is to grow the business and legacy, while also making it their own.

This shift away from individuality and toward collectivism, I think, ties perfectly with the second word: *loom*. A loom takes individual strands and binds them together to make a strong fabric or weave. The strands are interconnected and locked in place, and while very visible to anyone looking at said fabric, we tend to see the entire shape and not the individual strands.

This is an important image for the type of work we can do with heirlooms, in that they function to weave together times, generations, and narratives. In some ways, the greatest heirloom of all is life, handed to us by past generations that we then give to the next generation.

Use of Object in Practice

It is very relevant to see the role of an object as a way of activating memory and emotion, especially nostalgia, both for the living and the dead. If we expand on the discussions previously on physical space and communication, we see heirlooms can be a powerful element of communication with ancestors. The dead may recognize the object as originally belonging to them and be even more present. In the same way that we may culturally see bodily remains as imbued with presence, objects can also take on this quality. This is one reason why touch relics, those small objects pilgrims collected and physically touched to saint shrines, were regarded as containing the same spiritual quality as direct relics. Objects take on a spiritual element when so intimately connected to us, and this spiritual element lingers on after the death of the owner.

If we consider that the dead have gone through the major experience of dying, sometimes objects tied to their past can activate memories, and in that way create a connection to them. A good example of this is the ceremony conducted by Tibetan monks when determining if an individual is a reincarnation of a particular teacher. Objects are displayed before the candidate, usually a child, and the candidate selects the object most familiar to them, with an understanding that it used to be theirs in a past life. This ceremony is most often performed for identified individuals when they are children, because they would not have the necessary understanding of which object originally belonged to the deceased unless they were the reincarnated individual.[89]

Any experimental archaeologist will tell you that artifacts only give you so much information divorced from their context, and that you gain even more contextual information and insight through replicating the production of or regularly using the objects as they were meant to be used. This approach to research can be applied to ancestor veneration work as well with very strong results. My friend Finn and I were once discussing her grandfather's glasses

89. Geoffrey Samuel, *Introducing Tibetan Buddhism* (New York: Routledge, 2012), 146.

that she kept at her altar, and I commented that in some ways glasses were incredible heirlooms because she was literally seeing the world through the lenses of her grandfather. One reason we seem to be attracted to pilgrimage and visiting sites where we know our ancestors once lived is that we can simultaneously experience the place ourselves while also imagining what it was like for them. We stand in the same place as them, separated only by time. This same approach can be used with objects too; knowing that an object was used by one of our forebears allows us to step into their life to some degree.

Objects for Non-Blood Ancestors

So far, we have discussed heirlooms as having originated from blood ancestors, but what about non-blood ancestors? If you are working with a deity or spiritual ancestor, you may consider having a different space devoted to them with tools, accoutrements, or ritual objects. If you are working with land of origin as ancestor, inclusion of parts of that land or a representation of that land would be powerful, for example a stone or a sample of earth. If you are working with a precursor species, a fossil or figurine of that precursor species might be in order. If you are working with ancestors of lineage or profession, a representation of that individual(s) can be a powerful connector. For example, if you are a writer and you see William Shakespeare as ancestral to your craft, you might have a small bust of him. Indeed, literary or historical ancestors who are important to you can be represented by copies of their works. If you relate to specific characters in fiction as ancestral in some way, a statuette or some memorabilia of that character can be displayed. Whatever you decide to use in your devotions to these categories of spirits, again, it always comes back to intention and relationship; these objects are meant to be tools to bridge the gap and be worked as part of building relationships.

Some Examples of Objects and Their Use in Ancestor Work

Below are some examples of objects you might like to consider in your ancestral practice and, more importantly, how they can be conceptualized and thought about. This is not a list of must-haves; again, this list is more about relationships with and to. A common feeling with practitioners new to alternative spiritualities is the need to run out and buy all of the things so as to feel authentic in the practice, but in truth you don't need to buy anything. The following list contains many heirlooms handed down, gifts received, and natural objects collected as part of the process of building relationship.

Stones, Sand, and Earth

These objects can relate to blood relatives, ancestors of place, lineage, affinity, or even the land as ancestor. What I'm talking about here are specimens of sand, dirt, or stone that can be used as a proxy or stand-in for that place, or the people associated with that place. In the previous chapter we talked about grave dirt standing in for physical remains of particular ancestors, while in this regard the dirt or stone is used to connect to the land you know your ancestors dwelled on. (Of course, keep in mind that crossing international borders with dirt is usually a customs nightmare.)

If you go on pilgrimage—and we will discuss this a bit more later in the pilgrimage chapter—consider asking that space if you can take a part of it for use in your shrine. If that homeland is considered sacred to you or as an ancestor in itself, having a part of it can create a direct connection. This is particularly useful for ancestors we know nothing more about other than their place of origin, which we will all have eventually in our lineage. Spiritually, having a touchstone (literally, here—a stone you can touch) connected to a place allows the ancestor to have presence and is something you can physically connect with as well.

In hoodoo and other traditions like it, graveyard soil is a potent metaphysical ingredient, one that is useful for all manner of different magic. Expanding this a bit, we could see graveyard soil as a possible stand-in for personal remains, especially for those graves that are far away from where we live. Asking the ancestor whose grave you visit if it is okay to take some of the dirt to house in your shrine, you can utilize the dirt as a proxy for physical remains. However, proceed with some caution and respect, as in many places around the world, it is not permitted to take stones or dirt from certain sites. In Greece, for example, it is a criminal offence to take stones from ancient monuments, and in other places there are spiritual reasons not to take without asking or not take at all. If you are wanting to collect a stone from a place, make sure you are permitted to do so.

This is certainly not an isolated example; the spirits of place or the place itself may not wish for certain spaces to be disturbed but may offer alternatives to you. A few years ago, a good friend of mine traveled to Tibet to visit the holiest mountain connected to Shiva: Mount Kailash. I asked if he would bring me back a stone from that holy place for use in my personal devotions. He told me that when he was at the foot of the mountain, he asked the spirit of the place for a stone and was told no, but when he asked a bit further down the path, he was told yes. Remember, the land has agency just as much as we do and is populated just like our own segment of reality. Before taking any stone or object from a place, investigate the legalities and rules of that site, as many sacred and historical sites prohibit taking anything off the property for risk of damaging the site. If every tourist took a stone from a place, soon there wouldn't be any place left.

Toys

Toys are useful tools for ancestor work because of the intense emotional bond between the object and the individual. I keep toys from when I was a child as precious keepsakes of innocence and a time when life was all play. Housing a toy in the ancestral shrine evokes the childhood and innocence of both the individual and general ancestral community. We will talk more about offerings later on, but offering toys, especially if they are heirlooms passed down, speaks to a vital part of the individual's life. That vitality can add a different energy to the space.

Books

Books and the information inside of them are useful for ancestral work because of their ability to connect with the dead. First of all, books that belonged to the individual are objects that spent a great deal of time with them; their hands touched every page of the book, and books have an intimacy that is similar to some of the other object types listed here. Secondly, the ideas of the book tell us a lot about the individual, especially if it was one of their favorites. In ancestral devotion, an intimate way of connecting with specific ancestors is to read aloud passages from the text, be it fiction, nonfiction, or poetry. Favorite poetry is especially interesting as an offering, because while we read the piece, we may have our emotions stirred in the same way as our ancestors, and in that shared experience we build intimacy with them.

A very good friend of mine, who has been working with ancestors for many years now, commented on this section and reminded me of a conversation we had last year where he took it upon himself to read aloud a book his grandfather had been reading and left unfinished due to passing. My friend described how that act of reading to his ancestor felt incredibly healing by finishing something left unfinished. Sometimes it is the small things that can bring relief.

Articles of Clothing

Articles of clothing are interesting because they can tend to retain emotional and sensory imprints and feelings, and when wearing a particular article ourselves, we're inside our ancestor's life, in a way. Experimental archeologists will tell you that we gain information by living the everyday, and in a way, clothing allows us to do this as well. As an item we can incorporate into our everyday life, clothing can sometimes help bring out aspects of ourselves, or we might sometimes emulate our ancestors.

Clothing as an heirloom can be quite a powerful experience, especially if it is a garment that is passed down through the generations. For example, it is customary in some families to pass down a wedding dress or other article of clothing to each generation of women in the family to be married in. Other examples might include a beautiful silk scarf, a cardigan, or even a pair of shoes. Each of these items carries with them a different purpose and a different relationship than to the original owner. They allow us to connect in a more intimate way by preserving the garment.

Dishes and Drinking Vessels

I was recently helping my older sister and dad go through old boxes of items that were packed when we moved to Canada nearly thirty years ago. A lot of these items were dishes and glassware from my parents' old pub in Wales, but quite a few pieces belonged to my grandparents and had been kept hidden away for safety. I got to thinking about such treasured vessels and how they might one day be used in ancestral veneration. Do you have any crockery or glassware that stand out in your mind associated with certain ancestors?

Using certain mugs or glasses as ritual tools for offerings or libations, as well as keeping them as treasured heirlooms, can be an intimate and powerful way of showing respect to ancestors.

Jewelry

Jewelry has a personal intimacy different from some of the other examples listed here. First, pieces are often made from precious materials and have cultural value because of that. Second, they are usually tied to specific moments of importance: as heirlooms handed down from loved ones, lockets to hold small images or memories, and gifts for rites of passage, such as communion, sweet sixteen, graduation, marriage, or retirement. Third, they are intimate objects used to beautify or embody deeply held mores or ways of seeing the world. Fourth, they can often have religious or spiritual associations, such as prayer beads, religious pendants, or figures of spiritual importance. Like other personal belongings, jewelry pieces can be displayed or housed in your ancestral space and used as touchstones to connect with the individuals they belonged to.

Letters, Diaries, and Scrapbooks

One of the most direct and intimate forms of personal possession and relic is a diary or letters written by an ancestor. Though we may not always know context, we can read a lot into a letter, especially if it is written in the hand of the individual. We see their handwriting, we learn a little slice of their life, and we get a sense of how they presented themselves. In lieu of home movies, diaries and letters are little glimpses into a person's life. The same can be said for newspaper articles or other documents about the individual, but personal letters take on an intimacy that documents written about them lack. Diaries in particular are some of the most vulnerable places for a person to go, and you see aspects of an individual you may not have seen in other circumstances. Diaries are something I always struggle with because of how deeply intimate they are. Unlike scrapbooks, which are incredible documents that assist the creator in triggering living memories, diaries were not necessarily intended to be read by outsiders and so may contain deepest and sometimes darkest secrets.

A few years ago, I had a client who went through a process of decluttering. Part of the issue was an unhealthy sentimentality and attachment to objects that no longer served her and a feeling of guilt for getting rid of them.

One of the examples we worked with were her diaries from when she was much younger. She read through them and did not recognize the individual in the texts. For her, part of the work was to redefine herself, and so she wondered what to do with these diaries. Part of her wanted to hand them down to her children as mementos, but another, larger part of her didn't feel comfortable with anyone seeing the unhealthy place she came from. Through the work, my client shifted to a place of empowerment and made the decision that her diaries were her private space and not meant for anyone else. Instead, she created a scrapbook of the entries she was comfortable with to show the next generation.

Diaries must be cared for much more sensitively than other objects we include in our practices, because they are not just connection points, but spaces of vulnerability for individuals. My recommendation is that if you possess a diary of an ancestor that you wish to place in the sacred space, ask the ancestor how they feel about their words being so open, or house it in a discrete location so that it is not openly accessible to anyone who might visit you.

Another consideration is whether the diary should be read at all, in which case, communicate with your ancestors about whether they appreciate their words being read. This can form part of an ancestral tradition handed down within the family, and you can consider this question for your own preparations of what you want to leave behind to your descendants.

Military Heirlooms

Military heirlooms are a type of artifact connected to an intense, defining part of someone's life. Many of us probably have an heirloom, be it an object or a picture, of a grandparent or great-grandparent that fought in one of the World Wars. Visit any military family, especially those whose sons or daughters have been lost, and you will see a common reverence for the relics of that individual. Mementos such as a neatly folded flag, and especially the medals awarded, might be the only remains that a family was left with.

While researching my family history, I came across a photo placed online by my father's cousin in the UK of a great-uncle who shared my grandfather's name. Great-Great-Uncle James Stimpson was killed in France in 1918 at the tender age of twenty-four, and his body was not returned to England. I believe that my grandfather was named after this lost uncle of his, though no one in the family can verify that hunch. The photo that my cousin placed online was of a slightly blurry James in his Tommy uniform, looking proud and fresh faced. Knowing that this was the context of his demise, and that the family never had access to his body, makes mementos like these even more precious.

In the US, it is custom for a service member's coffin to be draped in a US flag, which is given to the family upon burial, and which often sits in a place of pride in military households. Whatever the article is, it takes on special meaning both for those who died and those who survived. Indeed, there are whole customs and codes connected to military articles that can be utilized as part of ancestral devotions that will not only be understood by the deceased veteran ancestors but can be utilized to build relationship with them as a living descendant.

Family Recipes

The recipe takes on many forms, such as a tangible item when written in a family cookbook or the end product of the created dish. The recipe, then, can simultaneously be an idea and an item, depending on the format. The recipe preserves the method of creating the foodstuff and is an intimate and sensual example of living history. One of the prized possessions of my family is my grandmother's cookbook, with extra recipes neatly handwritten and carefully pasted into the back. Family recipes take on double significance, because they are not only a document written by an ancestor, but they are also usually shared experiences. My great-aunt Florence's lemon curd recipe was a well-loved part of my father's childhood and something he's made my siblings and me throughout our lives. Family recipes take on a potency both as objects to be admired and viewed, and as an experience you can share with your ancestors and the living individuals in your life. Indeed, so beloved is this form of heirloom, etching recipes on tombstones has become a trend in North America.

This form of heirloom extends further than the remembered members of your own family. There is an abundance of historical food programs that show you how to make food from previous centuries, and as an act of offering, this can be a powerful nod to the ancestors who lived during those times, as well as a sensory experience of stepping into the past.

Watches and Clocks

A watch as a timepiece is an important symbol, but when it belonged to an ancestor, it takes on even more symbolic significance. A timepiece regulated the life of that ancestor and was literally around for all the important moments and even the less-than-memorable times. The slight ticking of that clock is a sound that was in the background of the ancestor, and likely the object was a constant plaything in their hands. Timepieces were also, for men at least, sometimes a proud status symbol or a piece of jewelry they used. For women, sometimes timepieces were badges of office, such as the medical brooch clocks that nurses traditionally wore. Larger clocks, especially heirloom antiques like grandfather clocks, were typically situated in important and central parts of the home, and many of the ones I know of function to regulate the family's communal life.

Journal Prompts

- What objects do you have in your possession that belonged to your ancestors?
  - List each of these objects, who they belonged to, and any stories attached to them.
  - What feelings and thoughts do these objects evoke for you?
  - What do you learn about your ancestors through the objects?
  - How does each object relate to a part of that ancestor's story?
- How do you relate to the different objects you wrote about above? How does your relationship to these objects impact your relationship to the ancestor who held them first?
  - For example, what is the difference for you between a multi-generational item versus an item from a single ancestor? What responsibility do you have to items that have been passed down through multiple generations like heirlooms, versus objects tied to a single ancestor's memory?

Chapter Thirteen

Offerings

Go to any spiritual space around the world and inevitably, with a few exceptions, you will come across offerings of some kind. Food, ritual objects, votive prayers, and sometimes the remains of sacrifice can be found left for the unseen forces of the world. What we see in offerings and other physical signs of spiritual practice is what is called in academia "material religion." When it comes to ancestor veneration, just like working with other kinds of spirits, the relationship is built and maintained through reciprocity. That reciprocity can take the form of tangible offerings. Because offerings come in so many different forms, instead of giving you a list of types of offerings from traditions around the world, I think it more appropriate for you to consider what offerings mean to you and let those ideas inspire their own conclusions. This chapter details what roles offerings can take, with comments about specific forms. Like many other elements of lived practice we're discussing in this book, offerings often carry with them deep cultural meaning and symbolism.

Defining Offering

For the purposes of this section, I define *offering* as anything intentionally given in thanksgiving, placation, or as a gift. Throughout the world, traditions have different rules about proper protocol, what offerings are considered appropriate, and the contextual circumstances surrounding the offering. We aren't going to discuss rules here, because as you build your own practice, the rules will be co-created by you and your ancestors. Instead, I want to highlight the word *intentionally* here, because as with everything, offerings sit in that place of connection between two or more individuals and constitute a complex social interaction. The very reason for protocol and rules surrounding offerings in particular traditions is both metaphysical and, in many ways, also cultural. These rules of engagement allow all parties to understand the offering and what it represents in the relationship, as well as the expected outcome.

To better understand this concept of offering, I think it's useful to break it down into its constituent parts so that when developing your own form of offering, you can learn to read the offering for what it is, understand on a deeper level the ritual as a form of communication, and ultimately develop an intuitive understanding of what constitutes an appropriate or inappropriate offering.

When I think of offerings specifically (and ritual in general), I tend to see the act of offering as composed of the following elements: the offering itself, the form of presentation, the delivery, the intention behind the offering, and what happens after the offering is received.

Notice in the above breakdown, I didn't mention belief. I noted intention but not belief. In many traditions, right belief (orthodoxy) is important, but in many ritualistic traditions, the focus is on right action (orthopraxy). For example, you can believe all you want that you're going to make a cake, but when actually cooking, you need to perform the recipe in specific, correct steps for the desired outcome. This is true, I think, for many ancestral traditions around the world; the emphasis is on the ritual aspects because they support the desired outcome, such as a positive relationship. Belief and worldview do inform ritual practice, as we've discussed, and are important, but the ritual aspect is the experiential and matters more.

So, why do we make offerings? As discussed in previous chapters, there are many beliefs about the purpose of offerings. Sometimes they are symbolic gestures meant to convey respect, while in other traditions they are necessities that literally feed and clothe the spirits of the dead. At the very least, making an offering is a statement that you are remembering the spirits you work with and have them in mind. The different types of offerings can be different statements, and they are often the punctuation marks for questions or requests.

Offering as Communication

An offering, like any other form of practice, has communicative aspects. When making an offering, ask yourself what you are communicating to the spirit world. How will an offering be received, and what will the reply be? What will the offering communicate about your desires, your intentions, and how you view your ancestors? Making an offering that is inappropriate, in my experience, damages relationships in the same way that giving a half-assed gift to our living friends and relatives can create resentment. But even a cheap gift that is well-thought-out can outweigh an expensive gift that is meaningless. I think of that episode of *The Office* where Secret Santa is being played, and the character Jim Halpert stuffs an inexpensive teapot with inside jokes and meaningful little gifts that ultimately proves more valuable to his love interest, Pam Beesly, than an expensive iPod.[90]

Offering as Personal Sacrifice

Sacrifice is an often-misunderstood word, especially when it comes to making offerings. To me, sacrifice is in many ways a declaration. I have been taught that the spirits I work with and my ancestors don't want to see me in rags, but at the same time, when an offering becomes a sacrifice, it is a declaration of my willingness to endure small discomfort for the greater benefits later. It is an honest and authentic underlining of my intentions. That is the true essence of sacrifice: the temporary experience of discomfort and the humbling of oneself to processes greater than yourself.

An offering as a sacrifice can be physically large or small, but it is always extremely meaningful, and rarely is it something that can be done with a laissez-faire attitude. The value of whatever we're offering and the discomfort of not taking it for ourselves speaks volumes to the spirits we work with, and that deepens relationship. The word *intentionality* is very relevant here; it doesn't matter so much what we intend to do if that intention doesn't translate to action. Again, a heartfelt gift outweighs a meaningless afterthought.

---

90. Charles McDougall, dir., *The Office*, season 2, episode 10, "Christmas Party," aired December 6, 2005, on NBC.

Offering as Propitiation

We have spoken about offering as a form of respect, but what about offering as a form of request? The term most often used for offerings that are made as a form of request is *votive offerings*, and they are usually things directly connected to the request being made. For example, going to a church, lighting a votive candle, and offering a prayer is an example of such an offering. Other examples could include the leaving of charms, donations, or food at sacred sites with the idea that you will not be retrieving said offering afterward. In ancient Greece, the shrine of the physician god Asclepios at Epidaurus was a popular site to visit when seeking the god's aid in treating illness. Worshippers would purchase from artisans at the sanctuary a stone or clay replica of a part of the body that was believed healed, and these would be left as votive offerings to the deity. Often, these offerings were left after the deity was believed to come in a dream as fulfillment of the ritual of healing.

If your interest in ancestral working is to develop relationships where the ancestors will act directly in your life, then apart from just communicating or showing respect, offering is a primary tool of earning desired results. How might certain offerings be given with a request for assistance or the blessings of the ancestor? How might communication directly with ancestors be achieved and supported through offering?

Offering as a Tool

Another aspect of this type of work is to introduce items that may not have belonged directly to the dead, but that can stand in for items that would have been part of the ancestors' experience on earth. Saints, deities, ancestors, and other spirits in multiple traditions are given approximations of tools and instruments as symbolic items to use in the world. These tools are usually placed with or next to the physical representation of these beings on earth, whether they are statues, enshrined objects, or other forms of representation. Most saints and deities, for example, are identified by their iconography, and their attributes are reflected in their tools or accoutrements. Shiva holds a trident, Saint Lazarus holds himself with a crutch, the Medicine Buddha holds a vessel of *amrit*, Hermes has winged sandals, Thoth holds his stylus, etc.

In ritualistic practice, these tools might be represented as full-size versions or smaller symbols in the form of charms or amulets. Consider that working with ancestors could be like working with saints: you approach the ancestors as a collective, asking for their unified blessings, or you approach ancestors whose skills and insight may suit your goal better. With these ancestors, you may wish to offer them tools to assist and empower their work here on earth. For example, if your great-grandmother was a renowned seamstress, you might consider asking her if she would assist in stitching things together for you and place into the shrine a dedicated sewing kit or a needle and thread. If you have a doctor or nurse in your lineage, you might offer a medical item. By placing this item with the intention that the ancestors may use it for a purpose, you concentrate the effect. It should be noted here, though, that the ancestors, communally or individually, may refuse to do the desired action because they have a broader scope of vision than us and see that it is not correct for us in the long term.

My family's history includes various professionals and skilled laborers, including nurses, publicans, fishermen, plumbers, and carpenters to name a few. If I need assistance catching something, I might place a fishhook or net devoted to my fishermen ancestors in the shrine; if I need healing, I might ask the ancestors as a collective and place into the shrine tools for those from the medical profession. Approaching individual or groups of ancestors in this way is a powerful means of not only humanizing them and equipping them with the tools of their trade, but also representing that history in the shrine. As with everything, though, this type of work comes only after you have built solid, healthy relationships with your ancestors, and forethought is needed if you are going to approach individuals.

Offering as a Form of Intimacy

Offerings are a manifestation of a social bond. To give something to someone else evokes for me those times in our history where a little food could often mean life or death. Hospitality is such a powerful aspect of many cultures, and with that hospitality comes a certain kind of relationship. Middle Eastern cultures are famous for their hospitality, and when invited into the home, a guest is considered under the protection of their host. Consider for yourself any gift-giving occasions or holiday that you are involved with and the social rules around what is appropriate to give. The most prized gifts of my life have often been the most intimate, and intimacy can be from expensive or inexpensive gifts.

Cooking food for any guest is one of the most intimate experiences. About three years ago, my Ile put on a party for the orisha Oshun and Yemaya. I was living with my parents at the time, and I devoted the day before to cooking up a load of tartlets and mini quiches. It was a wonderfully intimate process making this food, knowing that the next day it was going to be offered to the orisha and to all the assembled guests. At the party, we erected an ancestor shrine and offered some of the food to them, and the whole atmosphere was wonderfully connected. Over the last few years, I have had many other opportunities to cook for the orisha and for my ancestors, and those experiences cemented for me an understanding of how the simple act of cooking is a devotional and intimate act.

Food is probably what comes to mind when many people think of offerings. Food is sustenance, and in most areas of the world, a primary commodity. We can survive without gold, but we cannot survive without food. Offering food, whether large amounts or a simple spoonful, is often a form of sacrifice, and an incredibly intimate one. In my own practice, I tend to offer a spoonful of each of the things I eat in a meal, especially those meals I cook myself or at special occasions. There is nothing more intimate than serving the dead in this way.

When it comes to ancestor veneration practices, food as a symbol of wealth and life is a potent one. Just like with other spirits, offering the best kind of food is a show of respect. On a purely practical level, when dealing with the dead who once ate food, one can become creative with their offerings. Say your grandmother or great-grandmother was well known for her famous lemon curd recipe (as my great-aunt was), learning to cook that can not only help you relate to her but also show respect. During celebrations or anniversaries, particular foods can be used to heighten the experience and add intimacy.

Offering and Cosmological or Natural Force

In our discussion of sacred space, we talked about the shrine as a microcosm of a much larger cosmology. Offerings connect to or represent much larger aspects of the universe, and in this way become more powerful than they are outside the context of an offering. For example, the ritual of transubstantiation in Catholic tradition transforms the mundane wafers and wine into the sacred blood and body of Christ for the worshippers. Going through the ritual, the mundane is turned sacred—in the same way that offerings to deities or spirits in other traditions are transformed to be more than they were, now touched by greater cosmological forces. By placing the offering at the shrine of the ancestors, you connect the ancestral work with that much larger cosmology.

For example, a common ritual in Slavic countries and adjacent areas is to welcome guests with salt and bread, the offering of which bestows good fortune and blessings on the guest. Exploring this ritual deeper, we see bread and salt are both incredibly important commodities. Bread is a miraculous foodstuff; it takes effort to produce it, and once made, it is greater than the sum of its parts. Bread is one of the oldest prepared foods, and variations of it can be found all over the planet. Salt is equally important to humanity, as it is needed for our basic biological functions and is used for basic food preservation in many cultures. Both bread and salt are two specific substances linked with the rise of many civilizations. So offering these two substances to a guest might seem symbolic in our modern age, but at some point in the past, they were incredibly important offerings of life.

An offering connecting to natural or cosmological forces helps to bring those elements into the relationship, either for the recipient or because of the importance of their role in the relationship. Incorporating this into your ancestral work, you can ask yourself what culturally relevant symbols tie into greater forces that were important to your ancestors. What effect might incorporating that element have for your ancestors? If you offer plain water (a common offering for spirits cross-culturally), what might that water represent or symbolize? Depending upon the culture, it can mean anything from refreshing oneself after a journey to the essence of life itself.

Offering as Symbolic of Community

Are there certain symbols or goods that represent your community? In many examples throughout this book, we've talked about culturally relevant elements of ritual practice that strengthen ties between community members, affirm cultural identity, and instantly foster an inclusive environment of belonging. For example, in many cultures the offering of drink is part of social customs of hospitality and social bonding. Whether that drink is alcoholic or nonalcoholic, the act carries the same weight as sharing food and goes a long way to creating social bonding.

This act of food or drink sharing is frequently connected to religious ritual (such as the Christian sacrament of the Eucharist) and with remembering the dead. The offering of libations, which is when a food or drink is poured onto the earth or thrown up into the air, is believed to make that substance accessible to spirits. In my own culture, it is often a custom to toast the dead using alcohol, and sharing a drink in memory of the dead is an important part of social bonding.

Now, this is where offerings in the name of community can become nuanced and intentional, especially if you have a diverse heritage. Many years ago, I sat around a fire with a friend whose ancestry is both Anishinaabe and Irish. In her personal spiritual path, alcohol is an important offering for working with her Irish ancestors, and she toasts them as is custom. However, for her Anishinaabe ancestors, the relationship to alcohol has been devastating, and her people regard it as a poison. She expressed her journey to find a balance in her practice with this substance, and her mindfulness of how it is offered and to whom. Her own relationship to alcohol is informed by this insight into her ancestors' relationships to the substance. By being mindful and intentional with her use of offering, her relationship to different ancestor lineages became more nuanced and intimate.

Offering as Tangible Good

For many traditions, offerings are tangible goods for the spirits of the dead. Grave goods are universally understood to be able to be utilized or go with the dead as they embark on their journeys, and offerings of food or drink to the dead subsequently are believed to be accepted by the dead. In Asian communities, especially in the Chinese diaspora, the burning of joss paper products, such as spirit money or replica goods, is believed to go directly to the spirit world. Does your grandfather need a new suit or your grandmother a new car? Simply purchase joss paper replicas of the desired good and burn it to offer it to the ancestors. Then, the replica shows up in the spirit world. You particularly see wads of spirit money being sold and burned. This belief in the tangibility of material goods to the dead is widespread, particularly the view that food offerings nourish the dead and are not just symbolic. In Lukumi we have an ancestral rite of feeding the dead where large amounts of foods are prepared, offered to the ancestors, and then buried beneath the earth. The purpose of this is not symbolic; it is a ritual specifically to feed the dead. As mentioned above, I also offer a small spoonful of my meals to the dead so that they can be nourished as well. The understanding here is similar across the board: the food's essence is accessible to the spirit realm. In most cases, this food is then not consumed by the living because it is now connected to the realm of death. This relationship to making offerings is very different than traditions that offer food to deities. The understanding of the latter is that a deity partakes and then blesses the food, which is then shared with participants of the ritual.

Multipurpose Offerings

Reading through the above purposes of offerings, you get the picture that individual offerings could potentially serve multiple purposes. This is one of the dynamic aspects of offering that allows you to get creative with what and why you offer certain things. For example, votive offerings are things you intend to leave behind at sites or which will be disposed of eventually, such as food or drink, whereas types of offerings such as gifts, decorations, or permanent memorial markers are meant to last. Sometimes some offerings will serve multiple purposes; they become empowered and even more meaningful because of their dual roles.

Journal Prompts

- What does the concept of offering mean to you?
- How might offering be used by you in a veneration practice?
- What felt natural or unnatural around the concept of offering to the dead?
- What form of offering came to mind as you worked through this chapter?
- What questions do you still have around the concept of offering?

Chapter Fourteen
Ritual

Ritual is one of the key elements of spiritual and secular practice. We live in a world saturated with ritual. From the moment we get up to when we go to bed, our lives are filled with rituals, such as preparing ourselves for the day, dressing for sleep, interacting with others, and even making a cup of coffee. *Ritual* is defined broadly as any sequence of meaningfully performed actions involving words, gestures, actions, or objects.

For the purposes of spiritual practice, I would expand this to mean ritual is any intentional sequence of meaningful actions. Whereas belief is a mental activity, ritual is putting belief into action. My role here is not to provide you with a set of rituals to practice by rote, but to encourage you to develop meaningful rituals for yourself in relation to your ancestral practices. While reading this section, consider how your practice can incorporate ritual and what benefits intentional ritual can play in developing your relationship with your ancestors, furthering your goals, and supporting other aspects of your practice.

Purpose of Ritual

The purpose of ritual is to actualize our worldviews and beliefs, as well as perform tasks associated with our goals. Mundane ritual can be seen in all aspects of our lives and is essentially the choreographed performance of certain actions to achieve a goal. For example, the ritual of preparing for bed at night could include dressing in night attire, washing one's face, brushing one's teeth, making sure all the doors are locked, turning off the lights, and settling into bed.

The goal was to get to bed so you could sleep; all of the other pieces helped you prepare for that end. But the pieces needed to be in a particular order to support each other; you wouldn't be able to see in the dark if you turned your lights off first, for example. A similar example is in the ritual of cooking, which involves particular actions at particular times so that the recipe turns out as intended. This is essentially the dynamic of ritual: a goal is supported by the actions taken to actualize it. When you see ritual in this way, you can see that the only difference between spiritual or religious ritual and mundane ritual are the types of actions taken and the understanding of the actions used. All rituals utilize similar instruments to achieve an intended goal, such as words, gestures, choreographed movement, and a meaningful order.

As you embark on building a relationship with your ancestors through developing veneration practices, consider the types of rituals that might be incorporated into your work. Consider what your goals and needs are for your practice and how they intersect with those of your ancestors. Certain ritual types will serve your needs while others will be focused on your ancestors.

Role of Tradition in Rituals

A meme floating about social media recently got me chuckling. It talked about how "tradition" is really just dead people's way of peer pressuring us. The meme is not wrong; tradition very much tends to be peer pressure from the past. But, looking at this a little deeper, it is my observation that even if this was a bad thing (which I'm not certain it is), tradition is prone to always emerge in culture. We are creatures of habit, and as we go through our lives, we humans tend to synchronize with those around us to fit in. Tradition, therefore, is not just peer pressure, but as I've said elsewhere in this book, it is a connection point. When we engage in ritual that is grounded in tradition and was once engaged in by our ancestors, we join them in a lineage of action and experience ritual work they once performed while also developing our own relationship with the ritual. For those who have children, passing down rituals to the next generation perpetuates that cycle. It is why tradition is so highly prized—because it is unifying and a connector for multiple generations.

Ritual as Communication

Communication is an important part of this whole section, and it is in ritual that communication becomes an active element. What we do, when, with what, and how are all symbolically meaningful. I would even argue that ritual and ceremony are entirely linked with communication, because for ritual to be meaningful, it must be understood by others, whether that other is spiritual or material. So, with your rituals, what do they convey to the spiritual world and the world of the living? Are your ritual activities in alignment with other parts of your practice? Are there any misalignments with your practice that end up not making sense? For example, if you believe that your ancestors are in the earth and you ritualistically place offerings to them in an elevated position, is there dissonance between the belief and practice? And what are the potential implications of that?

The other piece to ritual as communication is how ritual builds relationship and understanding. Through ritual, we engage and interact with spirit, and it is through the subtle and experiential connection points that ritual provides that we learn to see life and our place in it in different ways.

Private and Public Ritual Experience

Ritual encompasses both private and public spaces, and we often know instinctively what is appropriate for a group experience and what should be personal and private. Likewise, while group ritual is often organized to facilitate multiple roles, it is crucial to know that each individual within a ritual context will come out of it having had their own unique experience. The power of ritual is that even within a shared experience, everyone will come away with their own relationship to the event. Personal and shared ritual is necessary for all of us, and often they work off each other. Take the holiday season for example: usually there are components of group ritual centered on the holiday and then personal responsibilities or actions taken in private, often stemming from the group experience.

Dynamics of Ritual

You may be reading this thinking, this is all well and good, but tell me how to do ritual! Ritual is all about doing, and so it is literally as simple as how you conduct yourself in your practice. For me, some of the simple rituals I perform with my ancestors are to offer them a plate of food when I cook, wish them good morning, and have a conversation with them. More broadly, ritualistic conduct impacts every way I interact with my spirits, from my spirit guides to my gods. Each set of spirits has different needs; each has a different way to approach them. This is not to be pedantic; it really does mirror how different human beings have different needs and social rules for how to engage with them. You know these rules exist whenever there feels like an unwritten social rule has been broken.

If you think of ritual as communication, then ritual in many ways is like a language that you learn to converse with and understand through. Every language has rules so that both parties understand each other, but every language also develops slang and short forms. The same is true of spiritual ritual. When I go to my ancestors in more elaborate settings, I create a temporary shrine, light a candle, recite a prayer, bow, and show respect. When I am at home in more casual moments, I might lovingly spoon out a little of my food into their offering bowl, light a candle, and set the food down while saying thank you and showing my appreciation.

Physicalizing Spiritual Expression

In the West, I have noticed there is a tendency toward minimalism and relegating spirituality to a form of philosophizing or mental gymnastics. I am not keen on this trend, because I have seen the way that physicalizing and enacting ritual plugs into forces that are not merely mental. The power of play and story demonstrates that for us as a species, there is a psychological benefit to dressing up and doing rather than just thinking. Thinking about horseback riding is very different from going horseback riding. A friend of mine once said, "You can think you know something until you actually go through it yourself; that's what ritual is, the experience of going through something personally." I completely agree with him, and physicalizing practice is all about that somatic, experiential understanding. Likewise, if you're just sitting there thinking about your ancestors and not actually doing anything, will they know what you're thinking? Maybe on some cosmic level they might, but just like with living humans, expressing love is more valued than just thinking about it. In many traditions around the world, especially Eastern traditions, the importance is placed on right practice rather than right belief. On a cosmic level, movement and action are reality, whereas thought processes are intangible.

Consistency

Rituals can be singular events, but often they are repeated again and again. When conducting ritual over and over, it is highly recommended to remain consistent with your approaches or actions. I'll use a simple example: when we communicate with each other, we follow culturally understandable rules of engagement that facilitate effective communication. In some cultures, maintaining eye contact and nodding are expected signs that we are engaged in the conversation. Have you ever spoken to someone and it just felt awkward? Or have you ever known someone who, every time you meet them, they come across as hot or cold and you don't feel you can trust them because of those inconsistencies? Therefore, in ritual practice, we must remain consistent in some way when interacting with our ancestors, because not doing so can lead to confusion. Likewise, remaining consistent in practice often leads to a feeling of security and builds trust. If you decide to make offering food to your ancestors a part of your routine, remaining consistent builds trust in the same way that remaining consistent with the living builds trust.

Sacred Space

In magical and spiritual practice, ritual relies on entering nonlinear and alternate reality, where the normal rules of life can be subverted or changed, and the way of interacting with others takes on different forms. Sometimes entering into that space is simply closing your eyes, taking a deep breath, and engaging in the ritual; other times it's about setting apart a separate space to work within.

I remember the first time I was involved in a large group ritual; I was sitting in a stone circle with sixty other people at midnight on a cool summer evening. We walked into the circle in procession and lied down with our heads facing outward and feet turned in. Musicians began to play, and we began a ritual of connecting with land spirits. That sacred space had been prepared and consecrated before we entered it, and when we entered that threshold, the normal rules of the mundane were supplanted by the rules of the ritual. This is essentially why sacred spaces are consecrated and set apart or differentiated somehow. When we exist in a mundane headspace, we can be limited in experiencing or meeting spirit, and so it takes removing ourselves temporarily from the world at large to create a meeting point with the spiritual.

The Symbolic Language of Ritual

As was written about above, ritual conveys meaning as well as performs actions with an intended goal. Every gesture, every word, every action converges to support the main point of the ritual and has within it subtle symbolic meaning. Sometimes customs evolve in such a way that the original meaning or intent of the action can be lost, but on a deeply subconscious level, we understand. For example, the custom in some cultures of shaking hands using the right hand was originally a signal to a stranger that you were not going to attack because the right hand was understood to be one's sword arm. Now we shake hands as a sign of respect and greeting, as most of us do not wear swords on our person anymore.

If you are performing a ritual of thanksgiving, you may decide to include praising your ancestors, an offering, and a declaration of thanks. The message of thanksgiving might become ambiguous if you don't say thank you or if you leave an offering and it isn't clear what the offering is. How might you convey a thank you in ritual if you don't explicitly state it? What symbolic elements clearly state thank you? In many ancient traditions, ritual offerings were usually connected to agreements or pacts with deities and spirits. For example, in the Greco-Roman world, petitioners used curse tablets offered to deities at sanctuaries as contracts to curse opponents. Often, the wording of these cursing tablets, which have been found in Greece and as far north as Britain, obligated petitioners to sacrifice specific animals to the god if the desired results were achieved.[91] The more you work with a set of spirits, in this case your ancestors, the more the rituals will become entrenched, the more your relationship will build, and the easier your gestures and actions will be understood.

Rules of Engagement

Ritual, whether large or small, follows rules of engagement, especially if multiple individuals are taking part. These rules of engagement facilitate the successful completion of ritual activity. The actors are all those taking part in the ritual experience, from the initiators to the bystanders and recipients. In

---

91. John G. Gager, ed., *Curse Tablets and Binding Spells from the Ancient World* (Oxford: Oxford University Press, 1999), 156, 241.

the case of our ancestor practices, the initiator would be you, and the recipients are the ancestors themselves. The actors each have responsibilities and roles within ritual activity. As the initiator of the ritual, your responsibility is to be prepared to engage with the ritual in an appropriate and respectful manner. The rules and expected conduct are established so that the ritual will run smoothly, those taking part will not clash and compromise the intention of the ritual, and all present can remain focused. Even if you think you are conducting the ritual alone, when engaging with the spiritual world, you are never truly alone. I have been involved in rituals that became chaotic in the past, and it was not fun to deal with the aftereffects. This applies to personal and private rituals, no matter how large or small; the purpose of rules of engagement and order of activities is so stuff can get done.

Openings and Closings

In most traditions, it is strongly advised that ritual activities have an opening and a closing, especially when the ritual involves working with spirits. A strong opening differentiates the ritual from mundane reality, and a clear closing ends the ritual, and the actors reemerge back into mundane reality. These openings and closings can be anything from a declaration, a cleansing, or the banging of a drum or bell. The important feature here is that there is a clear understanding of a ritual's start and end for all those involved. In my ritual connected to offering food, the prayer I speak contains both an opening and closing, while in less formalized rituals the lifespan of the candle I light demarcates the time of the ritual. The important detail here is that there is a clear boundary between ritual and mundane.

Spiritual Hygiene, Cleanliness, and Maintaining a Healthy Lifestyle

Personal hygiene is important regardless of the area of our life, but it is particularly important when engaging in spiritual work. Mental and physical hygiene are well understood, but spiritual hygiene is an integral element in spiritual practice. There are many ways we can maintain good hygiene for ourselves and our spaces, and it has been my observation that in many traditional cultures, rituals of hospitality are connected to guests cleansing themselves physically as well as emotionally and often spiritually.

All traditions around the world have some form of cleansing ritual or practice done regularly to maintain physical, emotional, and mental well-being. These cleansing rituals can be semi-regular or performed just before or just after specific ritual. Whether it is using water to wash, heat to sweat, perfumes or oils to anoint, smoke or incense to enwrap, sound to scare away, or a brush to sweep away the undesirable, modes of cleansing are everywhere. Why is this important? Just as maintaining physical hygiene is important for our physical, emotional, and social self-esteem, spiritual hygiene is essential for smoothly engaging in spiritual work.

When engaging in spiritual work, we might come across experiences or entities that leave us feeling drained or not our best selves. As we practice, if this spiritual residue is left and accumulates, it can start to seep into other areas of our life, particularly our mental health. A friend once likened a Lukumi practice called a *rogation*, a cleansing ritual provided by an initiated priest, to defragging a computer. Just like a computer, as we go through our lives, things can get out of order, and little errors can appear that need to be routinely corrected so the computer can work at its optimum. A rogation, and similar rituals, seeks to bring us back into an optimum mental and spiritual state by decluttering and defragmenting us. This is the essence of spiritual hygiene: maintaining good routines and practices that will bring us back to a place of unified center. This goes part and parcel with maintaining a healthy and balanced lifestyle so that we are in the best overall position to do the work.

Cleansing traditions can be anything from formal rituals to the laying of salt or water. One tradition I practice is using holy water to sweep myself down and remove anything spiritually unclean. Some traditions incorporate ritual cleansings as part of their everyday routine, such as the use of holy water or herbs in floor washes or using a broom to sweep away both physical and energetic detritus. By far, one of my most practiced forms of cleansing is a nice hot shower at the end of the day.

Journal Prompts

- What everyday rituals can you perform, and how might these rituals deepen relationships in your life?

- What cultural or familial rituals or traditions are important to you that can be brought into your practice?

- What are your experiences with ritual? Is ritual experiential for you, a chore to get through, or something else? What practical purposes do the rituals in your life serve for you?

- What times have you felt energetically bogged down? What helped to make you feel clear?

- In what areas of your life do you feel stressed, and how does that impact your energetic or mental hygiene?

- What rewards do you receive from maintaining yourself (spiritually, physically, emotionally)?

- What cleansing traditions exist in your life or your cultural background(s)?

Chapter Fifteen
Communication

One of the most drastic changes when someone dies is that we are no longer able to communicate and relate to the individual in the same way we did before. This is one reason why psychic mediumship is such a potent market, with individuals seeking out diviners, mediums, and conjuration of the dead so that communication can continue. In this section, we will explore various forms of communication with ancestors and how you might incorporate this important element into your veneration practice. We will also explore communication with different types of ancestors, such as conceptual and affinity.

As we move through this content, be mindful of your beliefs around communicating with spirits and the dead. If you are interested in developing ways of communicating with the ancestors, be mindful of your relationships with different forms of ancestor and what you would want to communicate about. This is offered as a starting point, and resources for further study are listed in the resources section. This is a huge topic and one that entire books have been written about, but what I'd like to present here is a list of topics and modalities that can get you started.

Ancestor Veneration as Ritual Communication

A crucial "aha" moment for me came when I began to realize that ritual is not just actions, but a form of communication. This realization completely revolutionized how I approach spirituality in general, let alone ancestor veneration.

As I developed a deeper understanding and appreciation for ritualistic actions and gestures, I came to understand that what we do in ritual practice is, among other things, a form of communication. I felt slightly disappointed, as though a certain part of the mystery of magic had been stripped away and I could clearly see the working mechanism beneath, but this understanding greatly empowered my ability to dive into ritual with even more intention.

I must be honest—this is not a new insight at all. As I began to realize and put two and two together, I spoke with my elders from various backgrounds, who all confirmed for me this aspect of ritual expression. As has been mentioned in this book before, human beings are creatures that seek out meaning and understanding. To understand one another, we communicate in a myriad of ways, and all our ways of communicating utilize signs and symbols. Our brains are literally hardwired to see patterns and form conclusions from those patterns. When we walk down a trail and see a footprint in the mud, we understand that someone else has probably preceded us. We see a hole in the ground, identify it as a boot shape, interpret it as belonging to another human being, take note of the direction it is pointing, and conclude that another human being walked on this trail previously, and they likely headed in the direction the print is pointing. This deductive form of reasoning is applied to most aspects of our life, including communication.

When we interact with someone, we aren't just listening to their words but simultaneously reading body language and facial expressions. If you meet someone at their home, you can look around and read information from their environment about them. You can infer based on their belongings, arrangement, and even cleanliness of the space, making conclusions about the individual that then affects how you perceive and interact with them.

Spiritual practice often includes relationships with incorporeal beings who utilize and rely on forms of communication other than just verbal. What I came to realize is that the elaborate forms of spiritual expression we see around the world, from the rituals performed, words spoken, offerings given, and spaces built, are all options available to us to interact with the spiritual world. Learning to communicate with an entire plane of existence that is very different from our own can be daunting, as there are different rules and logic that don't apply in our mundane world. I strongly encourage the reader going forward, when considering practices, to be mindful of viewing them as potential ways to communicate and deepen relationships.

Too often, I hear spiritual practitioners say things like, "Well, as long as my intention is there...," and I find that point of view unsatisfactory when it comes to the deepening of relationship in our practices. A common phrase often said by a well-known oriate and talked about in my Lukumi house is, "God is deaf, you need to speak up!" This phrase means we must be clear and understandable when addressing the spiritual world, because God or spirits might be able to read minds or they might not. Regardless, we have a responsibility to be clear and mindful with how we choose to communicate in the world, which is good advice for any situation really. This really gets to the point of seeing anything we do as a form of communication, and being mindful of how clear we are.

Consider some of the following questions and be mindful:

Journal Prompts

- What does the performance of a particular meaningful gesture or action communicate to the spiritual world?
- How does inclusion of particular elements, such as objects, colors, types of food, etc., affect relationships?
- How does the inclusion of particular elements affect the mood of the dead?

The Subtle Ways of Spirit and Synchronicity

It is my experience that spirits and ancestors communicate differently from what we are used to in our mundane reality; the language is subtle, often abstract. Spirit communication often employs the language of gesture, symbolism, synchronicity, dreams, divination, and other indirect forms. Communicating with them necessitates a paradigm shift away from language as we are used to it, and instead becomes the search for meaning in the seemingly meaningless. We explored this a little when we discussed ritual and offerings. Anthropologist Clifford Geertz said, "Arguments, melodies, formulas, maps, and pictures are not idealities to be stared at but texts to be read; so are rituals, palaces, technologies, and social formations."[92] What Geertz is getting at here is that meaning underscores understanding, and so developing the ability to read symbols unlocks meaning and thus understanding. By understanding that the world is filled with sign and symbol, we can become literate in reading those myriad signs used by spirit.

How does one go about developing an understanding of symbolic language? You start small; you start by looking at the world through different lenses and challenging your preconceived notions of your environment. Intuition becomes a piece to this, as our intuitive self can usually pick up on things our rational mind blocks out. Signs, omens, portents, and synchronicities all become ways the realm of spirit communicates. *Synchronicity* was coined by psychoanalyst Carl Jung, who defined it as the simultaneous occurrence of events that appear significantly related but have no discernible causal connection.[93] Synchronicity happens to us all, whether we're aware of it or not. How many times have we heard of situations where two lovers worked across the road from each other or knew the same people but only met years later in a different context? How many times have odd coincidences happened that point toward inexplicable connections?

It has been my experience that spirits and the unseen forces of the universe work in these subtle ways, which we are unaware of but that seemingly also have direct impact on our lives. I have found that the awareness of synchronicity in my life usually comes in retrospect. Once I put the puzzle pieces together, I can then step back and see the picture emerge.

Now, a warning here is quite necessary. As the saying (often erroneously attributed to Sigmund Freud) goes, "Sometimes a cigar is just a cigar."[94] It's very possible and likely that in our drive to understand, we might intuit meaning into something that doesn't have greater meaning. We must keep a degree of logic and rationality in developing this understanding. This

---

92. Clifford Geertz, *Negara: The Theatre State in Nineteenth-Century Bali* (Princeton, NJ: Princeton University Press, 1980), 135.

93. Laura K. Kerr, "Synchronicity, Overview," in *Encyclopedia of Critical Psychology*, ed. by Thomas Teo (Berlin, Heidelberg: Springer-Verlag, 2014), 1905–1908.

94. Garson O'Toole, "Sometimes a Cigar Is Just a Cigar," Quote Investigator, August 12, 2011, https://quoteinvestigator.com/2011/08/12/just-a-cigar/.

is where a healthy balance between intuition and rationality comes in. My friend Tiffany Lazic often teaches that when developing intuitive skills, we need to have a soft stare and focus. The example she uses when teaching is that when you look up at the stars, you often don't see stars when you look directly at them. Our peripheral vision sees what our direct stare seems to hide or make invisible. Intuition is like looking at stars; with a softer gaze, we can detect peripherally what has been there all along.

In my experience, and usually in retrospect, the puzzle pieces begin falling into place, and there is suddenly an "aha" moment of understanding. When I started to become aware of this phenomenon in my life, it was first as a creeping feeling almost like déjà vu. I would feel slightly anxious as I started to understand something was happening around me that I couldn't explain. I started calling this experience the "weave" because it felt like little threads of coincidence would form. The more this experience happened for me, the more I knew what to look for, and it continues to feel like something is happening and I'm just an accessory to it.

The closest frame of reference I have found to describe this experience is the Anglo-Saxon concept of *wyrd*. To the Anglo-Saxons, wyrd was an ever-unfolding moment of connection and relationship that was symbolized by a giant web. Everybody is connected through the web of wyrd, and through this multidimensional web of personal destiny and responsibility, we all interact with each other. In my understanding, synchronicity plays a huge role in wyrd. In becoming aware of the mechanisms of wyrd, I was able to understand when I am an active participant in whatever is happening and when I need to just stay out of the way.

One of the aspects of my spirituality in recent years has been to really pay attention to synchronicities and inexplicable circumstances. Everyone I have spoken to seems to have had situations or moments that are impossible to explain, but which suggest a guiding invisible hand or mechanisms that are subtle and hidden that we are not privy to. The more I work on paying attention to this in my life, the more I seem to experience and see.

What does this look like as a concrete example? In 2016, seven important men from my past who I had unfinished business with came back into my life through inexplicable means. Some of them I had hurt, some had hurt me, some I was holding onto in unhealthy ways, and one was holding onto me in an unhealthy way. I was able to gain closure with every single one of them. Years later, when I spoke with my godfather about it, he explained that it was my ancestors or spirits conspiring to bring about these occurrences as a way of healing and moving on. Now, when I say explicable, I mean truly odd. One of these men I spoke to on a dating app, and we didn't recognize each other at first. Another appeared as a mutual friend on social media. Individually, we can say these reunions were coincidence, but as a set, they were part of an important message I needed to hear that year: "Don't live in the past; you don't belong there."

As I moved through each encounter, I became more aware of the physical experience of this intuition. I would feel anxious and not know why. I'd get that sense of dawning awareness, that feeling of déjà vu, or a sneaking suspicion something was happening just off camera. When I re-met the person and realized who they were, I had an instinctive knowing that the encounter had greater meaning. Every time I engaged with them, I would feel closure or healing. Other such events have happened since, and each time it's a similar experience, but my ability to discern the signs and read the hidden aspects of reality around me has become honed. Consider when you have had moments of intuitive knowing in your own life and what they were like for you physically, emotionally, and psychologically.

Years ago, I relayed some of my wyrd situations to my godfather in Lukumi, who encouraged me to think of some of them in terms of blessings from ancestors. The reconnections I made in the above example all heralded opportunities for healing, and he reflected that this was not a coincidence. As we have discussed throughout this book, the incorporeal world can be very direct but more often is very indirect. It is a prominent view around the world that ancestors have an impact on our world, and I tend to believe that whether it was a god, my spirits, or my ancestors, some of the experiences I have had in my life were coordinated for my healing. If there is anything I have learned from a process like this, it is that sometimes you just need to get out of their way.

So, what does all this have to do with communicating with spirits? In considering that spirits in general tend to communicate non-directly, in my experience, this presents us with some opportunities and some issues. The opportunities presented are the expansion of how we can communicate; the problems are in discovering for ourselves the purpose of these new forms of communication.

Journal Prompts

- In what ways have blessings shown up in your life?
- Have you experienced synchronicity or coincidences that defy rational explanation? What was the feeling you got when you started to clue in to the fact that something bigger was happening?
- How sensitive are you to seeing hidden blessings in your life?
- In what ways do you receive hidden blessings from the universe? In what ways have you rejected or interfered with hidden blessings?

Forms of Communication

Developing intuition is just the beginning of further forms of communication. Let us explore a few broad categories of types of communication. This is not an exhaustive list, and there are suggestions for further exploration in the resources section to expand on what we are going to cover.

Divination

Simply put, divination is communication with the spiritual world through a systematic practice utilizing some tool or instrument, such as tarot cards or crystal gazing. Every culture has seemingly developed some form of divinatory practice. This is somewhat simplifying a very broad range of techniques and practices, but for our purposes, this definition will be used to differentiate it from other forms of communication.

Some of the most widespread divination tools here in the West are connected to a specific practice of divining called cartomancy, and include the tarot, Lenormand, Kipper, and oracle decks. Cartomancy relies on interpreting the symbols in the cards as they relate to each other and drawing conclusions about the inherent message. Other forms of divination that utilize this approach include the runes, tea leaf reading, ogham staves, bone casting, and other systems that rely on physical objects or pieces.

Astrology and geomancy, two systems you'll often see paired together, especially in India, rely on cosmological data pertaining to an individual to uncover hidden esoteric information. Another favored and powerful form of divination is bibliomancy, which is divination by using a book. Ask a question directed toward God, the spirits, or the ancestors and allow yourself to casually open a book or stick a pin between pages. The answer to your question will be the answer. In traditional folk magic in both Europe and North America, the Bible has been used as part of bibliomancy.

A form of divination not requiring a set tool is the awareness and proper reading of omens and premonitions in the environment around you. This is a very old form of divination, where events are understood to have secondary meaning and connection to seemingly unconnected events. In many ancient cultures, the reading of omens was a serious business and often part of established religion. Ancient Roman religion had state-sponsored augurs who read the signs of the world and made predictions from the gods. On a more general level, becoming aware of signs and meaning is something accessible to anyone, and when looking at our modern culture, a common trope in entertainment is for a character to "ask for a sign" from the spirit world and receive that message.

Interpretation of signs carries us toward the dream realm, a space of nothing but symbol. In many cultures, dreams are believed to be messages from the spirit world and are interpreted for their meaning. Even in modern psychotherapy, we see dream interpretation as an important window into the psyche, and we ascribe meaning to the rich tapestry of symbols that manifest. As a form of divination or communing with the dead, interpreting dreams relating to ancestors is a widespread practice.

I used to love collecting dream interpretation books, but I tend to favor a Gestalt approach to interpretation now. The psychotherapeutic Gestalt approach favors the dreamer understanding the symbols in the dream themselves, as opposed to looking for the meaning outside of us. The approach is simple: when you wake up, write down as much of a dream as you can and then go take a shower and have breakfast. Come back to what you wrote down about your dream, underlining any of the important words in what you've written. Create a list of those words, and looking at them by themselves, generate their meanings to you. Evaluate the list of meanings and see what the message that comes through to you is. I have found this approach to be very powerful.

There are many forms of divination; some of them are tied to specific traditions and others are open practices anyone can use. Some forms of divination are directed toward the Divine, while others are expansive enough to include other spirits. For our practice, if you include divination, choosing a modality that works for you and your ancestors is important. Consider also choosing a tool that can be dedicated only to the ancestors. If you choose to read Lenormand or learn how to read tea leaves as a form of communication, consider using a special cup or a particular deck as a way of demarcation and to solidify the channel between you and your ancestors. Consecrate the tool with your ancestors so that only they can come through this channel and you don't get spam calls from spirits with less-than-pure intentions.

Mediumship

Mediumship is any form of communication with spirit through a human interpreter, who receives the information or converses with the spirit themselves. Mediumship and full-on possession are often linked, but I am defining mediumship as when a human communicates with a spirit directly without the spirit taking possession.

Mediumship is found all around the world, and in most cultures the role of the medium is to be the bridge between the human community and the spiritual. The spiritual specialists of animistic traditions are understood to have direct connection with spirits and are often chosen due to bloodline or because they exhibit certain characteristics or experiences.

It is a common belief that mediumship is an ability that is inherited, often also with other forms of magical ability. In Celtic cultures the term would be *second sight*, an ability to view the Otherworld and those who dwell there, as well as sometimes the dead. Traditionally, those believed to have the second sight were sought after in the community as soothsayers or wise folk, and at other times also distrusted or feared.

In some cultures, the ability to perceive and converse with the spirit world can mark one out for special spiritual roles, such as a shaman or priest, while often abilities are said to manifest because of initiation into these roles. In the West, occult traditions such as Blavatsky and Olcott's Theosophy,

Spiritualism, and Allan Kardec's Spiritism all posit that anyone can develop these skills with enough practice and the proper mentorship. These three traditions specifically have had a huge impact on the current New Age movement's proliferation of psychic mediumship. In the United States we have the Spiritualist centers of Cassadaga, Florida, and Lily Dale, New York, and in the United Kingdom such centers as Findhorn and Arthur Findlay College. Publishers like Llewellyn Worldwide, Red Wheel/Weiser, Inner Traditions/ Bear & Company, and Hay House all have an assortment of books and materials on developing this skill.

But what is mediumship, and how does it manifest? The following definitions come from the Spiritualist tradition, which categorizes different abilities through the way information is perceived: clairaudience (to hear), clairsentience (to feel), clairparlance (to speak), clairalience (to smell), clairgustance (to taste), claircognizant (to know). I suspect that by quantifying the ability through particular sensory experiences, Spiritualist mediums are able to understand their experiences better. However, it is important to keep in mind that not all traditions understand mediumship this way, and they may have different ways to understand and translate experiences.

Channeling is a separate skill and is the ability to convey information through trance. The mechanism of trance is to access the incorporeal and deliver a message. Channeling is not the same as spirit possession, however, as the channel is a mouthpiece for information and not necessarily being inhabited by a spirit. Both Spiritualism and Spiritism involve channelers, and the Theosophical movement worked heavily through channeling information to receive what they considered divine revelation from their Ascended Masters. In contemporary times, there are many channelers working with spirits and sources of information throughout the world.

How information is received and interpreted very much depends upon the individuals experiencing it. Some mediums I know who smell information will usually intuitively know the significance of that smell or ask for verification. When performing readings for others, mediums may utilize several forms of clairvoyance to gain an awareness of the information or message coming through. Some mediums hear the deceased quite clearly, others see selections of images and symbols in their minds, while others receive coherent messages as thoughts.

Different traditions will take up this question of mediumship differently, and you may find that it is not necessary for you to develop at all in your ancestor veneration practice. While in the traditions I belong to it is encouraged to work with your spirits and become aware of the information they are flinging at you all the time, many individuals in these traditions also just rely on attending séances and *mesas*, and having readings with their spiritual godparents. (Mesas are the espiritismo version of séances, where espiritistas join together to recite prayers from the books of Allan Kardec and Catholic liturgy to communicate with and sometimes become possessed by spirit guides. They can then pass messages and perform healing on those gathered.)

Connected to but often distinct from mediumship is the phenomenon of controlled spirit possession. I hesitantly raise the subject of spirit possession for this book, not because I don't think it's an important aspect of communicating with the dead and an extremely powerful current in the world, but because I don't want readers to go out and try to get possessed. *Spirit possession* is when a spirit of some kind temporarily inhabits the body of a human being and can communicate directly through us.

It is a moving and deeply powerful experience to witness a spirit possession take place, let alone interact with the spirit who is in control. It is an integral component of many Indigenous religions around the world and can be found on all inhabited continents, especially South America, Asia, and Africa.[95] In some traditions, such as Tibetan Buddhism, oracles in both villages and cities take the form of individuals who are possessed by nature spirits. The Tibetan government-in-exile in Dharmsala, India, is serviced by several state oracles, each of whom are possessed by spirits who provide advice to His Holiness the Dalai Lama.

Discussion of this form of communication is much larger than this book, but from my studies, I must remark that there is an eerie similarity in most

---

95. Examples of specific traditions with spirit possession: South America (Orisha traditions, Palo [Cuba], Sanse [Puerto Rico], Vodou [Haiti], Espiritismo, Cult of María Lionza [Venezuela], Umbanda and Quimbanda [Brazil]); Africa (Sangoma [Southern Africa], Isese [Yorubaland], Odinani [Igbo], Bori (Hausa) [Northwest Africa], Islam); Asia (Tibetan Buddhism, Hinduism, Nat tradition [Burma], Phii tradition [Thailand], Cao Dai and Dao Mau [Vietnam], Muism [Korea], Shinto [Japan], Tengriism [Mongolia], Siberian Shamanism).

of the traditions I have experienced or studied. Often, it is only specific individuals in a community who have been initiated or who have a set of signs showing they could be possessed who become vehicles for spirits. In some traditions, such as various forms of espiritismo, the skills of mediumship and spirit possession are linked.

There is an abundance of traditional practitioners who can interact with the dead via possession or are possessed by their own spirits, who will speak to your ancestors on the medium's behalf. Now, a word of caution is needed. Scam artists proliferate on the internet and over the past few years have become a regular occurrence on social media, often with fake names. They easily prey on those who are desperate and genuinely wanting to connect with different forms of spirituality. Every other week I have a fake babalawo or an account using the name of a real spirit worker in my inbox using lines such as "Your ancestors wanted me to reach out to you!" These scam artists are very rarely actually part of these traditions and are piggybacking on the interest in ancestral veneration in the West to take advantage of the vulnerable. Always be skeptical of someone offering you a service you didn't ask for—or, to use a Welsh proverb: *Nid aur yw popeth melyn* ("Not everything that is yellow is gold").

Prayer

While in the Western world we think of prayer as being addressed to deities or saints, in most ancestral veneration traditions, it is common for prayers to be for the dead or to them. In the monotheistic Abrahamic traditions, there are several prayers and rituals for the dead, including the Catholic requiem, the Jewish *Kaddish*, and the Islamic *Ṣalāt al-Janāzah*, among others, which address the Divine on behalf of the soul of the deceased. While these formal prayers are rituals in themselves asking for the Divine's intercession, prayer broadly does not need to necessarily include the Divine and can incorporate what is meaningful to us and to our ancestors.

One of the most intimate moments of my life was visiting Canterbury Cathedral in the UK in 2010 and lighting a candle for my grandparents. While religion didn't play a huge role in my grandparents' life—or, rather, my parents have never said if it did or not—I felt it was an important gesture. Prayer can be what we make it and can be as simple as muttering words of thanks when thinking about the ancestors. In Lukumi, we have a prayer called the *mojuba*, a foundational prayer spoken before any formal occasion, which invokes God Almighty, the orisha, the biological lineage with as many names as one can remember, and the lineage of initiation. The mojuba is an example of a type of prayer that affirms the cosmological hierarchy, making sure no elder of importance is left uninvited.

Communication with Different Forms of Ancestors

The communication methods discussed so far have assumed you are connecting with similar forms of intelligence to our own, which is not unfair considering most ancestors we might want to connect with are deceased humans. However, as we've explored in previous chapters, depending on how you define *ancestor*, you may be working with a being or intelligence whose nature is considerably different. How might you communicate with a conceptual ancestor whose origin is fictional? What form of communication does an ancestor like the sky or the sea use? How or if you communicate with these conceptual ancestors depends very much on the relationship you have with them. Consider the nature of said ancestor and then reflect on how that ancestor already shows up in your life.

Communication with conceptual ancestors, in my experience, often takes more abstract forms. For example, some of my fictional ancestors who have been impactful in my life communicate through the medium of their existence. As I reread or rewatch the media they exist within, their stories communicate new truths to me because I am approaching these characters at different points in my own journey. In specific ways, I might rewatch or reread the entire work, or I might relate to moments of the character's journey. One specific method I like to use when I am looking to a fictional ancestor for guidance is to perform bibliomancy, where I take a book they exist within, ask my question, and let my mind casually flip through the pages until I land on a passage.

With some conceptual ancestors, such as the sky or the sea, you might communicate with these places through the gods associated with them, or you might physically go and spend time in those spaces to connect. Go to the seashore and spend time connecting with this vast presence, seeking answers to questions or communicating with the spirit of place.

Human affinity ancestors can be communicated with through the various divination and mediumship modes presented above, but there are other ways to communicate with these individuals. If the ancestor is known to you through their written legacy or their story, you might communicate in a similar form of bibliomancy as stated above. You might employ for some of these ancestors listening to recordings of speeches or interviews and randomly skipping to certain points in the recording.

Journal Prompts

- How do you view communication with the dead or with spirits? What images come up for you? What questions do you have about communicating with the dead?

- What feelings come up for you when thinking about communicating with spirits?

- Have you had experiences of communication with the spirit world? Was this communication intentional or unintentional? What impact did this have on you?

- If you could talk to your dead, what would you say? What would you want to hear?

Chapter Sixteen
Pilgrimage

As we began part two with exploration of building a local sacred space for your veneration practice, we will now explore how your veneration practice can include traveling outside of your local space and making pilgrimage to the sites of importance to your ancestors. Pilgrimage as a concept is often presented in religious terms, and the popular image is of going to some sacred site, but the definition of pilgrimage over the past few years has expanded, and people all over the world are finding deeper connection by embarking on journeys of self-discovery and relationship.

Pilgrimage is something we all do, whether we know it or not. Whenever we embark on a meaningful physical journey of transformation, we are engaging in pilgrimage. In this chapter, we will discuss various forms of pilgrimage and how it can relate to deepening ancestral practice. We will discuss what it is, its features, and some examples of how those features have evolved. While we focus a great deal on ancestors of blood in this book, we will also discuss ways that pilgrimage applies to conceptual and lineage ancestors.

Historically, most traditions, especially the larger multi-region religious faiths, have had journeys to sacred sites or holy lands as a major event of faith. In Europe in the medieval age, pilgrimage was one of the few unifying forces that all members of society could take part in equally, and important routes and destinations such as the Santiago de Compostela in Spain, the

Holy Land, or Cruach Phádraig in Ireland are still very important. One of the English language's most important pieces of literature, Geoffrey Chaucer's *The Canterbury Tales*, is set during a group pilgrimage to Canterbury. By far two of the largest pilgrimages to take place in the world include the Hajj of Islam, which before the pandemic saw upward of two and a half million each year, and the Hindu Kumbh Mela, which pre-pandemic drew millions, sometimes as many as 100 million devotees depending upon the year. Pilgrimage, whether involving millions or just an individual, has both social and individual significance. Pilgrimage, unlike other forms of travel such as a vacation, is all about transformation and relationship.

How does this relate to ancestral veneration? The human need to connect with one's roots is strong and can help to define one's place in the world. Pilgrimage of ancestry is so widespread that we might not even recognize it as such. Talk to any group of tourists visiting a place, and often you will find at least one person who is visiting because their ancestors originated in or were connected to that spot.

What might an intentional journey hold for you when centered on the ancestors? How might you come out changed by such an experience? What would your goals be for such a journey? I think of the times in my life when I have had the chance to walk in the footsteps of my forebears and experience a small portion of their lived reality. By stepping outside of our modern comfort zones, we engage in a journey with our ancestors as companions and guides.

Defining Pilgrimage

Will Parsons and Dr. Guy Hayward, the original founders of the British Pilgrimage Trust (BPT) and a truly dynamic pair who have had a big impact on how I see pilgrimage, define it as a purposeful journey on foot to holy, wholesome, and special places.[96] The BPT is a beautiful organization that seeks to explore and return pilgrimage as a facet of British culture through the re-founding of pilgrimage routes and by promoting infrastructures that support modern pilgrims on their journeys.

---

96. "About the British Pilgrimage Trust," The British Pilgrimage Trust, Wordpress, accessed August 2, 2022, https://britishpilgrimage.org/the-bpt/.

The institution of pilgrimage, specifically to Catholic sites in England, was abolished when King Henry VIII broke away from the church in Rome. While many of the pilgrimage routes being developed through the partners of the BPT are religious in nature, Will and Guy speak a great deal in their work about the spiritual importance of a general form of pilgrimage. Many of their own pilgrimages have explored the relationship between journey and subject, whether the destination is a cathedral or the physical location that a song was first composed. This gets to the heart of why I like this definition, because it expands the idea of pilgrimage to include any subject of specialness to us. The emphasis of pilgrimage "on foot" by the BPT is, in my understanding, to underscore the relationship of the pilgrim to the nature of the journey, but I think also to reduce the potential distraction that modern technology can have.[97] For our purposes, especially in visiting far-off locations where your ancestors came from, taking a plane or driving is a necessity.

Many of the BPT team members and partners have themselves explored the concept of pilgrimage in secular ways or for secular goals. The Indian British activist Satish Kumar, well known for his eight-thousand-mile peace walk to the capitals of the four major nuclear powers, speaks often about life as pilgrimage, a constant venturing forth into uncomfortable unknowns.[98] Stepping into the unknown and all the possibilities surrounding it can lead people to life-changing transformation, built around the context of the journey. When applied to ancestral relationships, this definition creates many possibilities.

Important Elements of Pilgrimage

Unlike a vacation, where the purpose is to relax and unwind, pilgrimage is often embarked upon with a specific set of goals in mind. Sometimes those goals change or are placed into larger fields of perspective because of experiences on the journey, but there is always an intention to achieve a goal. In many ways, a pilgrimage is like a quest to obtain or find a treasure of some kind. For example, Frodo Baggins in *The Lord of the Rings* didn't go to Mordor

---

97. "About the British Pilgrimage Trust," The British Pilgrimage Trust.

98. Satish Kumar, *No Destination: Autobiography of a Pilgrim* (Cambridge, UK: Green Books, 2021), 79–119.

to take in the sights; his quest was to return the One Ring to Mount Doom, and his journey took on some important attributes of pilgrimage.

Observation versus Interaction

The kind of mindset one embarks on a pilgrimage with is important for the kinds of experiences they will have along the way. Just like how intention will color goals, mindset will color how circumstances are viewed as they are encountered. When embarking on a pilgrimage, are the events seen as interactive or things to observe? Does the individual include themselves in the process as an active part of the event, or do they remove themselves from interacting with the event? When one goes to a museum, they are observing and learning; when one goes to a living history museum, one is immersed in an interactive experience. The difference between observing and interacting can have profound effects on how we relate and what we take away.

To expand on the important difference between observation and interaction, I think the main difference between tourism and pilgrimage is that tourism is only ever observational, while pilgrimage is interactional and always leaves us transformed. Yes, while away on holiday we might encounter new experiences that enrich us and give us new points of view, but we encounter these new experiences as an outsider looking in. Pilgrimage has a tendency of shaking us to the core and challenging our constructed status quo. This relates back to the I-It and I-Thou relationships of Martin Buber. When we relate to an experience as I-It, we don't need to take any responsibility for the challenges it presents. When we relate to pilgrimage as I-Thou, I think we allow ourselves to relate to the potential of change and embrace those challenges.

In this point of view, pilgrimage does not necessarily have to be a long-distance journey; it can be an emotional or social journey. One of my favorite presenters is the British Anglican vicar and television host Rev. Peter Owen Jones, who has explored pilgrimage and lifestyle in various projects. In *How to Live a Simple Life* (2010), Jones turned his back on consumerism and embarked on a 180-mile journey on foot from his home outside of Lewes in Sussex to visit Satish Kumar in Devon. Jones planned to embark on his journey by emulating Franciscan friars, who vow to only accept the charity of strangers. Through the journey, Jones met with challenges that would normally be so simple to rectify if he was carrying money.

Jones met with Franciscan friar Brother Phillipe Yates of Grey Friars in Canterbury, who said, "There are two principles that underlie Franciscan life; the first is poverty, and the other is fraternity. Our poverty says to the world 'I'm not going to rely on myself, my resources…to provide all that I need. I'm going to allow God to provide those needs through other people because that is how I am going to build up that fraternal relationship.' It is not about self-sufficiency, because sometimes that self-sufficiency creates us as an island separated from others."[99]

What I interpret the brother's words to mean here is how often we rely solely on ourselves out of a place of fear and scarcity. We can fixate on controlling everything in our life to give us security, but in doing that we become alone, and our relationships break down. As Brother Phillipe said, "By giving others the opportunity to be generous," we can create those fraternal relationships.[100] I have seen this in my own life, having grown up in a family where receiving from others was always conceptualized as accepting charity and, thus, others' pity. Being able to accept from others is a humbling experience and a life-changing one. Living comfortably and in a place of security is an important developmental goal, but as it relates to the idea of pilgrimage, that false sense of control often puts us into an observational rather than interactional state.

Journey

Journey in pilgrimage is an important aspect of the transformative nature of the experience. How one journeys, who and what they meet along the way, and the sacrifice of both comfort and time all have implications on the result. In many traditions, pilgrimage is organized into certain routes with infrastructure and secondary sites along the way to frame the experience. In other traditions, pilgrimage is understood to require a certain level of discomfort, and the journey reflects this. The road as a space of interaction is deeply interesting and worth talking more deeply about. Many traditions

---

99. Peter Owen Jones, *How to Live a Simple Life*, episode 2; directed by Graham Johnston and Rob Cowling; London: BBC, May 7, 2010.

100. Jones, *How to Live a Simple Life*, episode 2.

speak about journey and the road as a place of potentiality and destiny. In Joseph Campbell's monomyth theory, which seeks to demonstrate similarities in hero journeys show up in comparative myth, the metaphorical road is the linking point between all the parts of the hero's adventure, and the space where both villains and allies enter the picture. It becomes a liminal space of possibility as it leads the heroes to the places and people that stimulate transformation.[101] The road is both an intimate and a shared space, because while we all have our own individual destinations, others may join us in or depart from that journey, and we don't have control over who we meet on the road or where the road leads. Sometimes the road we're on may end and we need to take another route, and rarely are roads straight lines.

Giving Up Control, Surrender, and Trust

In *The Lord of the Rings*, Bilbo Baggins says to his young nephew Frodo, "'It's a dangerous business, Frodo, going out of your door…You step into the Road, and if you don't keep your feet, there is no knowing where you might be swept off to.'"[102] This quote has always struck me, because for Bilbo, we know that was his experience. By removing ourselves from our comfortable surroundings of home and entering new physical spaces, we enter new psychological and social spaces. We're no longer able to fully control the experience, and this invites those invisible hands to effect change. This does not mean being led blindly; there is most definitely agency in this process, but it's agency in relationship with and informed by something bigger than yourself. It's an exercise of trust building between yourself and the subject of your pilgrimage, or often the road itself.

Arrival and Encountering the Subject

The penultimate moment of a pilgrimage is the arrival at the place, or the arrival at the final place. After embarking on the journey, enduring the road, you arrive at the intended destination. You partake in the ritual of that space, meditate on the subject, and contemplate the journey you've just arrived from. Oftentimes, it's at this point that a blessing or token will be given or

---

101. Joseph Campbell, *The Hero with a Thousand Faces* (New York: Pantheon Books, 1968).

102. J. R. R. Tolkien, *The Fellowship of the Ring: Being the First Part of the Lord of the Rings* (New York: William Morrow, 2022), 74.

received. In Christian pilgrimage and many other traditions, sites would often issue a badge or token to mark completion of the pilgrimage and give you something to carry on your way. Often, these badges or tokens will hold spiritual power as well as the social mark of distinction of completion.

The Return Home

The final, most important aspect of pilgrimage is the return home. After embarking on the quest, overcoming the challenges the quest provided, and fulfilling the goal, we return back to our comfort place transformed. We return with a slightly different gaze, having changed in the process of pilgrimage. We create a new normal and a new comfort zone. Joseph Campbell in his monomyth theory speaks about the importance of the return as an invitation to embark on the next journey.[103] Returning changed and with new eyes, one is able to make more-informed choices about their relationship to the world and to themselves. If we consider ancestral practice in this return, as we embark on pilgrimages to encounter and honor the ancestors, we return with another piece to our own story.

A Selection of Pilgrimages

With the elements of pilgrimage discussed above, how might pilgrimage look in an ancestral practice? Many of us are already well prepared to engage in pilgrimage, even if we don't realize it. Many of our religious rituals are in fact pilgrimages but enacted on a smaller scale. Many of us engage in "walks down memory lane," which are mental pilgrimages to uncover or discover. Below are some examples of pilgrimages you might embark on or form for yourself.

Aboriginal Songlines and Folk Tradition

Previously, we discussed the Aboriginal Australian concept of the Dreaming, the collection of laws, stories, ceremonies, and shared knowledge that guide the community in their everyday and spiritual lives. One of the rituals employed by Aboriginal Australians in their practices to honor and enter into the Dreaming is a ritual called a songline. Songlines are routes or

---

103. Campbell, *The Hero with a Thousand Faces*, n.p.

pathways following the ancient trails made by the Dreamtime creator ancestors who shaped the physical landscape in their movements. Songlines are
a multifaceted ritual technology that is also used to store information, and
through the oral memory method of loci, information is associated with certain land features that are recalled via walking the length of the route. When
embarking on the journey of the route, at specific spots along the way, particular songs or dances are performed, which contain information through
movement and verses. The information is maintained by initiation into the
songline and careful repetition of the exact order. Through walking the songline, the information is perpetuated and maintained. While the concept of
the songline is Aboriginal in nature, the essence of it is found throughout the
world in different forms.

In many ways, this concept of the songline operates similarly to how folklore and story operate in most other cultures. Folk tradition tends to embed
information into the landscape to both explain the landscape feature and
utilize the method of loci. If you look at any community, local legend will
often be used to educate about the culture, beliefs, and history of that place.
The songline is a very specific form and one with particular rules and cultural connotations, but I definitely see how it can be useful for other peoples
in other places in harnessing the relationships between landscape and story.
Dr. Lynne Kelly speaks a great deal about songlines in her work and gives
detailed accounts of how her own developed songlines have affected her relationship with the subjects she includes.

Inspired by the songline and Kelly's own use of the modality, one exper-
iment I have taken upon myself is to use this method as a way of memo-
rizing family history, albeit through proxy with a map and not a walked
route. Through my family history research, I have generated a route map of
the movement of my family across the face of Britain and Ireland, as much
as I can find. Starting in Norfolk, John O'Groats, County Clare, Devon, and
Wales, I have traced as my family migrated each generation, eventually leading to my parents meeting in the north of England. Looking at a map, I start
at the origin points and move around the country to different towns, stating the name of the ancestor. I am adapting this method so that it becomes
more like a prayer I can recite. Tracking this history in this way has given me
greater appreciation for how many roots I have in those isles.

Visiting Graves

An intimate form of pilgrimage and ancestor veneration is to track down and visit graves of individual ancestors or burial grounds that contain the remains of family members. Sometimes due to history or oppression, there are very few records for some groups in society, and burial grounds become even more culturally important. The physical connection to remains, as written about in previous chapters, is a potent one. Leaving the UK at an early age and coming to Canada, all the graves of my ancestors were inaccessible to me. When I visited home for the first time in 2010, some of the places I visited were graves or locations where ashes had been scattered, and the experience was deeply meaningful to me. On the same trip, I had the good fortune to visit Dieppe, France, and the Canadian War Cemetery. There were fresh flowers and even handwritten letters attached to some of the graves from still-living siblings or friends. Even as I write this, I feel deeply emotional at the thought of walking in the footsteps of so many other visitors to that cemetery, knowing they came to pay their respects.

Religious Pilgrimage

Religious pilgrimage when it comes to ancestor veneration can often be about embarking on the pilgrimage in the name of an ancestor. While the pilgrimage might not necessarily be for you, you may choose to go to a site that had significance for your deceased, and to enact the ritual for them. For example, I had the opportunity to visit Canterbury Cathedral, an incredibly important site in Anglicanism. Among other pieces that made this visit so important was that I decided to light a candle that was set up in the nave in honor of my family and pray for them. Many of them were Anglican, and it appears more than a few were involved in the church somehow. You can make this even more intimate by journeying to a shrine of a particular saint, god, or spirit who was connected to your ancestor(s) in some way. You could embark on religious pilgrimage as a way of spreading ashes, or to follow through on a vow to pray for them.

Return to Homelands and History

Making pilgrimage to an ancestral homeland is probably one of the more widespread examples for individuals reading this book. You might be hearing a call to return to a home that was your family's, or to visit a space that can educate you about them. I am sure we all know someone who went on a transformative journey to visit the lands of their ancestors and came back different, changed, somehow more fulfilled.

This form of pilgrimage does not necessarily need to be a long distance, or even to another land. Dotted everywhere there are an abundance of living history museums and sites connected to the past. Visiting any of these spaces with the intention of experiencing a facsimile of what life looked like can give us deeper appreciation for how our ancestors may have lived. What are some time periods you are drawn to, and how did your own ancestors fit into those times?

Pilgrimage of Idea

The *pilgrimage of ideas* is a secular form of pilgrimage that honors an idea, concept, song, or story. In an interview, Parsons and Hayward spoke about a pilgrimage they undertook to pay respect to the victims of the 1853 Hartlake Bridge disaster in Kent. Thirty Romani and Irish hop pickers were killed when a horse caused the cart they were riding on to tip and throw many into the river. Parsons and Hayward embarked on a six-day walking journey to visit the bridge and sing "Hartlake Bridge," a folk song about the disaster. They visited the memorial to the victims, and while stood singing, happened to meet a couple who were descendants of some of the victims. The intent of the pilgrimage was to return the song to its location, and Hayward said later he realized they were also, quite by accident, able to return the song to the lineage by teaching it to the couple they met.[104]

In this way, there are many pilgrimages we can embark upon that include our affinity ancestors. Have you ever visited an important place connected to your profession? Have you ever, with intention, wanted to visit a place with significant meaning to you? One of the crowning jewels in my life experiences was visiting an exhibition at the Victoria and Albert Museum in London, which showcased the Walpole Collection. Among the collection's pieces was a selection of items that once belonged to the noted Tudor alchemist and

---

104. Dave Smith, Will Parsons, and Guy Hayward, "Druidcast—A DruidCast Episode 130," January 19, 2018, in *Druidcast—The Druid Podcast*, podcast, 1 hour, 8 minutes, https:// druidcast.libsyn.com/druidcast-a-druid-podcast-episode-130-0.

magician Dr. John Dee. As a member of the occult community, Dr. Dee has always held a special interest for me as a very early figure in English magic. I was able to stand within a foot of his famous black mirror and other objects close to him. That was a pilgrimage of ideas; I could connect with him in a slightly different and more intimate way than just reading about him in books.

Journal Prompts

- How might you bring the pilgrimage of ideas into your ancestor work?

- What ancestors, in any sense of the word, would fit into this form of pilgrimage? Where would you go?

- What pilgrimages have you already undertaken, and in what ways were these journeys different from regular travel? What was the lasting impact of these journeys on your life?

- What would you hope to gain from a pilgrimage related to your ancestors?

Conclusion

I set out to write this book because I saw a need. So many people seem to be interested in connecting with ancestors but don't know how to do it. While it is powerful to uncover stories through genealogical research, it is also so easy to just leave them as stories. This book was written to break down the fourth wall separating us as living people from the dead—to build a practical and intentional practice that invites the ancestors of any kind into an authentic spirituality.

In part one, I asked you to consider what you believe and how you see the ancestors. In part two, I asked you how your beliefs and worldview will affect how you communicate and collaborate with the ancestors through ritual. This book was not designed to be definitive; there are so many other pieces I feel have been left out, but it was designed to challenge. I hope that as you read this conclusion you come away with as many questions as you started with, but now with ideas on how to seek out the answers.

As you build your relationship to your ancestors, you are not merely relating to individuals but a whole community going back into the depths of time. You are finding yourself in that community and sharing in a web of responsibility so large it encompasses the entire planet. Up until now we have been focused a great deal on relationship, intentionality, and process. We have talked about the way tradition can be utilized and forged to create spaces of encounter and communication. Now, we end on the idea of legacy, for as you engage in this important work for yourself and perhaps for your communities, you yourself stand as an ancestor-in-waiting. You stand at the foot of the ancestral tree of life and death, bound to one day join those in the great tree's branches as your descendants look up at you.

Your work now, whether it will be remembered a hundred years from now or not, will have impact. While many are interested in ancestral work to discover themselves, the relationships you build with your biological or affinity ancestors will impact your relationships to the living. This impact is what I see as *legacy*, a fifth foundational word I will leave you with. One's legacy is hard to control; most of us will be forgotten as individuals eventually, but our individual roles merge to form the context of the world yet to come. Our collective legacy is the world our children and grandchildren inhabit. And as our descendants savor that beautiful fruit, perhaps they will make an offering to us in thanksgiving as they listen to the ancestral whispers whistling through the branches of the tree of life and death.

Resources and Further Reading

Below are some resources on various topics for further study. This is not an exhaustive list but offered to provide some further direction for subjects that I believe are worth your time to investigate. Included are links, books, and individual practitioners or content creators whom I have drawn a great deal of inspiration from in my own work.

Part One

Below are topics that appeared throughout part one with additional resources to explore, especially major topics such as the process of death and grief. I highly recommend exploring these topics further on your own, as they will supplement the material in part one.

Death and Grief: While we only touched on these subjects throughout the book, I feel it is important for anyone engaging in this work to explore these topics on a deeper level.

- *On Grief and Grieving* (coauthored with David Kessler) and *On Death and Dying* by Elisabeth Kübler-Ross. She was the preeminent writer on grief and mourning.
- Caitlin Doughty is a funeral professional and founder of the Order of the Good Death. Caitlin has published several books and runs a wonderful YouTube page with documentaries about death and the funeral industry.

- *As the Last Leaf Falls: A Pagan's Perspective on Death, Dying & Bereavement* by Kristoffer Hughes
- *Personal Grief Rituals: Creating Unique Expressions of Loss and Meaningful Acts of Mourning in Clinical or Private Settings* by Paul Martin
- *Death: A Graveside Companion* by Joanna Ebenstein

Prehistory and Precursor Species: Below are some titles relevant to the exploration of prehistoric and precursor ancestors. New discoveries about the beings that evolved into us are being uncovered all the time, as are discoveries of what the world was like thousands of years ago.

- *The Rise and Reign of the Mammals: A New History, from the Shadow of the Dinosaurs to Us* by Steve Brusatte
- *Otherlands: Journeys in Earths Extinct Ecosystems* by Thomas Halliday
- *Origin: A Genetic History of the Americas* by Jennifer Raff
- *Decolonizing "Prehistory": Deep Time and Indigenous Knowledges in North America* edited by Gesa Mackenthun and Christen Mucher
- *The Evolution of the Human Head* by Daniel E. Lieberman

The Natural World as Ancestor: As we spoke of in chapter four, connecting with the land, sea, and sky as ancestor takes understanding these realms not through personifications but as they are. Below are some books that I have found useful in learning more about the natural world or which explore in greater depth how to incorporate that work into your practice.

- *Root & Ritual: Timeless Ways to Reconnect to Land, Lineage, Community, and the Self* by Becca Piastrelli
- *The Heartbeat of Trees: Embracing Our Ancient Bond with Forests and Nature* by Peter Wohlleben
- *Finding the Mother Tree: Discovering the Wisdom of the Forest* by Suzanne Simard
- *Braiding Sweetgrass: Indigenous Wisdom, Scientific Knowledge, and the Teachings of Plants* by Robin Wall Kimmerer

- *Entangled Life: How Fungi Make Our Worlds, Change Our Minds & Shape Our Futures* by Merlin Sheldrake

Fictional Ancestors: I have found the following to be useful in exploring the relationship of ancestors who are fictional and how I can relate to them.

- *Superhero Grief: The Transformative Power of Loss* edited by Jill A. Harrington and Robert A. Neimeyer
- *Characters in Fictional Worlds: Understanding Imaginary Beings in Literature, Film, and Other Media* edited by Jens Eder, Fotis Jannidis, and Ralf Schneider
- *Starship Therapise: Using Therapeutic Fanfiction to Rewrite Your Life* by Larisa A. Garski and Justine Mastin

Family Research: The best resource I can give to help you in your journey of family research is:

- Cyndi's List: www.cyndislist.com

Family Dynamics and Storytelling: The following writers have an abundance of material on family dynamics, systems theory, and exploring your family narrative. Many also have television or web series devoted to these subjects. Next to their names are book titles I find particularly useful:

- John Bradshaw (*Bradshaw On: The Family* and *Family Secrets: The Path to Self-Acceptance and Reunion*)
- Brené Brown (*Atlas of the Heart; I Thought It Was Just Me (But It Isn't): Making the Journey from "What Will People Think?" to "I Am Enough"*)
- Mark Wolynn (*It Didn't Start with You: How Inherited Family Trauma Shapes Who We Are and How to End the Cycle*)
- Debbie Ford (*Why Good People Do Bad Things: How to Stop Being Your Own Worst Enemy*)
- *Healing Storytelling: The Art of Imagination and Storymaking for Personal Growth* by Nancy Mellon

Working with the Story of Conceptual Ancestors: Below are some of my favorite writers whose works influence how I connect with conceptual and fictional ancestors. Many are part of the archetypal psychology movement. While some of these books are centered on particular archetypes or figures, their methods can be applied to your work with any form of conceptual ancestor.

- Carol S. Pearson (*Awakening the Heroes Within: Twelve Archetypes to Help Us Find Ourselves and Transform Our World*, *The Hero Within: Six Archetypes We Live By*, and *Persephone Rising: Awakening the Heroine Within*)
- Clarissa Pinkola Estés (*Women Who Run with the Wolves: Myths and Stories of the Wild Woman Archetype*)
- Jean Shinoda Bolen (*Gods in Everyman: Archetypes That Shape Men's Lives* and *Goddesses in Everywoman: Powerful Archetypes in Women's Lives*)
- Robert L. Moore (*King, Warrior, Magician, Lover: Rediscovering the Archetypes of the Mature Masculine*, *The Warrior Within: Accessing the Knight in the Male Psyche*, and *The King Within: Accessing the King in the Male Psyche*)

Indigenous Projects and Reconciliation: The following resources support reconciliation efforts between settler and Indigenous communities around land and relationship.

- One of the best resources showing the traditional lands of Indigenous peoples across the world: https://native-land.ca
- The Canadian government's listing of Indigenous place names: https://www.nrcan.gc.ca/indigenous-geographical-names-data/24317
- *Working with and for Ancestors: Collaboration in the Care and Study of Ancestral Remains* edited by Chelsea H. Meloche, Laure Spake, and Katherine L. Nichols

Part Two

For the resources for part two, I have chosen to include recommended further reading as well as the names of prominent practitioners who put out good content through their websites or social media that is relevant to the subjects we've covered. This is not an exhaustive list, but one I hope will provide some direction for you.

Conceptualizing Practice: In chapter 8, we talked a great deal about some of the considerations you could approach your living practice with. I have found the following resource useful in exploring these considerations more.

- *Invention of Tradition and Syncretism in Contemporary Religions: Sacred Creativity* edited by Stefania Palmisano and Nicola Pannofino

Sacred Space: In chapter 9, we discussed the creation of shrines and sacred spaces for your ancestor practice. Below are some further titles that expand on these concepts.

- *Astrology and Cosmology in the World's Religions* by Nicholas Campion
- *Spontaneous Shrines and the Public Memorialization of Death* edited by Jack Santino

Psychological Relationship with the World: I would like to offer some more resources on this topic to flesh out this important aspect of how we relate.

- *Cave Paintings and the Human Spirit: The Origin of Creativity and Belief* by David S. Whitley
- *Memory Code: The Secrets of Stonehenge, Easter Island and Other Ancient Monuments* and *Memory Craft: Improve Your Memory with the Most Powerful Methods in History* by Lynne Kelly
- *From Signal to Symbol: The Evolution of Language* by Ronald Planer and Kim Sterelny
- *Man and His Symbols* by Carl Jung, and M.-L. von Franz, Joseph L. Henderson, Jolande Jacobi, and Aniela Jaffé

Color: These resources are to explore the history and use of color as it relates to spirituality and ritual.

- *The Secret Lives of Color* by Kassia St. Clair
- *The Brilliant History of Color in Art* by Victoria Finlay

Physical Representation: To more deeply explore the ideas raised in this chapter, I suggest some titles below on iconography, symbol, and representing the spiritual.

- *Death, Memory & Material Culture* by Elizabeth Hallam and Jenny Hockey
- *Cave Paintings and the Human Spirit: The Origin of Creativity and Belief* by David S. Whitley
- *Depicting Deity: A Metatheological Approach* by Jonathan L. Kvanvig
- *An Introduction to Iconography* by Roelof van Straten, translated by Patricia de Man
- *An Illustrated Encyclopaedia of Traditional Symbols* by J. C. Cooper

Objects of Power: While objects and use of objects is spoken about throughout the book, below are some specific handbooks to explore heirlooms and symbolism more.

- *Life After Death?: Inheritance, Burial Practices, and Family Heirlooms* edited by Marcia Amidon Lusted
- *Jewels: A Secret History* by Victoria Finlay
- *Threads of Life: A History of the World Through the Eye of a Needle* by Clare Hunter
- *The Woman's Dictionary of Symbols and Sacred Objects* by Barbara G. Walker
- *Signs & Symbols: An Illustrated Guide to Their Origins and Meanings* by Miranda Bruce-Mitford

Offerings: Understanding that my readership will come from diverse backgrounds, below are some resources as a jumping-off point for your own research, whether to be inspired for your own work or to just see examples.

- Max Miller, a foodie historian who writes on history of food from around the world and who runs the YouTube channel "Tasting History with Max Miller"
- *Ritual Offerings* by Aaron Leitch
- *Sharing with the Gods: Aparchai and Dekatai in Ancient Greece* by Theodora Suk Fong Jim
- *An Edible History of Humanity* by Tom Standage

Ritual: Below are some resources that speak to nonspecific forms of ritual and the origins of human ritual practice.

- *The Power of Ritual in Prehistory: Secret Societies and Origins of Social Complexity* by Brian Hayden
- *Ritual Theory, Ritual Practice* by Catherine Bell
- *The Power of Ritual: Turning Everyday Activities into Soulful Practices* by Casper ter Kuile
- *Ritual Gone Wrong: What We Learn from Ritual Disruption* by Kathryn T. McClymond
- *The Ritual Process: Structure and Anti-Structure* by Victor W. Turner
- *Routledge Encyclopedia of Religious Rites, Rituals, and Festivals* edited by Frank A. Salamone

Communication: Below are some books on various forms of divination or psychic skills, as well as organizations that facilitate training in these skills.

- *The Fortune-Telling Book: The Encyclopedia of Divination and Soothsaying* by Raymond Buckland
- *Psychic Witch: A Metaphysical Guide to Meditation, Magick & Manifestation* by Mat Auryn
- *Signs: The Secret Language of the Universe* by Laura Lynne Jackson

- There are an abundance of courses and foundations that teach mediumship skills. Some of the oldest in the West belong to the Spiritualist tradition, which operates sites such as Arthur Findlay College (UK) and Lily Dale Assembly (NY). When seeking out courses or groups, be sure to check the credentials and history of the group.

Pilgrimage: As the scope of this book is large, I have selected a couple of generalized titles for those interested in pilgrimage as a general idea. I have found these two titles are useful to explore the various ways pilgrimage is taken up around the world, both religious and secular.

- *Shrines and Pilgrimage in the Modern World: New Itineraries into the Sacred* edited by Peter Jan Margry
- *Pilgrimage: From the Ganges to Graceland: An Encyclopedia* by Linda Kay Davidson and David M. Gitlitz

Magic: We did not touch on magic too often in this book because there are other books devoted specifically to ancestral magic. Magic and ritual practice have often been linked, and folk traditions often encompass magical traditions as well. Focusing in on this aspect would have been a whole book in itself, and so instead, below are some of my favorite more general books on magic as resources for you to explore.

- *Mastering Magick: A Course in Spellcasting for the Psychic Witch* by Mat Auryn
- *The History of Magic: From Alchemy to Witchcraft, from the Ice Age to the Present* by Chris Gosden
- *Visual Magick: A Manual of Freestyle Shamanism* by Jan Fries
- *The Magic of Pathworking: A Meditation Guide for Your Inner Vision* by Simon Court

Ancestral Healing: We spoke of ancestral healing throughout the book, but I specifically did not write a section on it because so many aspects of ancestral healing are in my eyes conditional on cultural understandings of who and what the ancestors are, which impact their needs for healing. These titles offer thought-provoking approaches to ancestral healing from multi-spiritual approaches and perspectives and are not grounded in specific traditions.

- *Ancestral Medicine: Rituals for Personal and Family Healing* by Daniel Foor
- *Pagan Portals—Ancestral Healing* edited by Trevor Greenfield
- *What Kind of Ancestor Do You Want to Be?* edited by John Hausdoerffer, Brooke Parry Hecht, Melissa K. Nelson, and Katherine Kassouf Cummings

Queer-Specific Resources: As a queer-identifying person, I have found the following resources helpful in my queer ancestral work. I place these resources here specifically, as the queer community is often overlooked in alternative spirituality circles, and there is a growing corpus of works that explore this aspect of spirituality. Many of these resources directly mention queer ancestral work or are useful for this.

- *Cassell's Encyclopedia of Queer Myth, Symbol, and Spirit: Gay, Lesbian, Bisexual, and Transgender Lore* by Randy P. Conner, David Hatfield Sparks, and Mariya Sparks
- *Queer Magic: Power Beyond Boundaries* edited by Lee Harrington and Tai Fenix Kulystin
- *Gay Witchcraft: Empowering the Tribe* by Christopher Penczak
- *Sacred Gender: Create Trans and Nonbinary Spiritual Connections* by Ariana Serpentine
- *Queering Your Craft: Witchcraft from the Margins* by Cassandra Snow
- *Gay Spirituality: Gay Identity and the Transformation of Human Consciousness* by Toby Johnson
- *Queer Spirits: A Gay Men's Myth Book* edited by Will Roscoe
- *Reclaiming Two-Spirits: Sexuality, Spiritual Renewal, and Sovereignty in Native America* by Gregory D. Smithers

BIPOC-Specific Resources: These are resources that speak to BIPOC experiences, both issues and approaches.

- *Voices from the Ancestors: Xicanx and Latinx Spiritual Expressions and Healing Practices* edited by Lara Medina and Martha R. Gonzales
- *Fleshing the Spirit: Spirituality and Activism in Chicana, Latina, and Indigenous Women's Lives* edited by Elisa Facio and Irene Lara
- *Connecting to Our Ancestral Past: Healing through Family Constellations, Ceremony, and Ritual* by Francesca Mason Boring
- *Asian American Dreams: The Emergence of an American People* by Helen Zia

Bibliography

"About the British Pilgrimage Trust." The British Pilgrimage Trust. Wordpress. Accessed August 2, 2022. https://britishpilgrimage.org/the-bpt/.

Adams, Kathleen M. "Club Dead, Not Club Med: Staging Death in Contemporary Tana Toraja (Indonesia)." *Southeast Asian Journal of Social Science* 21, no. 2 (1993): 62–72. http://dx.doi.org/10.1163/030382493X00116.

Angelou, Maya (@DrMayaAngelou). "Whatever you want to do, if you want to be great at it, you have to love it and be able to make sacrifices for it." Twitter, July 23, 2015, 3:50 p.m., https://twitter.com/drmayaangelou/status/624305657898930176.

Artbound. Season 10, episode 3, "Día de Los Muertos/Day of the Dead." 2019, KCET, 56:17. https://www.kcet.org/shows/artbound/episodes/dia-de-los-muertos-day-of-the-dead.

Aubinet, Stéphane. "The Craft of Yoiking: Philosophical Variations on Sámi Chants." Master's thesis, University of Oslo, 2020. https://www.duo.uio.no/bitstream/handle/10852/77489/PhD-Aubinet-2020.pdf?sequence=1&isAllowed=y.

Bayly, Susan. *Caste, Society and Politics in India from the Eighteenth Century to the Modern Age*, 3rd ed., vol. 4. Cambridge, UK: Cambridge University Press, 2001.

Bosi, Roberto. *The Lapps*. Translated by James Cadell. Westport, CT: Greenwood Press, 1976.

Bower, Bruce. "Stencils Rival Age of Europe's Cave Art." *Science News* 186, no. 10 (November 2014): 6. http://www.jstor.org/stable/24366970.

Boyd, James W., and Ron G. Williams. "Japanese Shintō: An Interpretation of a Priestly Perspective." *Philosophy East and West* 55, no. 1 (January 2005): 33–63. https://www.jstor.org/stable/4487935.

Bregman, Ona Cohn, and Charles M. White, eds. *Bringing Systems Thinking to Life: Expanding the Horizons for Bowen Family Systems Theory*. Hoboken: Taylor & Francis, 2012.

Bryant, Clifton D., and Dennis L. Peck, eds. *Encyclopedia of Death and the Human Experience*. London: SAGE, 2009.

Buber, Martin. *I and Thou*. Translated by Ronald Gregor Smith. Edinburgh, UK: T. & T. Clark, 1937.

Campbell, Joseph. *The Hero with a Thousand Faces*. New York: Pantheon Books, 1968.

Clarke, Philip. *Where the Ancestors Walked: Australia as an Aboriginal Landscape*. Crows Nest, N.S.W.: Allen & Unwin, 2003.

Crawford, Suzanne J., and Dennis F. Kelley. *American Indian Religious Traditions: An Encyclopedia*. Vol. 1. Santa Barbara, CA: ABC-CLIO, 2005.

Cush, Denise, Catherine Robinson, and Michael York. *Encyclopedia of Hinduism*. London: Routledge, 2010.

Davidson, H. R. Ellis. *The Road to Hel; A Study of the Conception of the Dead in Old Norse Literature*. New York: Greenwood Press, 1968.

Davis, Bret W. ed. *The Oxford Handbook of Japanese Philosophy*. Oxford; New York: Oxford University Press, 2020.

Elliot, Andrew J., and Markus A. Maier. "Color and Psychological Functioning." *Current Directions in Psychological Science* 16, no. 5 (October 2007): 250–54. https://psycnet.apa.org/doi/10.1111/j.1467-8721.2007.00514.x.

Elster, Ernestine S., Eugenia Isetti, John Robb, and Antonella Traverso, eds. *The Archaeology of Grotta Scaloria: Ritual in Neolithic Southeast Italy*. Los Angeles: Cotsen Institute of Archaeology Press, 2016.

Emick, Jennifer. *The Book of Celtic Myths: From the Mystic Might of the Celtic Warriors to the Magic of the Fey Folk, the Storied History and Folklore of Ireland, Scotland, Brittany, and Wales*. Stoughton, MA: Adams Media, 2017.

Eyers, Pegi. *Ancient Spirit Rising: Reclaiming Your Roots & Restoring Earth Community*. Otonabee, Ontario, Canada: Stone Circle Press, 2016.

"The Fascinating Death Ritual of the Toraja People | SLICE." SLICE. You-Tube video, 25:25. August 21, 2022. https://www.youtube.com/watch ?v=EuN5W6_jQK8.

Fong, Jack. *The Death Cafe Movement: Exploring the Horizons of Mortality*. Cham, Switzerland: Springer International PU, 2018.

Foor, Daniel. *Ancestral Medicine: Rituals for Personal and Family Healing*. Rochester, VT: Bear & Company, 2017.

Formoso, Bernard. "From Bones to Ashes: The Teochiu Management of Bad Death in China and Overseas." In *Buddhist Funeral Cultures of Southeast Asia and China*, edited by Paul Williams and Patrice Ladwig, 192–217. Cambridge, UK: Cambridge University Press, 2012.

Foster, Michael Dylan. *The Book of Yōkai: Mysterious Creatures of Japanese Folklore*. Illustrated by Kijin Shinonome. Oakland, CA: University of California Press, 2015.

Gager, John G., ed. *Curse Tablets and Binding Spells from the Ancient World*. Oxford: Oxford University Press, 1999.

Gates, Henry Louis, Jr., and Evelyn Brooks Higginbotham, eds. "Chisholm, Shirley." In *African American Lives*. New York: Oxford University Press, 2004.

Geertz, Clifford. *Negara: The Theatre State in Nineteenth-Century Bali*. Princeton, NJ: 1980.

Graham-Dixon, Andrew. *The Art of Russia*; London: BBC, 2009.

———. *Treasures of Heaven*. Directed by Paul Tilzey; London: BBC, 2011.

Greene, Heather. "Japanese Temples Are Holding Funerals For Unwanted Dolls." *Religion Unplugged*. The Media Project. November 5, 2021. https://religionunplugged.com/news/2021/11/5/japanese-temples-are -holding-funerals-for-unwanted-dolls.

Guthrie, Russell Dale. *The Nature of Paleolithic Art*. Chicago: The University of Chicago Press, 2005.

Hart, George. *A Dictionary of Egyptian Gods and Goddesses*. New York: Routledge, 2012.

Harvey, Graham. *Animism: Respecting the Living World*. London: Hurst & Co. 2005.

Harvey, Graham, ed. *The Handbook of Contemporary Animism*. London: Routledge, 2013.

Hughes, Kristoffer. *The Book of Celtic Magic: Transformative Teachings from the Cauldron of Awen*. Woodbury, MN: Llewellyn Publications, 2014.

Ingle, Cyndi. "About Cyndi Ingle." Cyndi's List of Genealogy Sites on the Internet. Accessed November 26, 2022. https://www.cyndislist.com /aboutus/.

James, William. *The Varieties of Religious Experience: A Study in Human Nature*. Scribere Semper et Legere, 2021.

Johnson, Harold R. *Firewater: How Alcohol Is Killing My People (And Yours)*. Saskatchewan, Canada: University of Regina Press, 2016.

Johnson, Sveinbjorn. "Old Norse and Ancient Greek Ideals." *Ethics* 49, no. 1 (October 1938): 18–36, https://www.jstor.org/stable/2988773.

Jones, Lindsay, Mircea Eliade, and Charles J. Adams. *Encyclopedia of Religion*. Detroit, MI: Macmillan Reference USA, 2005.

Jones, Peter Owen. *How to Live a Simple Life*. Episode 2. Directed by Graham Johnston and Rob Cowling, London: BBC, May 7, 2010.

Kelly, Lynne. *The Memory Code: The Traditional Aboriginal Memory Technique That Unlocks the Secrets of Stonehenge, Easter Island and Ancient Monuments the World Over*. Sydney, N.S.W.: Allen & Unwin, 2016.

Kelly, Lynne. *Memory Craft: Improve Your Memory Using the Most Powerful Methods from around the World*. Crows Nest, NSW: Allen & Unwin, 2019.

Kenna, Margaret E. "Icons in Theory and Practice: An Orthodox Christian Example." *History of Religions* 24, no. 4 (May 1985): 345–68. https://www .jstor.org/stable/1062307.

Kerr, Laura K. "Synchronicity, Overview." In *Encyclopedia of Critical Psychology*. Edited by Thomas Teo, 1905–1908. Berlin, Heidelberg: Springer-Verlag, 2014.

Kimmerer, Robin Wall. *Braiding Sweetgrass: Indigenous Wisdom, Scientific Knowledge, and the Teachings of Plants*. Minneapolis, MN: Milkweed Editions, 2020.

Klinkhammer, Amy. "Kennewick Man's Bones Reburied, Settling a Decades-Long Debate." *Discover Magazine*. February 21, 2017. https://www.discovermagazine.com/planet-earth/kennewick-mans-bones-reburied-settling-a-decades-long-debate.

Kübler-Ross, Elisabeth, and David Kessler. *On Grief and Grieving: Finding the Meaning of Grief Through the Five Stages of Loss*. New York: Scribner, 2014.

Kumar, Satish. *No Destination: Autobiography of a Pilgrim*. Cambridge, UK: Green Books, 2021.

Langdon, John H. *Human Evolution: Bones, Cultures and Genes*. New York: Springer, 2022.

Lindow, John. *Norse Mythology: A Guide to the Gods, Heroes, Rituals, and Beliefs*. New York: Oxford University Press, 2002.

Marchi, Regina M. *Day of the Dead in the USA: The Migration and Transformation of a Cultural Phenomenon*. 2nd ed. New Brunswick, NJ: Rutgers University Press, 2022.

McDougall, Charles, dir. *The Office*. Season 2, episode 10, "Christmas Party." Aired December 6, 2005, on NBC.

Merkur, Daniel. "Breath-Soul and Wind Owner: The Many and the One in Inuit Religion." *American Indian Quarterly* 7, no. 3 (Summer 1983): 23-39. https://doi.org/10.2307/1184255.

Michael, R. Blake. "Foundation Myths of the Two Denominations of Vīraśaivism: *Viraktas* and *Gurusthalins*." *The Journal of Asian Studies* 42, no. 2 (February 1983): 309–22. https://doi.org/10.2307/2055116.

Mildner, Vesna. *The Cognitive Neuroscience of Human Communication*. New York: Psychology Press, 2015.

Mori, Hiroaki, Yukari Hayashi, Barrie McLean. *The Tibetan Book of the Dead: The Great Liberation*. National Film Board of Canada, 1994, 45 min. https://www.nfb.ca/film/tibetan_book_of_the_dead_the_great _liberation/.

Nooy-Palm, Hetty. *The Sa'dan-Toraja: A Study of Their Social Life and Religion*. The Hague: Martinus Nijhoff, 1979.

Obayashi, Hiroshi, ed. *Death and Afterlife: Perspectives of World Religions*. New York: Praeger, 1992.

Ono, Sokyo. *Shinto: The Kami Way*. In Collaboration with William P. Woodard. Boston: Tuttle Publishing, 1962.

O'Toole, Garson. "Sometimes a Cigar Is Just a Cigar." Quote Investigator. August 12, 2011. https://quoteinvestigator.com/2011/08/12/just-a-cigar/.

Penn, Thomas. *Winter King: Henry VII and the Dawn of Tudor England*. New York: Simon & Schuster Paperbacks, 2013.

Pérez, Elizabeth. "Portable Portals: Transnational Rituals for the Head across Globalizing Orisha Traditions." *Nova Religio: The Journal of Alternative and Emergent Religions* 16, no. 4 (May 2013): 35–62. https://doi. org/10.1525/nr.2013.16.4.35.

Pettersson, Rune. "Cultural Differences in the Perception of Image and Color in Pictures." *Educational Communication and Technology* 30, no. 1 (March 1982): 43–53. https://doi.org/10.1007/BF02766547.

Placido, Barbara. "'It's All to Do with Words': An Analysis of Spirit Possession in the Venezuelan Cult of María Lionza." *The Journal of the Royal Anthropological Institute* 7, no. 2 (June 2001): 207–24. https://doi.org /10.1111/1467-9655.00059.

Plato. "Phaedo." Translated by G. M. A. Grube. In *Classics of Western Philosophy*. Edited by Steven M. Cahn. 8th ed., 47–79. Indianapolis, Indiana: Hackett Publishing Company, 2012.

Morten Rasmussen, Martin Sikora, Anders Albrechtsen, Thorfinn Sand Korneliussen, J. Victor Moreno-Mayar, G. David Poznik, Christoph P. E. Zollikofer et al. "The Ancestry and Affiliations of Kennewick Man," *Nature* 523 (2015): 455–458, https://doi.org/10.1038/nature14625.

Rose, Carol. *Giants, Monsters, and Dragons: An Encyclopedia of Folklore, Legend, and Myth.* New York: W. W. Norton, 2001.

Samuel, Geoffrey. *Introducing Tibetan Buddhism.* New York: Routledge, 2012.

Samuels, Elyse, and Adriana Usero. "'New York City's Family Tomb': The Sad History of Hart Island." *The Washington Post.* WP Company. April 27, 2020. https://www.washingtonpost.com/history/2020/04/27/hart-island -mass-grave-coronavirus-burials/.

Schwarzer, Ralf, and Peter A. Frensch, eds. *Personality, Human Development, and Culture: International Perspectives On Psychological Science.* Vol. 2. Hove, UK: Psychology Press, 2010.

Smith, Dave, Will Parsons, and Guy Hayward. Druidcast—A DruidCast Episode 130. January 19, 2018. In *Druidcast—The Druid Podcast.* Podcast. 1 hour, 8 minutes. https://druidcast.libsyn.com/druidcast-a-druid-podcast -episode-130-0.

Stang, Charles M. *Our Divine Double.* Cambridge, MA: Harvard University Press, 2016.

Starhawk, M. Macha NightMare, and the Reclaiming Collective. *The Pagan Book of Living and Dying.* New York: HarperCollins, 2013.

Starr, Mirabai. *Wild Mercy: Living the Fierce and Tender Wisdom of the Women Mystics.* Boulder, CO: Sounds True, 2019.

Stavish, Mark. *Egregores: The Occult Entities That Watch Over Human Destiny.* Rochester, VT: Inner Traditions, 2018.

Tann, Mambo Chita. *Haitian Vodou: An Introduction to Haiti's Indigenous Spiritual Traditions.* Woodbury, MN: Llewellyn Publications, 2012.

Thomas, W. Jenkyn. *The Welsh Fairy Book.* Illustrated by Pogány Willy. London: Abela Pub., 2010.

Todd, Malcolm. *A Companion to Roman Britain.* Malden, MA: Blackwell Pub, 2007.

Tolkien, J. R. R. *The Fellowship of the Ring: Being the First Part of the Lord of the Rings.* New York: William Morrow, 2022.

Vernot, Benjamin, Serena Tucci, Janet Kelso, Joshua G. Schraiber, Aaron B. Wolf, Rachel M. Gittelman, Michael Dannemann, et al. "Excavating Neandertal and Denisovan DNA from the Genomes of Melanesian Individuals." *Science* 352, no. 6282 (April 2016): 235–39. http://www.jstor.org /stable/24744207.

Williams, Paul, and Patrice Ladwig, eds. *Buddhist Funeral Cultures of Southeast Asia and China*. Cambridge, UK: Cambridge, University Press, 2012.

Index

A

affinity ancestors, 47–49, 55, 66–69, 91, 94, 97–99, 106, 175, 203, 216, 226, 230

AIDS, 104, 105, 107, 108, 128

Anglo-Saxon, 57, 62, 122, 143, 207

animism, 14–17, 28, 136, 154, 167, 211

Anishinaabe, 190

Australia, 40, 58, 143, 146, 160, 167, 223

B

baptism, 30

Bardo Thödol, 30

Bible, 13, 62, 166, 167, 210, 215, 216

Brazil, 106, 213

Buddhism, 3, 17, 23, 24, 29, 30, 37, 47, 77, 150, 154–156, 162, 163, 173, 213

C

Caribbean, 5, 69, 106, 124, 128

cascarilla, 138

caste, 53, 63, 144

Catholicism, 106, 121–124, 134, 154, 155, 167, 189, 213, 214, 219

Celtic, 5, 102, 211

China, 15, 16, 21, 32, 37, 77, 78, 85, 146, 148, 156, 190

Christianity, 3, 12, 13, 17, 29–31, 33, 36, 62, 91, 96, 154, 157, 161–163, 166, 167, 190, 223

church, 13, 29, 33, 121, 122, 134, 156, 161, 162, 186, 219, 225

clan, 53, 144, 165

cognitive, 93, 147, 152, 153, 157, 168

conceptual ancestors, 56, 66, 67, 72, 97–99, 203, 215, 217, 234

Cree, 55, 207

D

death café, 76

Denisovans, 51

Día de los Muertos, 75, 104, 121, 134

divination, 7, 19, 22, 23, 32, 38, 57, 66, 76, 79, 92, 149, 154, 203, 205, 209–211, 216, 237

Dreamtime, 58, 223, 224

Druidry, 5, 102, 226

dualism, 17, 18, 21, 191

E

Egypt, 20, 21, 28, 29, 33, 36, 57, 145, 148, 149, 155, 159

Espiritismo, 5, 6, 22, 69, 70, 106, 123, 126, 138, 148, 150, 213, 214

F

folklore, 3, 16, 33, 48, 56, 59, 60, 107, 224

G

genealogy, 39, 62, 87–90, 229

genetics, 44, 45, 51, 232

genogram, 90

Gede Lwa, 39

ghosts, 38–40, 50, 83

Greco-Roman, 23, 198

graves, 32, 33, 83, 107, 109, 110, 146, 163, 167, 175, 190, 225, 232

Greek, 12, 23, 33, 36, 49, 147

grief, 2, 40, 73–77, 99, 231–233

Grotta Scaloria, 52

H

Haitian Vodou, 4, 39, 106, 150, 213

hamingja, 35

Hildegard of Bingen, St., 19

Hinduism, 3, 5, 6, 17, 24, 47, 57, 85, 126, 133, 150, 154, 155, 159, 164, 213, 218

HIV, 53, 54, 104

Hopi, 66, 157

I

Indigenous, 15, 17, 31, 39, 40, 53, 56–58, 64, 65, 69, 95, 96, 106, 109, 110, 120, 143, 146, 156, 162, 167, 213, 232, 234, 240

Indonesia, 30, 31

Ireland, 94, 121, 144, 190, 218, 224, 226

Islam, 17, 29, 31, 36, 164, 166, 167, 213, 214, 218

J

Japan, 15–17, 57, 85, 213

Jesus, 12, 134, 156

Judaism, 17, 36, 123, 166, 178, 181, 214, 226, 236

Jung, Carl, 22, 48, 206, 235

K

kachina, 66, 67, 157, 161

Korea, 85, 156, 213

L

lineage ancestors, 39, 44–47, 49, 62, 71, 82, 86, 95,
    98–100, 144, 174, 175, 187, 190, 194, 215, 217, 226,
    232

M

magic, 1, 3, 5, 38, 59, 66, 80, 102, 141, 146, 175, 197, 204,
    210, 211, 227, 234, 237–239

María Lionza, 106, 213

medieval, 61, 62, 142, 143, 163, 217

mediumship, 83, 203, 211–214, 216, 238

Mexico, 104, 121, 134

mitochondrial Eve, 43, 44, 51

monsters, 15, 38–40, 60

mysticism, 17–19

myth, 33, 36, 55, 56, 59, 60, 62, 71, 72, 164, 222, 234, 239

N

Native American, 29, 109

Neanderthal, 51

Neopaganism, 4, 29, 34, 75, 91, 125

New Age, 21, 22, 69, 124, 212

Nondualism, 17, 18

Norse, 29, 33, 35, 36, 49, 57

O

ofrenda, 104, 134, 135, 160

Orisha, 5, 22, 23, 78, 84, 133, 149, 150, 188, 213, 215

P

Paganism, 3, 14, 124

Palo, 213

pets, 67, 69, 147, 198, 220, 221, 232, 238

Pixar, 2, 28, 29, 39, 134, 160

possession, 38, 106, 149, 154, 164, 178, 180, 181, 211–214

precursor species, 51, 64, 174, 232

psychology, 18, 50, 86, 141, 147, 148, 152, 156, 196, 206,
    208, 222, 234, 235

psychotherapy, 4, 5, 48, 89, 210

psychotropic, 19

Q

queer, 3, 5, 94, 103, 108, 239

R

reincarnation, 21, 27–31, 34–36, 168, 173

relics, 132, 151, 162–165, 171, 173, 178, 179

Rome, 33, 49, 50, 61, 62, 78, 154, 155, 210, 219, 226

Russia, 49, 162

S

Sámi, 32, 40

sacred space, 114, 131–136, 138, 149, 154, 168, 169, 171,
    179, 188, 197, 217, 235

saint, 12, 13, 19, 47, 48, 49, 151, 157, 161–163, 173, 186, 187, 214, 215

Scotland, 94, 96, 97, 121, 144, 165

Shinto, 15, 57, 213

silent café, 75, 76, 90

songline, 223, 224

Southeast Asia, 31, 37, 77

spirit guides, 69, 70, 123, 196, 213

Spiritism, 5, 69, 212

Spiritualism, 2–7, 15, 17, 22, 56, 69, 96, 116, 124, 126, 127, 131, 136, 137, 144, 148, 168, 174, 196, 203, 207, 212, 214, 229, 236, 238–240

T

Theosophy, 22, 211, 212

Tibetan Buddhism, 29, 30, 161, 162, 173, 176, 213

Torajan people, 30, 31, 159

Tudors, 60, 61, 226

U

Upanishads, 24

W

Wales, 3, 4, 59, 61, 94, 102, 121, 144, 163, 177, 214, 224

West Africa, 22

wyrd, 207, 208

Y

Y-chromosomal Adam, 43, 44, 51

yokai, 15, 16

To Write to the Author

If you wish to contact the author or would like more information about this book, please write to the author in care of Llewellyn Worldwide Ltd. and we will forward your request. Both the author and publisher appreciate hearing from you and learning of your enjoyment of this book and how it has helped you. Llewellyn Worldwide Ltd. cannot guarantee that every letter written to the author can be answered, but all will be forwarded. Please write to:

Ben Stimpson
℅ Llewellyn Worldwide
2143 Wooddale Drive
Woodbury, MN 55125-2989

Please enclose a self-addressed stamped envelope for reply,
or $1.00 to cover costs. If outside the U.S.A., enclose
an international postal reply coupon.

Many of Llewellyn's authors have websites with additional information and resources. For more information, please visit our website at http://www.llewellyn.com.